Vicious Cycle

VICIOUS CYCLE

Presidential Decision Making
in the American Political Economy

Constantine J. Spiliotes

Texas A&M
UNIVERSITY PRESS
College Station

The paper used in this book meets the minimum requirements
of the American National Standard for Permanence
of Paper for Printed Library Materials, Z39.48–1984.
Binding materials have been chosen for durability.
∞

For a complete list of books in this series,
please see the back of the book.

Library of Congress Cataloging-in-Publication

Spiliotes, Constantine J., 1963–
Vicious cycle : presidential decision making in the American political
economy / Constantine J. Spiliotes—1st ed.
p.   cm.—(Joseph V. Hughes, Jr., and Holly O. Hughes series in the
presidency and leadership studies ; no. 9) Includes bibliographical
references and index.
ISBN 1-58544-142-2 (cloth : alk. paper)
1. United States—Economic policy. 2. Presidents—United States.
3. Presidents—United States—Decision making. 4. Political planning—
United States. I. Title. II. Series.
HC103.S72 2002
338.973—dc21
2001002485

For my parents,
James N. and Constance Spiliotes
And for my wife,
Michelle Welsh Spiliotes

Contents

Figures

Tables

Preface

Simply stated, this book is about understanding why presidents make the decisions that they do when working within a critical policy-making domain, the American political economy. I provide a theoretical framework for broadly explaining the tradeoffs that presidents accept in pursuing partisan and electoral objectives while simultaneously seeking to soundly manage our nation's macroeconomy. In doing so, I suggest that a president's ability to respond to political incentives in the policy-making arena is powerfully shaped by the institutional imperatives each one faces as America's chief macroeconomic policy maker.

The manner in which this *institutional responsibility* has developed in the White House over the course of the past century provides important clues as to why presidents are constrained in their ability to fully pursue their political objectives once in office. I argue that, when viewed through the filter of a president's institutional responsibility for sound macroeconomic management, these political objectives are recast in ways that lead to presidential decision making that is not easily explained by existing models of presidential behavior. Presidents must reconcile the dictates of their institutional position with their roles as party leader and electorally driven political actor; it is the political tradeoffs implicit in these multiple presidential roles that *Vicious Cycle* attempts to explain.

The book has a secondary purpose. It represents an attempt to open a dialogue between scholars working in the field of political economy and scholars engaged in research in presidential studies. These fields have a wealth of insights to offer each other, but as I note in subsequent chapters, they have thus far failed to realize the full potential for each to complement the research agenda of the other. I realize that this enterprise, in particular, runs the risk of provoking many while satisfying few, yet I am undaunted in my belief that these disciplines have much to offer each other, if only clearer paths of rapprochement can be defined. My hope is that this study will clear away some of the brush from a path or two, on the way to more fruitful intellectual exchanges in the future.

To this end, part I of the book establishes the broad theoretical and empirical parameters of the study in order to better view the conditional nature of presidential decision making through the lens of institutional responsibility for effective macroeconomic management. Chapter 1 introduces the theoretical parameters of presidential decision making in the American political economy. Chapter 2 takes a close look at the first half of the twentieth century in order to uncover the origins of the stable institutional framework within which presidents have pursued their partisan and electoral macroeconomic objectives in the postwar world. The chapter does so through a consideration of competing explanations for institutional development in the presidency. The chapter ultimately highlights the role of ideas as a catalyst for the promulgation of new institutional authority for presidential decision making. Models of positive political economy all assume a stable macroeconomic policy-making environment in which a president from either party may pursue preferred targets for inflation and unemployment. Chapter 2 highlights the underlying institutional dynamics of this policy-making environment and, in doing so, suggests why competing explanations are insufficient for understanding its institutional evolution.

Chapter 3 proceeds with the construction and estimation of an econometric model designed to capture tradeoffs in partisanship and institutional responsibility. Building upon the book's consideration of current econometric models in positive political economy, the chapter offers a direct test of presidential decision making rather than relying on indirect inferences from movement in the model's other parameters. In essence, this approach opens the black box of presidential decision making to close inspection. From archival sources I construct a dependent variable that directly measures the decisions presidents make on the macroeconomy. The resultant time-series (1953–96) is then used to estimate a model of presidential decision making in the American political economy. I use a variety of data on the institutional, electoral, and macroeconomic environments in which presidents operate in order to estimate a probabilistic model of how a president's institutional responsibility shapes tradeoffs in the pursuit of partisan and electoral incentives, under varying political scenarios.

Part II tests the theoretical insights on institutional responsibility and conditional decision making derived from the aggregate models in chapter 3 through a close consideration of the postwar archival record on presidential management of the macroeconomy. In order to highlight these concepts in the historical record, the case studies proceed in two phases; this plan allows for a separate consideration of the impact of partisan and electoral incentives on presidential decision making. The choice of case studies on Presidents Eisenhower, Johnson, Carter, and Reagan offers variation across several analytic dimensions—temporal, partisan, electoral, and institutional. Chapters 4 and 5 look at how the imperatives of institutional responsibility interact with the incentive for partisan decision making faced by presidents in the macroeconomic policy-making environment. The four case studies analyze the first term of each president (when partisan and electoral incentives are strongest) in order to better explain how and when presidential behavior shifts from the expected partisan behavior. In each case, the archival record speaks with minimal interference from me or from reference to other authors' interpretations of the period under consideration. The primary source documents allow for a first-hand reconstruction of the presidential decision-making episodes under analysis.[1]

After establishing the way in which institutional responsibility mediates response to a partisan incentive for presidential decision making, the book takes a second cut at the four case studies in chapter 6. The goal here is to search the archival record for presidential responses to a political business cycle–style electoral incentive. I trace the election-year macroeconomic decision making of each of the four presidents in order to determine whether any did indeed rapidly expand the macroeconomy without regard to partisanship or institutional responsibility. The presidential intention would be to ride a wave of prosperity and voter approval to reelection.

Finally, the broader message with which the book concludes in chapter 7 is that the shift from party accountability to institutional accountability has been driven in part by a transformation in the nature of the American presidency. The institutional responsibility model extends this theoretical insight to the macroeconomic policy-making domain. Institutional responsibility causes a president's decision making to be powerfully shaped by a conflicting desire to serve as party leader and win office, while still fulfilling the institutional mandate to be the nation's chief macroeconomic policy maker. Understanding how presidents resolve this inherent conflict between political incentives and institutional constraints is central to this study and to accurately modeling presidential behavior.

Acknowledgments

My interest in the presidency and political economy owes a great deal to the time I spent at the University of Chicago. I would like to thank John Mark Hansen, Lloyd Rudolph, John Padgett, and Gerald Rosenberg for their guidance on this project and for providing me with a first-rate grounding in

American politics and political methodology. I owe a special debt of gratitude to John Mark Hansen for the direction, motivation, and friendship he has offered me both on this project and in my general development as a political scientist. I would also like to thank members of the American Politics Workshop at the University of Chicago for all of their constructive feedback on this study. I hope that it will continue to serve as an incubator for creative scholarly work in American politics for years to come.

I would also like to express my gratitude to the many professional colleagues who have been willing to read portions of this study as it evolved over time. In particular, the following individuals have helped strengthen the ideas in this book: Harold Bass, Daniel Carpenter, John Coleman, George Edwards, Anna Greenberg, Karen Hult, Michael Krukones, Ann Chih Lin, Thomas Nichols, Catherine Shapiro, James Shoch, Gordon Silverstein, John Sloan, John Theis, and Stephen Weatherford. I owe a special thanks to Stephen Weatherford for his longstanding interest in this study and for his extremely helpful comments on the complete manuscript.

My colleagues at Dartmouth College have also been instrumental in strengthening the ideas in this study. I would like to thank Linda Fowler, David Kang, Nelson Kasfir, Lynn Mather, Denis Sullivan, Dirk Vandewalle, Lynn Vavreck, and Richard Winters for their constructive feedback on the project. I would also like to thank Dartmouth colleagues who participated in the Government Department's colloquium series for their comment on portions of the manuscript. In addition, the help of several research assistants was crucial to the timely completion of this book. I would like to thank Gregory Boison, Sophia Delano, Brian Fleming, Sarah Kelly, Jennifer Parkinson, and Jacqueline Rose for their hard work as part of the Presidential Scholars program at Dartmouth. I owe Jacqueline Rose a special debt of gratitude for her outstanding contribution during a critical phase of the manuscript's development. Finally, many thanks to Kathleen Donald and Darsie Riccio for their superb administrative support of my research.

Several organizations provided generous funding for this project. I would like to thank the Andrew Mellon Foundation for two separate research grants. The Eisenhower World Affairs Institute provided generous support during my research visit to the Eisenhower Library in Abilene, Kansas.

I would also like to thank James Pfiffner, who brought my work to the attention of Texas A&M University Press, and the Press's editors, whose efforts have made the production of this book a smooth and enjoyable process, despite my occasional efforts to the contrary.

Some of the material presented in this book has appeared previously in article form in, "Partisanship and Institutional Responsibility in Presidential

Decision Making," published in the September, 2000, issue of *Presidential Studies Quarterly.*

Finally, I would like to thank my wife, Michelle Welsh Spiliotes, who has been a full partner in my every undertaking over the past seventeen years. Like so much in my life, this book would not have been possible without her advice, support, attention to detail, laughter, and patience. I owe a tremendous debt of gratitude for her tireless efforts on my behalf.

Part I
*Toward a Theory of
Institutional Responsibility
in Presidential Decision Making*

INTRODUCTION

In formulating his macroeconomic policy response to the 1954 recession, President Dwight Eisenhower remarked to his Cabinet that the time had come for "liberal action to stimulate the economy."[1] Several months later, as the recession continued, Eisenhower wrote in his personal diary that "I am convinced that the dangers of doing nothing are far greater than those of doing too much. By which I mean that everything the government can do to increase the spending power of the country . . . will, at least until there is a decided upturn in economic activity, be a good thing."[2] Eisenhower found himself in the decidedly non-Republican policy-making position of focusing on unemployment, under conditions of unified Republican government. Responding to the intense criticism from the conservative wing of the Republican Party that Eisenhower received for his macroeconomic policies, Henry Cabot Lodge, one of Eisenhower's closest political advisers, admonished the president that "you must not become the tin can tied onto the Republican tail this year."[3]

President Jimmy Carter found himself in a similar partisan predicament in the late 1970s, when forced to focus on inflation under conditions of unified Democratic government. In discussing his anti-inflation program in October, 1978, Carter commented that "further progress in reducing unemployment will depend on our success in reducing the rate of inflation. The budget that will be submitted in January will give top priority to moderating inflation."[4] It was the Republican macroeconomic logic expressed by Carter that led domestic policy chief Stuart Eizenstat to warn the president that the administration's preoccupation with inflation "gives the impression that you have adopted GOP thinking regarding the relation between federal spending and inflation in a high unemployment economy."[5]

These two anecdotal examples of presidential decision making should not strike the reader as particularly unusual. For decades, presidents have struggled with the need to stabilize the macroeconomy during moments of inflationary spiral and recessionary downturn. That decisions about these tradeoffs in inflation and unemployment involve partisan Republican and Democratic considerations is also to be expected, given the dynamics of our two-party system. Thinking about the nature of these tradeoffs as they have played out in the postwar world, however, provides an important opportunity for reconsidering presidential decision making in the American political economy.

Political economists have studied the dynamics of the "vicious cycle" for decades, through study of the political business cycle and partisan macroeconomic stabilization policy. This book builds on that research tradition and melds it with institutional research on presidential decision making in order to provide a close systematic examination of how presidents pursue tradeoffs between partisan and electoral goals, and the concomitant mandate for sound macroeconomic management. Thus, this book's contribution is a richer and more nuanced understanding of how presidential behavior as conditional partisanship actually functions. This study provides a clearer picture than we currently possess of *when* and *how* presidents shift between partisanship and the fulfillment of other macroeconomic objectives. In explicating this theory of conditional partisanship, the book underscores the ways in which the institution of the presidency acts as a filter on the pursuit of political incentives, shaping and directing the ways in which presidents pursue their macroeconomic objectives. I refer to this filtering effect throughout the book as the impact of *institutional responsibility* on presidential decision making. Much more will be said in subsequent chapters on the nature of this important institutional effect and how it constrains presidential response to partisan and electoral incentives present in the policy-making environment.

Theoretical Perspectives on Presidential Decision Making in the American Political Economy

In general, presidential decision making, as an area of substantive scholarly research, strikes an uneasy balance between the parsimony of studying a particular presidential decision and the complexity of mapping the organizational dynamics that assist in the making of that decision. Given this fundamental tension, and thus the potential scope of any model constructed to fully represent its workings, arriving at a general understanding of presidential decision making is an especially vexing task. As Karen Hult (1993) notes, this undertaking is further complicated by the fact that the dynamics of presidential decision making, both in terms of the internal structures and external environments shaping the decisions, vary substantially both within and across presidential administrations.

Simply deciding on what one means by presidential decision making and thus on the appropriate unit of analysis are difficult questions in themselves. One may consider the components that go into a presidential decision in terms of policy makers providing information, defining problems, structuring choices, generating alternatives, and communicating viewpoints. As both Hult (1993) and Paul Light (1991) note, analysis of a decision may also encompass both policy advice about the substantive content of a particular option and political advice about that option's possible impact. This is a complex definition to be sure, yet one that usefully confirms possible subsequent areas of analysis.

Given the myriad components of presidential decision making, how might one begin to generalize about the wide variety of decision-making systems and resultant outcomes visible across the presidential landscape? This book uses a combination of econometric modeling of data on presidential decisions and empirically rich case studies, developed through extensive archival research at several presidential libraries, to develop a theory of conditional partisanship in the American presidency. The theory's central goal is to employ the idea of institutional responsibility in order to account for the impact of both institutional constraints and strategic incentive-driven behavior on presidential tradeoffs between partisan objectives and management of the economy.

In developing these important ideas, the book also considers broader paradigmatic issues, such as the role of rational choice as a possible bridge between presidential studies and political economy, and the importance of the link between ideas and institutions in shaping presidential behavior.[1] My intention is that this combination of theoretical and empirical research will foster a more integrated understanding of presidential behavior, one that will appeal to both presidential scholars and political economists.

Unfortunately, a fundamental cleavage (or tension) has emerged in the literature on presidential decision making in the 1990s, one between decision making viewed as a function of presidential style, and the same behavior posited as an interaction between political incentives and institutional structures. Steven Shull (1999) provides a concrete example of this tension, as these competing perspectives coexist uneasily in an end-of-the-century assessment of presidential decision making undertaken by almost two dozen leading presidency scholars. Shull's comprehensive volume nonetheless underscores the immense difficulties that scholars of the presidency face in attempting to move toward a more organic notion of presidential behavior.

Regarding the presidential style approach, Terry Moe (1993) notes that traditional notions of the presidency pass the institutional structures of decision making through a presidential filter. The office of the presidency is viewed as highly malleable, with its structures continually redefined by subsequent presidents, as a function of an individual president's personality, values, beliefs, background, and style; presidents essentially fashion the structures of the institution in their own image.[2] The result is a highly particularized (or perhaps balkanized) understanding of presidential decision making across administrations, one that is largely resistant to theoretical generalization. To the extent that the presidential style approach may be generalized, it usually suggests that presidents select their decision-making apparatus from among a number of recognized types—formal, competitive, collegial, and so on—that best meet their needs. Charles Walcott and Karen Hult (1995) have referred to this theoretical perspective (in the specific context of presidential advising) as a *personal contingency* approach.

A number of scholarly works written in the 1970s and 1980s adopt this personal contingency (or management style) approach to explaining presidential decision making. For example, Alexander George (1980) employs a cognitive psychological approach to presidential behavior, defining it in part as a function of "character-rooted needs" and "psycho-dynamic patterns for adapting to stressful experiences." The author theorizes about presidential decision making by noting that "much of value can be learned by studying presidents from the standpoint of the fit or lack of fit between various components of personality and the different role and situational requirements of the enormously complex job of being president."[3]

Both Alexander George (1980) and Richard Tanner Johnson (1974) match these presidential personality needs with the appropriate decision-making typologies—formalist, collegial, competitive, and so forth—and map them on an administration-by-administration basis. Similarly, Roger Porter (1980) and Stephen Hess (1988) note the importance of presidential style for understanding both the way in which decision-making systems are structured and the types of presidential decisions they are likely to generate. More recently, Shirley Anne Warshaw (1997) depicts the organizational structure of domestic policy staff as a function of the level of activism that presidents express for their domestic policy agendas. The author categorizes post-Watergate domestic institutional arrangements according to whether particular presidents can be considered activists in domestic policy making (Reagan, Clinton) or not (Ford, George H. W. Bush).[4] This approach to understanding presidential advising and decision making is reminiscent of James David Barber's (1972) active and passive, positive and negative typologies for understanding presidential character or style. Most recently, Alexander George and Juliette George (1998) and Fred Greenstein (2000) update the paradigm's conceptions of leadership and performance.

In sum, these scholarly works on presidential behavior all share a common analytic thread. They posit variation in the structure and function of presidential decision making across administrations (and thus our ability to understand specific decisions) as a reflection of the management style of an individual president, as shaped by a number of prior personal cognitive and experiential factors.

In contrast, since the publication of Terry Moe's "The Politicized Presidency" in 1985 (but perhaps for quite a bit longer), the field of presidential studies has been criticized for lack of analytic rigor.[5] Moe (1997) argues that, because the traditional methods of presidential scholarship are rooted "in history, in the uniqueness of presidential personality, in the rich complexity of politics and context," the result is a lack of a logically rigorous body of theory. With institutional structures for decision making continually redefined by subsequent presidents' personalities, values, beliefs, backgrounds, and styles, the result is a body of scholarship that is highly resistant to abstraction, parsimony, and theory building.[6]

To remedy these perceived deficiencies in scholarship on the presidency, Moe suggests a two-pronged recourse to rational choice theory and the new institutionalism. Rational choice strips away the "dizzying complexity of the real world" and avoids an "endless proliferation of relevant variables" in order to build "simple, clear, logically tight models that seem to capture just the essence of what is going on."[7] The new institutionalism complements this approach by encouraging scholars to think of presidents "as types of institutional actors whose incentives are structured in particular ways (due to their institutional locations), and who can thus be expected to behave in a characteristic manner."[8] Moe (1997) and Moe and Wilson (1994) conclude that rational choice theory has been somewhat unevenly applied across the spectrum of presidential studies, with the most promising applications emanating from congressional scholarship (e.g., scholars studying the presidential veto). Most importantly, Moe notes that rational choice models may encounter significant difficulties when applied to some domains of presidential scholarship. As will be discussed shortly, this caveat applies to research on political economy as well. Prevailing models in this research tradition are both theoretically and empirically problematic.[9]

As an outgrowth of Moe's critique, an alternative approach to the study of presidential decision making has evolved, one that draws its rationale from economics, new institutionalism, and organization theory. Works in this tradition share a common critique of the presidential style perspective, claiming that it hinders systematic explanation of the political phenomena under study (Ragsdale and Rusk 1999; Moe 1993; Hult 1993). Moe in particular notes that this *methodology of personalism* attaches explanatory value to virtually everything that might influence the specific decisions of the unique human being occupying the office. This empirical overload in turn has the unfortunate effect of encouraging "explanation through history, description, anecdotes and educated judgment."[10] Hult adds that the fit between the literature on presidential decision making and social science methodology is an uncomfortable one, dominated by evaluation and prescription.[11]

This alternative approach accepts the premise that presidential structures and their decision outcomes are largely a function of strategic presidential response to incentives in the external political environment (Moe 1985, 1993; Moe and Wilson 1994; Kernell 1997; Hult 1993; Walcott and Hult 1995). In this sense, the works draw from the insights of rational choice, although some works (e.g., Walcott and Hult 1995) incorporate aspects of network theory into their research as well. As Hult (1993) notes, this approach is more parsimonious in terms of variable selection and focuses more exclusively on the relationship between presidential decision making and the external political environment. As a result, the decision-making system is cast as a function of the president's need to respond to varied exogenous incentives for policy choice, rather than as an expression of a particular cognitive and experiential background. Walcott and Hult conclude that in this analytic perspective, presidents, "rather than bringing unique bundles of style and substance to the presidency, are treated instead as rational decision makers, who seek to protect and enhance their power and effectiveness."[12]

Several authors see this need to consolidate presidential power and effectiveness as resulting in an ever-expanding White House staff, one that is highly centralized, specialized, and politicized (Moe 1985, 1993; Moe and Wilson 1994; Kernell 1997; Hart 1987). Moe (1985, 1993) notes that the increasing centralization of the White House staff shapes a decision-making apparatus that is highly responsive to the political needs of the president. Walcott and Hult (1995) accept this basic premise and then add an organizational component to the analysis by focusing on the White House advisory networks that link actors at several levels, particularly below the top echelon of staff. Their goal is to show how the complexity of White House advisory networks acts as a constraint to presidential decision making by shaping both perceptions of, and responses to, the external political environment.

So where does this cleavage in current research leave us in our understanding of the dynamics of presidential decision making? The rational choice perspective has had an undeniable impact on how scholars conceptualize the problem. It has allowed more efficient theorizing about presidential behavior across administrations and moved us away from *sui generis* explanations of the presidency. Most importantly for understanding decision making, it tells us that to explain variation among presidents, we must necessarily explain the impact of the external political environment on the form and function of institutional structures for decision making. Thus, it is the relationship between *exogenous* political incentive and *endogenous* institutional structure that directly affects presidential decision making.

This book takes the above premise a step further by arguing that this interaction is manifested (and thus most efficiently studied) in an effect often referred to in the presidency literature as *institutional responsibility;* this effect acts as a filter on presidential response to partisan and electoral incentives. The interaction does so by producing an institutional incentive for responsible decision making. Presidential response to this incentive may occur at the moment when current theories would predict that presidents focus on exogenously generated incentives for decision making, such as reelection or legislative consensus with core partisans in Congress (Spiliotes 2000). *The result is a disjunction between policy expectation and presidential decision.*

Presidents may still pursue partisan goals and reelection, but the strategies employed to do so, and the decisions emanating from them, are constrained by their institutional mandate for sound macroeconomic management. Presidential decisions regarding partisan and electoral objectives are thus necessarily recast in light of the need for effective stabilization of the economy; a president's political success becomes intimately tied to success in fulfilling this institutionally defined role. This is precisely the circumstance illustrated by the Eisenhower and Carter anecdotes in my introduction to part I of this book. Both presidents are seen struggling with the difficult political tradeoffs implicit in trying to satisfy party and electorate, while exercising sound stewardship of the economy. This book explores the nature of that ongoing struggle by more precisely defining the contours of institutional responsibility, both in terms of its origins and its imperatives for presidential decision making in the context of macroeconomic policy making. This study thus helps us to better conceptualize the president's role in theories of conditional partisanship suggested by the political economy research of the past several decades.

Presidential Decision Making and Political Economy

One may ask why the scope of this book should be limited to stabilization policy, and particularly to decision-making tradeoffs in levels of inflation and unemployment. Indeed, M. Stephen Weatherford and Lorraine McDonnell make a compelling case for broadening the study of economic policy making to include issues of allocation and distribution rather than for adopting a more traditional narrow research focus on stabilization policy. The authors also note, however, that stabilizing the economy is a "necessary evil" for presidents, particularly during times of macroeconomic crisis.[13] I will argue that this notion of "decision making as necessary evil" most closely links presidential response to political incentives with the idea of institutional responsibility. During times of recessionary downturn and inflationary spiral, presidents are forced to make decisions that most clearly bring the constraints of their institutional position into focus. As Paul Mosley (1984) notes in the comparative context of Great Britain and the United States, leaders often have no option but to act, however ineffective their decisions may be, or risk detrimental policy, partisan, and electoral consequences. These constraints in turn exert tremendous force on presidential behavior in the policy-making environment. So the narrow focus on stabilization in this study is intentional. It provides an efficient means of isolating the presidential behavior of interest.

Political economists have long theorized that two key political incentives, partisanship and reelection, motivate presidential decision making in the macroeconomic policy-making arena. Scholars working in the rational partisan and political business cycle research traditions have employed these fundamental assumptions about presidential behavior to construct sophisticated models of both the American and international political economies. As such, in the realm of political economy, they come closest to Moe's notion of a rational choice model of presidential behavior. These models are rigorous and parsimonious in specification, abstract and generalizable in their results. They therefore serve as the perfect methodological foil for presidential studies. This rational choice literature, along with additional insights from the new institutionalism, provides the basis for exploring the idea of institutional responsibility. Through this type of synthesis, we can define a more generalizable understanding of an otherwise familiar policy-making terrain, so that the Eisenhower and Carter anecdotes that introduced part I of this book can be integrated into a broader theoretical understanding of presidential behavior.

Before turning to the political economy literature, however, I must be clear that this book *makes no claims to uncovering the vicious cycle implicit in the functioning of our macroeconomy;* as shown herein, political economists have studied its dynamics under various names consistently for decades. My goal in revisiting the relevant political economy literatures is simply to establish a framework in which to turn the theoretical lens on one institutional actor, the president. Thus, the goal of this study is to theorize systematically about how the president struggles with the difficult political tradeoffs implicit in the postwar cycling of inflation and unemployment. This is not a question currently addressed in the literatures on political economy and on presidential decision making; it therefore presents important theoretical and empirical lacunae to be filled.

One type of political incentive for presidential decision making is found in research on rational partisan theory. The basic partisan cycle model has been developed primarily through the work of Douglas Hibbs (1977, 1983, 1986, 1987, and 1994), Nathaniel Beck (1982a, 1982b), and Henry Chappell, Jr., and William Keech (1986a, 1986b). Following Hibbs (1977, 1986, and 1987), the American partisan cycle model theorizes that Democratic and Republican administrations are ideologically polarized and accordingly pursue macroeconomic policies designed to serve the socioeconomic interests of their core partisan constituencies. Hibbs (1977) notes the close connections between the Democratic Party, organized labor, and lower income and occupational status groups, while the Republican Party is depicted as highly responsive to the interests of business and upper income and occupational status groups. Hibbs (1986, 1987) argues that as a result of these divergent clientele, Democratic administrations are likely to pursue expansionary policies targeting lower levels of unemployment while tolerating relatively higher levels of inflation. In contrast, Republican administrations target lower levels of inflation, at the risk of increasing the level of unemployment. These partisan cleavages in macroeconomic policy making are said to persist throughout the duration of the four-year cycle, hence the idea of a partisan cycle in which presidential decisions on macroeconomic policies targeting unemployment and inflation are largely a function of partisan affiliation. Beck (1982a, 1982b) is critical of the early work on the partisan cycle model, arguing that Hibbs greatly overestimates the magnitude of partisan effects on the level of unemployment. More importantly, he claims that individual administration is a better predictor of the unemployment rate than is partisan affiliation.

Chappell and Keech (1986a, 1986b) resolve some of the initial debate over partisan cycles by noting that both Hibbs and Beck focus on aggregate macroeconomic outcomes rather than on policy instruments. Chappell and Keech (1986a) argue that this approach is misleading, as it does not account for the lags between policy implementation and outcome or for exogenous shocks to the macroeconomy that may obscure systematic partisan cleavages in decision making. Chappell and Keech (1986a) suggest that partisan cycles should first be evident in the paths of policy instruments, before any inferences can be drawn from movement in macroeconomic indicators. Chappell and Keech (1986b) extend this analysis to a spatial model of two-party competition in which political constraints on the issue space result in administrations pursuing a range of macroeconomic outcomes that fall somewhere between a pure Downsian vote-optimizing strategy and a pure partisan cycle strategy. Voters are faced with clear partisan choices, yet the administration's need to win swing votes constrains the distinctiveness of those choices toward the ideological center.

Finally, Hibbs (1994) builds on his earlier work by testing a revised partisan cycle model. He finds that, while partisan cleavages in aggregate demand policy do exist (i.e., Democrats are more expansionary than Republicans), earlier empirical work erred in imposing immutable partisan objectives on that policy.[14] Hibbs (1994) concludes that partisan preferences for macroeconomic outcomes are actually variable and also respond forcefully to the acceleration of inflation.[15]

As an extension of the partisan cycle model, the partisan business cycle model attempts to combine theoretical insights about changes in voter uncertainty and the accuracy of rational expectations calculations with the partisan and electoral incentives facing institutional actors such as the president and Congress. The goal is a more empirically realistic model of macroeconomic policy making in the business cycle. The partisan business cycle model has been developed largely through the work of Alberto Alesina (1987, 1988, 1991), Alesina and J. Sachs (1988), Alesina, John Londregan, and Howard Rosenthal (1993), and Alesina and Rosenthal (1989, 1995). Alesina (1987, 1988) follows Hibbs (1977, 1986, 1987) in theorizing that parties care about policy content, particularly as it affects core partisan constituencies.

In contrast to Hibbs, however, Alesina (1987, 1988) argues that the unemployment-inflation (Phillips curve) tradeoff is a short-term one, due to the ability of rational forward-looking wage-setters to anticipate surprise inflationary expansion by the policy maker. Economic agents recognize the electoral incentive facing the administration; they counter their own pre-election uncertainty about the partisan identity (and hence Phillips curve preferences) of the next president by setting the nominal wage sufficiently high to eliminate any incentive for the new president to generate surprise inflation upon assuming office. The result of this rational expectations behavior is not the consistent long-term partisan cleavages predicted by Hibbs. Instead, a partisan business cycle results, in which recessions are observed during the first two years of Republican administrations, while Democratic administrations exhibit above average growth and higher inflation in the first half of their terms. In the second half of both types of administrations, no substantial differences in unemployment and output are observed. Thus, the partisan business cycle posits that partisan cycles in macroeconomic outcomes are a transitory phenomenon, largely confined to the first two years of a presidential administration.

Building upon this initial model of the partisan business cycle, Alesina and Rosenthal (1989, 1995) and Alesina, Londregan, and Rosenthal (1993) integrate the cycle into a full-scale model of the American political economy. The macroeconomic side of the model employs the same rational expectations argument as Alesina (1987, 1988) regarding the ability of forward-looking wage-setters to dissipate the partisan cycle over time. The expanded model, however, also focuses particular attention on the role of voters and midterm elections as a means of introducing institutional considerations into the model. In Alesina and Rosenthal (1989), the macroeconomic outcomes of the partisan business cycle are placed in an institutional context in which voters first choose between two polarized presidential candidates in the general election, in keeping with the idea of partisan cleavages during the first half of an administration. Voters then use midterm elections to counterbalance the president's partisan macroeconomic behavior by strengthening the opposition in Congress. Alesina and Rosenthal (1989, 1995) follow Chappell and Keech (1986a, 1986b) in highlighting the importance of swing voters and their pivotal moderating influence on the extremes of both parties' macroeconomic behavior. This circumstance facilitates the practice of institution balancing at the midterm election. The logical conclusion drawn from this process of institution balancing is that divided government has a moderating effect on a president's partisanship.

Scholars have also theorized that presidents make use of their unique institutional authority over macroeconomic policy making to opportunistically manipulate the business cycle for electoral gain. A large body of econometric literature on the resultant "political business cycle" has yielded mixed empirical results, based upon analysis of patterns of movement in economic indicators. The political business cycle model posits an incumbent who is solely motivated by the desire for reelection. The president, showing little regard for ideological consistency, manipulates macroeconomic policy in order to rapidly boost the economy prior to reelection. The model's theoretical structure leaves no doubt that the president, rather than the party's other institutional actors, is working the policy levers of the political business cycle. The president's strategic calculus is to provide voters with a positive macroeconomic rationale for granting a second term in office.

William Nordhaus (1975) and C. Duncan MacRae (1977) provide early representations of the political business cycle. Nordhaus (1975) notes that, due to a lag in the tradeoff between unemployment and inflation, the short-term impact of presidential tinkering with the macroeconomy is realized primarily in increased economic growth. In essence, presidents can enjoy the short-term benefits of decreased unemployment in an election year and not have to confront the lagged increase in inflation until shortly after reelection. This phenomenon represents a powerful incentive for strategic behavior by the president. For the United States, Nordhaus detects traces of the political business cycle in the annual unemployment rates for five postwar presidential election years. He concludes that a president's term in office (regardless of partisan affiliation) has a predictable pattern of macroeconomic policy making, one that begins with relative austerity in early years and ends with booming economic growth just before reelection. MacRae (1977) also looks at the pattern of inflation and unemployment in the United States for roughly the same postwar period and detects a similar political business cycle effect for two presidential election years.

Bruno Frey (1978), Frey and Friedrich Schneider (1975, 1978, 1979), and Edward Tufte (1978) all expand upon the original model. Frey and Schneider (1978) test a political business cycle model for the postwar United States and find that the likelihood of presidential reelection is significantly improved by an increase in the growth rate of private consumption. Frey and Schneider theorize that when the probability of reelection is low presidents expand the economy in order to enhance their chances of winning. The authors add the provocative theoretical coda that incumbents pursue partisan policies when reelection is likely, regardless of the relative popularity of the measures in the electorate.

Tufte (1978) also finds political business cycle activity in the postwar period, citing a downturn in the unemployment rate in the year preceding a presidential election and a subsequent upturn in the rate approximately twelve to eighteen months after the election. Tufte posits that these cycles are driven by an increase in transfer payments (e.g., Social Security, veterans benefits, and so forth) in the year preceding a presidential election. These transfers directly and immediately affect real disposable income, providing presidents with the quickest path to voters' pocketbooks. Tufte concludes his depiction of the four-year cycle by noting that incumbents often undertake deflationary policies as their first priority after reelection.

Following this initial development of the political business cycle model, researchers began to question both the theoretical specification and empirical findings of the model. David Golden and James Poterba (1980), William Keech (1980) and James Alt and K. Alec Chrystal (1983) raise a number of issues about the viability of political business cycle models. Golden and Poterba (1980) estimate models for fiscal policy, monetary policy, and transfer payments and find no convincing evidence of political business cycle behavior by the president. They tie this result to the limited ability of presidents to directly manipulate the macroeconomy, even if their preference for such an outcome is strong. Keech (1980) analyzes similar empirical data and also finds limited evidence that presidents can engage in what he terms a cyclical vote-optimizing strategy. Finally, Alt and Chrystal conclude their analysis of the model with the often-quoted remark, "No one could read the political business cycle literature without being struck by the lack of supporting evidence."[16]

Given the mixed empirical results of full-scale political business cycle models, cyclical research has fragmented into fiscal and monetary branches. For example, David Lowery (1985) tests for a postwar cycle in the budgetary surplus/deficit and finds no conclusive evidence of political business cycle activity. In contrast, Beck, Kevin Grier, and John Williams find varying levels of cyclical activity in the movement of M1 (Beck 1987; Grier 1989) and interest rates (Williams 1990). While the authors conclude that presidential elections seem to enhance macroeconomic performance in the short term, the authors have difficulty linking the monetary cycle to presidential manipulation of monetary policy instruments.

Finally, Kenneth Schultz (1995) attempts to improve the political business cycle's mixed empirical results by respecifying the strategic interests of key institutional actors. Schultz employs data for Great Britain (1961–92) to argue that the incentives facing incumbents vary from one election to the next. He ties this variation to the degree of electoral security enjoyed by the incumbent. Incumbents facing difficult reelection battles have a much greater incentive to induce electorally profitable macroeconomic cycles than do those who are secure in their positions. Schultz's insight that the incentives shaping incumbent behavior may vary over the course of an administration works well with the idea that presidential preferences react to changing political incentives and constraints over the course of a four-year term.

Despite the intellectual appeal of these models, for several reasons they have not fully supplanted more traditional presidential scholarship on economic policy making. Although these models describe the dynamic relationship between electorate, presidential decision, and macroeconomic outcome from a powerful econometric perspective, they have responded to empirical tests with mixed results. In fact, most of the effort expended on them in the 1980s and 1990s has focused on respecification of general parameters, without marked improvement in the results.

The inconclusive empirical results generated by estimation of these models illustrate a fundamental conceptual problem. The models' three key components (vote, decision maker, and economy) are unbalanced in terms of the respective emphasis focused on each component. As Lowery (1985) notes, political scientists (due, in part, to the constraints imposed by quantitative data analysis) have almost exclusively dedicated their energies to the first component (the vote), studying how and why voters respond to economic stimuli. Similarly, economists have focused on the third component (the economy), engaging in theoretical and econometric refinements of the relationship between decisions about levels of macroeconomic instruments and aggregate macroeconomic conditions.

The underlying problem for the rational choice approach employed in these models is that the president's decision making behavior must be inferred from the models' parameters or included as part of the initial set of assumptions made in order to proceed with model estimation. Although movement in macroeconomic policy instruments and indicators is detected, presidential decision making, which intervenes to transform the models' partisan and electoral inputs into macroeconomic outputs, is essentially concealed in the proverbial black box. Political incentives may indeed be significant determinants of presidential decision making, but the models theorize about these incentives by looking only at movement in aggregate economic indicators, not at the decisions themselves. I will address this issue later in the study by incorporating the insights of extensive archival work on presidential decisions into the econometric model presented in chapter 3.

Nonetheless, the literature in positive political economy provides an important starting point for our consideration of how a president's institutional responsibility for the macroeconomy interacts with the partisan and electoral incentives for behavior that are present in the policy-making environment. Most importantly, these models establish that the nature of a president's response to partisan and electoral incentives is *conditional*. The models (particularly the recent ones) underscore the idea that presidential preferences over target levels of inflation and unemployment are variable rather than fixed. At some moments during their administrations, presidents may have the ability to single-mindedly pursue macroeconomic policy outcomes that favor their core partisan constituencies. At other moments, it may become clear to the president that narrowly pursuing partisan objectives at the expense of other broad macroeconomic concerns is a losing electoral strategy. After all, a president's broad heterogeneous reelection constituency ultimately encompasses a greater cross section of the populace than a single partisan base. The president may then select a decision-making strategy that emphasizes macroeconomic targets and instruments that are *not* in keeping with core partisan objectives. As will be argued later in this study, it is at these moments that the relationship between partisanship and institutionally responsible decision making is at its most tenuous. Still, at other times presidents may respond to the electoral incentive in a very straightforward manner; they may simply choose a short-term boost to the economy along the lines suggested by the decision-making calculus of the political business cycle.

The key intuition to take from these models is that the president pursues a variety of partisan and electoral objectives in a relatively stable macroeconomic policy-making environment. The question of how this stable policy-making environment developed during the first half of the twentieth century, and thus facilitated the postwar partisan macroeconomic cycling described in the models, is addressed at length from theoretical and historical perspectives in chapter 2. First, however, a bit more must be said about the theoretical parameters of institutional responsibility.

Presidential Decision Making and Institutional Responsibility

We have now seen several competing approaches to presidential decision making. On balance, these approaches provide useful insights but result in some difficulty for anyone attempting to generalize about presidential behavior. At bottom, there appears to be an intellectual divide between presidency scholars and political economists. As a result, the potential of these two research traditions to inform each other has largely gone unrealized in political science, due in part to significant disagreement over theoretical scope and analytic method.

As we have seen in the literatures discussed above, presidential scholars and political economists traditionally ask very different questions about the same presidential phenomena, empirically testing hypotheses with a broad range of methodological tools. Instead of fostering a vibrant intellectual catholicity in the study of the presidency and political economy, however, the two research traditions have spent several decades largely speaking past each other. Presidential scholars claim that research in political economy is too theoretically abstract, mathematical, and intellectually austere, ultimately failing to capture the rich and dynamic empirical reality of presidential behavior and institutions. Political economists counter that presidential scholarship is too anecdotal, lacking in analytic rigor and systematic theory building.

My hope is that the theoretical framework of institutional responsibility developed in this study will connect presidential studies and positive political economy in ways that lead to a more comprehensive theoretical and empirical picture of presidential behavior. As I argue elsewhere (Spiliotes 2000), political economy research, such as work in rational partisan theory and the political business cycle, produces econometric models that are constructed upon useful but fundamentally limiting assumptions about presidential behavior. Given their overwhelming focus on technical precision in econometric modeling, positive political economists have traditionally had little motivation to undertake the sort of archival work engaged in by presidential scholars, work that would allow for more empirically rich and nuanced assumptions about presidential behavior.

Thus, the detailed and extensively documented archival work presented in this book is undertaken with a specific goal in mind. I will argue, using insights from the archival record, that when the filter of institutional responsibility is applied to rational choice models of presidential decision making, presidents can be viewed making significant and sometimes surprising tradeoffs in policy objectives. These tradeoffs are of particular interest to presidency scholars because they are often at cross-purposes with the partisan and electoral incentives driving models in positive political economy. The president's need to be seen as a responsible macroeconomic manager recasts the electoral incentive from partisanship and/or stimulation to largely one of macroeconomic stabilization.

From a decision-making perspective, this circumstance underscores the conditional nature of presidential behavior suggested by some positive political economy models, yet it also provides us with an opportunity to more directly study the actual parameters of presidential behavior. While accepting the conditional nature of presidential behavior as a given from prior research in political economy, this study is more centrally concerned with the actual *when* and *how* of presidential strategies implicit in conditional decision-making behavior. In employing the filter of institutional responsibility, this study demonstrates that empirically rich assumptions about presidential behavior (of the sort employed by presidency scholars) can thus have a significant impact on systematic research in political economy.

A Theory of Institutional Responsibility

Several scholars have argued that presidents, by virtue of the ever-increasing responsibilities inherent in their office, are sometimes required to take autonomous action (Moe and Wilson 1994; Kernell 1997). These decisions may be highly incompatible with the interests of other institutional actors. Moe and Wilson note that for presidents, their heterogeneous national constituency "leads them to think in grander terms about social problems and the public interest, and to resist specialized appeals. . . . They are more fundamentally concerned with governance."[17] So, while presidential behavior is in one sense shaped by response to political incentives, it is at times motivated by the need to make decisions that are not in keeping with a purely strategic rational calculation. This perspective is a reflection of all presidents' need to respond to formidable public expectations and to seek control over the structures and processes of government that will enable them to better meet those expectations (Kernell 1997; Moe 1985).

Paradoxically, presidents demonstrate strong leadership by doing what is *unpopular* in a given circumstance. As Moe and Wilson note, presidents need to "show the way" by charting new paths for the populace, even when these paths do not appear to be the most strategically appropriate. The authors conclude that to fulfill their institutionally defined role, presidents "have to demonstrate their true mettle by being selectively *unresponsive* and showing their autonomy."[18] John Burke (1992) similarly notes the importance of institutionally defined roles for presidential behavior. Thus, although presidential behavior may be fine-tuned to strategic political needs, there are also times when presidents instead respond to an institutional incentive for autonomous (and even unpopular) action.

Scholars studying the institutionalization of the American presidency often note that during the postwar period the president has developed a number of policy responsibilities that were not contemplated for the institution prior to the Great Depression and the New Deal (Cohen 1997; Ragsdale and Theis 1997). Several of these scholars have focused on the development of the president's responsibility for the nation's macroeconomic health during the Great Depression and following the adoption of the Employment Act of 1946 (Stein 1988, 1996; Walcott and Hult 1995; Keech 1995; Frendreis and Tatalovich 1994; Anderson and Hazleton 1986; Sundquist 1981; Rossiter 1960). These scholars suggest that since presidents are assigned primary statutory responsibility for the nation's economic health, they are compelled by their institutionally defined role to act to stabilize the economy in the face of inflationary spiral and recessionary downturn (Stein 1988, 1996; Anderson and Hazleton 1986; Sundquist 1981; Rossiter 1960). This institutional growth in the American presidency has largely had the effect of strengthening the president's hand in pursuing policy-making objectives. The expanded institutional authority has given the president a host of new policy-making instruments with which to respond to the partisan and electoral incentives present in the political environment.

In light of these augmented presidential powers, public expectations of institutional responsibility are increasingly central to strategic presidential behavior (Keech 1995; Frendreis and Tatalovich 1994; Anderson and Hazleton 1986; Edwards 1983). In contrast to the incentive-driven behavior depicted in both the political business cycle and rational partisan theories, institutional responsibility suggests that any incentive for presidential decision making is closely tied to the response of the institution in dealing with the macroeconomy. It reflects the interests of a president's institutional position and partisan or electoral needs.

This transformation in presidential behavior is the result of a need to meet heightened public expectations for stabilization, brought on by the president's central institutional responsibility for the macroeconomy. In these circumstances, the expectations of the heterogeneous national constituency exert pressure on the office holder's policy making, thus reinforcing the president's need to be seen as institutionally responsible for the macroeconomy. The electoral incentive is still present, but it has been recast to reflect a president's relative success at macroeconomic stewardship. Reelection to a second term does not truncate this institutional filter on the electoral incentive; if anything, it should magnify the effect. In a second term, presidents are much more concerned with how history will hold them accountable for the office.

Institutional arrangements (as touched on in the partisan business cycle literature) such as divided government may further influence the pull of institutional responsibility. Under divided government, it is much more difficult for the electorate to hold the president responsible for the condition of the economy, particularly if blame can be affixed to the opposition in Congress. In contrast, unified control is particularly symbolic for raising the electorate's expectations of institutional responsibility for fighting inflationary spiral and recessionary downturn.

In sum, institutional responsibility may significantly shape the options for presidential response to exogenous political incentives, such as reelection and partisanship. *The result is that the vicious cycle, often captured in models of positive political economy, can be recast as a cycle in which presidential decision making fluctuates between the vicissitudes of partisan and electoral fortunes. The nature of this decision making is significantly shaped by the imperatives of a president's institutional position.* Unpacking the theoretical and empirical parameters of this presidential behavior is the central task of this study, one that will complement our current understanding of the dynamics of the macroeconomic policy-making system.

Given these considerations, I construct a model of presidential decision making at the intersection of presidential studies and positive political economy. I offer a consideration of postwar macroeconomic stabilization policy in order to answer the question of how the institutionally defined imperatives of the American presidency shape presidential decision making in an incentive-driven policy-making environment. To answer this question, the book employs the idea (underutilized as a theoretical construct in previous studies of presidential decision making) of *institutional responsibility* in the presidency. This represents a decision-making nexus in which the presidential mandate to make responsible policy often shapes the ways in which core partisan and electoral constituencies will be served. Presidents may even engage in tradeoffs that temporarily appropriate the decision-making logic of the opposition, if it is determined to be beneficial to their institutional position and electoral needs.

Understanding the impact of institutional responsibility on decision making is therefore crucial to unlocking the logic of presidential behavior in the *vicious cycle*, both in terms of capturing the cycling in the macroeconomy and in understanding the decision-making logic that presidents employ in addressing those conditions. This study thus allows the reader to better grasp the dynamics of presidential decisions on the macroeconomy, decisions that may involve fiscal austerity during a reelection year or massive public works spending in conjunction with balanced budget rhetoric. Political incentives alone cannot explain these behaviors; the answers require a close consideration of how the institutionally defined policy-making role of presidents fundamentally shapes their response to those incentives.

In developing the idea of institutional responsibility, I bring a systematic and methodologically rigorous theoretical framework to bear on the historically rich archival work often associated with presidential studies. As a by-product of this approach, the book also engages the broader methodological debate raging among American politics scholars over the uneasy relationship between presidential studies and rational choice. My intention is that this study serve as an example of how presidential studies can be more effectively integrated into broader research traditions in the social sciences.

The Evolution of the President as Macroeconomic Policy Maker, 1908–46

The two statements below were written a mere twenty-five years apart, but they are light-years apart in their implications for the institutional responsibility of the president. The first statement, from 1921, is by President Warren G. Harding: "There has been vast unemployment before and there will be again. There will be depression and inflation just as surely as the tides ebb and flow. I would have little enthusiasm for any proposed remedy that seeks either palliation or tonic from the Public Treasury."[1] The second statement is from the Employment Act of 1946, signed into law by President Harry S. Truman: "It is the continuing policy and responsibility of the Federal Government to use all practicable means consistent with its needs and obligations and other essential considerations of national policy . . . to coordinate and utilize all its plans, functions and resources . . . to foster and promote free competitive enterprise and the general welfare . . . and to promote maximum employment, production, and purchasing power."[2]

This chapter provides an understanding of how the macroeconomic mission of the presidency was transformed in such short order, from an institution with no interest in moderating the boom and bust of the vicious cycle to one with ongoing postwar institutional responsibility for the nation's economic health.

It is critical to note for the models estimated in chapter 3 that the positive political economy models discussed in chapter 1 all assume that postwar presidents function in a relatively stable institutional environment, one that provides them with the fiscal authority to pursue their macroeconomic agendas. Yet the models also depict the partisan content of policy decisions as being variable across presidential administrations; Democratic and Republican presidents consistently make divergent policy decisions when acting to stabilize fluctuations in macroeconomic conditions. I explain these results here by placing the political phenomena of postwar institutional stability and partisan decision making in the broader context of a president's augmented institutional responsibility for macroeconomic policy making. In doing so, I establish an institutional framework within which to situate the model of presidential decision making tested in subsequent chapters.

Competing Explanations for Institutional Development

Given these theoretical assumptions, two key institutional questions can be formulated for analysis. First to be considered is the question of how the presidency developed this institutional responsibility for macroeconomic policy making. Second is the question of how this responsibility evolved over time into a postwar institutional arrangement for macroeconomic policy making that is largely stable across presidential administrations and that leads to policy decisions exhibiting various levels of partisanship over time.

As previously mentioned, this chapter answers these questions through a consideration of the crucial period of institutional development for macroeconomic policy making that occurred during the years between 1908 and 1946. This period saw the presidency transformed from an institution possessing virtually no authority over macroeconomic policy to one that was gradually legislated ongoing responsibility for implementing policies designed to address the nation's economic health. It will be shown that by the time the development of this institutional responsibility was complete in 1946, the macroeconomic policy debate had shifted from questions of institutional responsibility (clearly belonging to the president) to consideration of the partisan content of the policies produced by that fixed institutional arrangement. Establishing this fixed institutional arrangement for the postwar period will allow for the assessment in subsequent chapters of the political and economic parameters of conditional partisan decision making in the appropriate institutional context.

Before turning to this period, however, a consideration of several theories of institutional development in the presidency will highlight the deficiencies in these explanations for the rise of presidential responsibility in macroeconomic policy making. I then propose an alternative explanation of this institutional growth to better explain the expansion of presidential responsibility for performance of the macroeconomy. This theory improves upon the others by explicitly linking the development of presidential responsibility for macroeconomic policy making—and the institutional structures that translate that responsibility into policy decisions—to macroeconomic paradigms.

In this chapter, I use the words "logic," "paradigm," and "calculus" interchangeably to represent any system of macroeconomic thought that offers the president a means of thinking about decision making. I will, however, avoid the more ambiguous (and loaded) term "ideology" in this instance. These concepts should be broadly understood to signify an overarching intellectual construct or paradigm of the functioning of the macroeconomy (e.g., budget balancing, stagnationism, Keynesianism, and so forth), within which political actors define a range of acceptable policy decisions, given the need to address particular macroeconomic outcomes (e.g., inflation, recession, and depression).

Most theories of institutional development ignore the nexus between institution and paradigm, focusing instead on the administrative struggle between the presidency and Congress for control of institutional prerogatives. I argue in this chapter that the development of a president's institutional responsibility for macroeconomic management is actually due more to the impact of ascendant macroeconomic paradigms than to interbranch conflict over institutional control of the policy-making apparatus.

Following these theoretical considerations, I use the idea of institutional responsibility to empirically reinterpret the 1908–46 period in three sections. The first section covers the years 1908–32 and focuses on the Progressives' campaign for a federal budget based on the logic of balanced budgets, economy, and efficiency. This section demonstrates that once this interaction of paradigm and institution was formalized in the Budget and Accounting Act of 1921, it shaped institutional development and macroeconomic policy decisions for the next decade in ways that cannot be explained by recourse to the other theories.

The second section of the empirical work presented in this chapter encompasses the years 1933–39 and considers the relationship between the development of New Deal institutions for macroeconomic policy making and changing conceptions of macroeconomic logic in the presidency. In particular, this section reinterprets the executive branch reorganization movement of 1937–39, in light of the need for policy makers to select from among the competing macroeconomic paradigms of the time.

Finally, the third section of the chapter studies the reconversion debate during the years 1940–46. The section demonstrates that the development and acceptance of stabilization theory dominated paradigmatic considerations, shifting the macroeconomic policy debate permanently away from issues of institutional responsibility (now firmly situated in the presidency) and toward the partisan content of presidential decision making. This reinterpretation of the reconversion debate makes explicit the genesis of the institutional stability ushered in by the Employment Act of 1946. It thus establishes the necessary institutional framework for the aggregate models estimated in the next chapter.

For each of the three sections in the narrative below, I draw extensively from the wealth of historical monographs documenting the period, rather than present addition archival material of the type presented in chapters 4, 5, and 6. My goal is simply to provide a persuasive reinterpretation of an already heavily documented institutional history. The chapter provides a cogent theory of institutional development that accounts for each of the critical periods mentioned above. I depict the rise of institutional responsibility for macroeconomic policy making as the product of an ongoing interaction between evolving macroeconomic paradigms for decision making and institutional structures designed to achieve those ends. This evolution has had a profound impact on how we understand the incentives and constraints shaping presidential decision making in the American political economy.

Theories of Institutional Development

There are three general types of theoretical explanation that can be applied to the development of a president's institutional responsibility for macroeconomic policy making. These are labeled herein as theories of *administrative control, presidential organization,* and *political development.* The basic tenets of each are discussed below.

Theories of administrative control argue that as the reach of the federal government into the private sector expands, the growth and control of the administrative state is solidified in the executive branch through an increasing rationalization of bureaucratic functions, directly or indirectly under the control of the president (Marini 1992). Scholarship in this tradition (e.g., Marini 1992 and Pemberton 1979) depicts the growth of institutional responsibility in the presidency as occurring at the expense of the legislature, usually as the result of an interbranch struggle over institutional prerogatives.

Interpretations within this rubric vary in assigning political motives to the growth of administrative control. Some scholars talk about the rise of a "managerial" presidency, in which the bureaucratic rationalization of institutional structures is primarily a function of the desire for increased administrative economy and efficiency in overseeing a rapidly expanding repertoire of governmental functions (Hart 1987; Hess 1988; Karl 1963). This approach views key moments of institutional development, such as the adoption of the federal budget system in 1921, the creation of the Executive Office of the President in 1939, and the establishment of the Council of Economic Advisers under the Employment Act of 1946, as part of an ongoing process that makes government function in a more rational and efficient administrative fashion. The development of the president's institutional responsibility for a particular policy domain is depicted as an administrative necessity rather than as a political strategy.

In contrast, other theories of administrative control view these same developments as part of a strategic attempt by the president to institutionalize control over the policy-making arena in a way that increases the probability of being able to implement a particular political agenda. John Marini (1992) and William Pemberton (1979) emphasize a struggle between the president and legislature for control of the policy-making apparatus in which both sides are cognizant of the strategic importance of institutional responsibility for realizing preferred policy decisions. Further, Pemberton notes that the institutional tools of fiscal policy, such as the budget, are viewed as a means by which the president can control the influence of outside interests on Congress and the bureaucracy.[3] In this way, the president maintains an institutional advantage in the implementation and management of macroeconomic policy initiatives.

Regardless of the degree to which theories of administrative control ascribe managerial or strategic motives to the development of the president's institutional responsibility, they possess a common deficiency. These theories cannot account for the institutional form that the president's responsibility for macroeconomic policy making takes at a given historical moment. They only depict the reach of the president's institutional responsibility in terms of the rate at which that responsibility has accrued over time, through legislative struggles over the right to control newly evolving policy-making areas. In essence, the theories provide content-neutral explanations.

Theories of administrative control allow one to gauge the strength of a president's institutional responsibility without being able to explain the implications of that responsibility for policy decisions. For example, the preparation of a budget implies certain policy decisions for the president that would not necessarily be the case given other mechanisms of institutional control. Similarly, the Council of Economic Advisers produces policy options for the president that often differ from those emanating from other advisory bodies. The point missed by these theories is that institutional structures for macroeconomic policy making, and the institutional responsibility governing them, spring from ideas about the macroeconomy that direct their development. It is not a question of who possesses administrative control but is instead one of why that control is defined in a particular way, to the exclusion of competing conceptions, and of what a particular conception implies for the range of possible macroeconomic policy decisions.

Theories of presidential organization, in contrast, explain presidential decisions by reference to presidential style or character. Following Neustadt (1990), Barber (1972), and Hess (1988), they posit the institutionalized form of presidential responsibility as being a function of the unique organizational style of individual presidents. Theories of presidential organization are prevalent among scholars studying institutional patterns in the New Deal. For example, following Hess (1988) and Richard Polenberg (1966), some scholars explain the disjunction between the chaotic organization of early New Deal measures and the subsequent reorganization of the executive branch in 1939 by reference to the evolution of Franklin Roosevelt's style of presidential management. Thus, these scholars view the development of the president's institutional responsibility for macroeconomic policy making over time as being determined by the managerial style of successive presidents.

The drawback to theories of presidential organization is that they permit one to talk only about individual presidents rather than about the presidency as an institutional construct. Scholars are constrained to *sui generis* explanations of institutional development during particular presidential administrations. Thus, one is prevented from generalizing effectively about the relationship between the presidency and institutional development over time. Since a general theory of the evolution of institutional responsibility is the goal of this chapter, theories of presidential organization are not particularly useful for developing a causal explanation. If, as is argued here, macroeconomic paradigms direct the development of institutional responsibility, the need to transcend a particular president's behavior is imperative.

Theories of political development, according to Stephen Skowronek (1982), depict the growth of institutional authority as an act of "creative destruction." The political development perspective traverses the same state-building terrain as theories of administrative control, yet it posits a very different process of institutional development. For example, Skowronek claims that the growth of administrative controls in the executive branch was not intended to make the state more efficient and that this process of institutional development should not, therefore, be viewed simply as a gradual accretion of appropriate responses to environmental problems. Instead, he argues, as do theories of political development in general, that the growth of the president's institutional responsibility in the early part of the twentieth century actually resulted from a fundamental disjunction between emerging administrative capacities and a well-articulated, established institutional order. The result was the construction of "a qualitatively different kind of state."[4]

Despite this fundamental difference, theories of political development, like theories of administrative control, view the struggle between political actors for control of prerogatives, during the transition from old order to new, as the central mechanism of institutional development (Skowronek 1982; Weir, Orloff, and Skocpol 1988). Although theories of political development posit a sharp disjunction between old and new institutional structures, the new structures are nonetheless constrained by the old order, as the institutional actors from the latter struggle to redefine their institutional prerogatives and status in the emerging order.[5]

Unfortunately, theories of political development are agnostic about the impact of new institutional responsibility on presidential decision making. Although their depiction of the disjunction between institutional orders points to a gap in policy-making continuity that could allow for the introduction of new institutional responsibility, these theories are unclear as to what would drive this development, be it macroeconomic logic and related institutional structures or some other paradigm. Capturing the essence of policy decision without this mediating theoretical link is problematic. Thus, theories of political development describe a plausible political struggle for control of institutional prerogatives but do not offer an understanding of how either the emerging or old order shapes the development of nascent institutional responsibility. Most importantly, the results of these political transformations are not clearly defined in terms of policy decisions.

Margaret Weir's work (1992) also falls under the political development rubric yet moves in the direction of the idea of institutional responsibility. Unlike other political development theorists, Weir more deliberately connects macroeconomic paradigms to institutional structures for policy making and to the policy decisions emanating from them.[6] She links the three constructs through the concept of a "policy sequence," in which "institutional development renders some interpretations of problems more persuasive and some prospective policies more politically viable than others." Institutional development narrows a president's policy options in ways that guide policy decisions in a particular direction. This ongoing process further evolves institutional development along that path.[7] The difference between Weir's approach and the one I suggest below, however, is that for her, institutions are the mechanisms that direct macroeconomic paradigms and policy decisions. In contrast, this study argues for a different policy sequence, one in which paradigms shape the development of new institutional structures and the policy decisions that result from them.

An Alternative Explanation of Institutional Development

We can best conceptualize postwar institutional stability and partisan decision making as being shaped by the interaction of a prevailing macroeconomic logic or calculus within evolving institutional structures for presidential decision making. By macroeconomic logic, I am referring to paradigmatic ways of thinking about the functioning of the macroeconomy, examples of which would include Keynesianism, supply-side economics, budget balancing, stagnationism, and so forth. These logics or paradigms are usually favored by one political party in opposition to the other (and thus my use of the phrase "partisan logic" interchangeably). They provide strong decision-making cues to the president, both in terms of macroeconomic cause and effect and in terms of guidelines for establishing institutional structures designed to pursue those ends. By institutional structures, I am referring to any statutory power, advisory network, decision-making procedure that allows the president to pursue the stabilization goals of a particular macroeconomic logic.

With these definitions in mind, I reinterpret the critical period of development of the president's institutional responsibility for macroeconomic policy making from 1908 to 1946, as it is revealed in the ongoing interaction between decision-making paradigm and institutional structure in the presidency. My narrative pays particular attention to key junctures in that evolution, notably the Budget and Accounting Act of 1921, the Reorganization Act of 1939, postwar reconversion policy, and the Employment Act of 1946. The process of evolution depicted below explicitly links presidential decision making in the American political economy to the manner in which presidents conceptualize macroeconomic policy and to how a particular paradigm, once ascendant in an administration, shapes the institutional structures designed to produce those policy decisions. This distinctive process of institutional development has resulted in a stable postwar arrangement for macroeconomic policy making with enhanced presidential powers to aid in the pursuit of partisan and electoral objectives. This new institutional configuration accommodates moments of partisanship and institutional responsibility in presidential decision making. Understanding presidential fluctuations between those two decision-making nodes is central to a more synthetic notion of presidential behavior.

I suggest in the narrative to follow that prior to each key moment of institutional development, macroeconomic conditions exert pressure (e.g., through the electorate, business and labor lobbying, and the like) on the federal government to expand its fiscal reach through ameliorative measures. Contending macroeconomic paradigms provide political actors with potential policy-making logics oriented toward solving the macroeconomic policy problems at hand. Policy makers debate both the need to take action and the macroeconomic paradigm best suited to the task. Ultimately, one macroeconomic logic prevails in the debate, and compatible institutional structures are legislated in order to implement desired policies. These contending macroeconomic paradigms set the old institutional order on its head (with some similarity to the process described in Skowronek 1982) by forcing policy makers, who are looking for promising policy solutions to pressing macroeconomic problems, to promulgate new institutional responsibility. Different macroeconomic paradigms envision particular types of solutions, so the institutional structures that develop in response to them are constrained to defining specific types of policy options. Absent the ascendancy of a new macroeconomic logic, however, conditions are insufficient to alter the balance of institutional responsibility at any given moment.

Under this process of institutional development, the successive decision-making paradigm or logics most influential in the period increasingly concentrate institutional responsibility in the presidency. Thus, it is the ascendancy of a succession of macroeconomic paradigms, rather than the interbranch struggles over the institutional control of new policy-making areas usually cited for this period, that propels the development of the president's institutional responsibility for macroeconomic policy making.[8]

The period 1908–46 saw the presidency transformed from an institution possessing virtually no authority over macroeconomic policy to one that was gradually legislated ongoing responsibility for implementing policies designed to address the nation's economic health. By the time the development of this institutional responsibility was complete in 1946, the macroeconomic policy debate had shifted from questions of institutional responsibility to consideration of the content of partisan policies produced within a fixed institutional arrangement. As noted above, the establishment of this fixed institutional arrangement for the postwar period allows one to study the political and macroeconomic parameters of partisanship in presidential decision making in the appropriate institutional context.

Karen Orren and Stephen Skowronek (1999), Sidney Milkis (1999), and John Coleman (1996) all provide support for this notion of the postwar institutionalization of partisan fiscal policy making, within the broad paradigmatic dictates of the Keynesian stabilization logic. It is this same stable policy-making regime upon which rational choice models of presidential behavior such as the rational partisan and political business cycle models are built. In this postwar period, both parties agreed upon the shape and boundaries of the policy-making environment but sought to control that environment with divergent partisan notions of stabilization and decision-making logics geared to the interests of their core partisan constituencies. Understanding why and when presidents are willing to make tradeoffs between partisan logics is central to our understanding of institutional responsibility.

The Politics of the Balanced Budget

The first two decades of the twentieth century were a time when the president's institutional responsibility for macroeconomic policy making was minimal, both in terms of paradigms promoting it and institutional structures formalizing it. This circumstance is attributable to two causes. First, the idea of macroeconomic policy as it has been understood since World War II did not exist. The federal government's approach to its role in the economic affairs of the nation minimized its responsibility for cushioning the peaks and valleys of the business cycle.[9] Second, the little institutional responsibility for macroeconomic policy making that did exist on the federal level belonged to Congress. With no federal budget per se, the Treasury acted primarily as bookkeeper, compiling a book of estimates to track federal expenditures and receipts. These estimates were, in turn, submitted directly to Congress without any coordination or clearance by the president. Scholars have debated the effectiveness of this arrangement, some depicting it as a process that resulted in "conflict, duplication, inefficiency, and irresponsibility."[10] In contrast, others have argued that this arrangement was actually quite suitable "in a time when balanced budgets were the rule and revenues were usually sufficient . . . to cover the costs of government."[11] Regardless of which interpretation one accepts, the fact remains that the president possessed neither the institutional responsibility nor the institutional structures to expand the federal government's role in the macroeconomy. This deficiency was reinforced by the lack of a prevailing macroeconomic logic to suggest greater presidential energy in dealing with the business cycle.

The state of policy-making affairs changed, however, when Progressives initiated a call for greater acceptance of a balanced budget paradigm to govern decision making at the federal level. In terms of institutional structures, the implication of this new logic was the development of an executive budget system. I have suggested that macroeconomic conditions were the catalyst for the acceptance of new logics and institutional structures. Indeed, the Panic of 1907 altered the manner in which policy makers conceptualized federal spending. Deficits from 1908 to 1910 embarrassed Republicans, who had traditionally raised tariff rates in order to accommodate increased federal expenditures without incurring debt. The deficits, however, put new pressure on policy makers to control federal spending and, in particular, drew attention to the way in which the existing decentralized congressional budget process limited their control over spending.[12] The result of this progressive push for balanced budgets was an initial shift in institutional focus, however tentative, toward presidential responsibility for macroeconomic policy making. This paradigmatic shift was solidified in 1909, when Congress requested that President William H. Taft appoint a commission to investigate and report on ways to more effectively balance future budgets.[13] The president's nascent institutional responsibility was further encouraged in that same year when a congressional statute called on him to submit recommendations for a program to meet an anticipated financial shortfall. In response, the president for the first time instructed department heads on proper policy for the submission of estimates to Congress.[14]

Progressives touted balanced budgets and the adoption of an executive budget system as a desirable means of realizing economy and efficiency in government; they claimed that the key to alleviating federal deficits was to lower the cost of government. An executive budget system was seen as the institutional mechanism best suited to accomplish this goal, through a more efficient collection of information, a rationalization of duplicative administrative procedures, and a centralization of planning for federal finances. The resultant elimination of governmental waste would increase the likelihood of restraining federal expenditures.[15]

On a normative level, Progressives believed that the balanced budget decision-making paradigm, institutionalized through an executive budget system, would ameliorate a number of ills associated with the country's growing nationalism, industrialization, and urbanization. Administrative economy and efficiency would depoliticize the macroeconomic policy-making process by eliminating partisan divisiveness, pork barrel spending, and political bossism.[16] The Progressives took their lead in this respect from the municipal budget movement. The latter had developed at the turn of the twentieth century as municipal debt grew during periods of control by machine politics. Local governments viewed the budget as a key reform for lessening the deleterious effects of political patronage.[17]

Through this interaction of macroeconomic paradigm and institutional structure, the balanced budget logic, with its dual emphases on economy and efficiency, translated into institutional reform that placed the president in charge of the budgetary process. This interaction provided an institutional responsibility for macroeconomic policy making that was previously nonexistent. *Through the production of a federal budget that tracked both revenues and expenditures, a new mechanism of fiscal control was made available to the president.* The new paradigm also called for the reorganization of appropriations committees in Congress into streamlined jurisdictions for prompt and coordinated consideration of budget requests and for an audit of financial transactions of the executive branch by an agency with primary responsibility to Congress.[18] *Thus, the balanced budget paradigm implied greater institutional responsibility for the president and a specific set of new institutional structures designed to reinforce that authority.*

Within this developing framework of macroeconomic logic and institutional structure, President Taft, employing the recommendations of his Commission on Economy and Efficiency, attempted the first major institutionalization of presidential responsibility for macroeconomic policy. While the commission put out twenty reports covering a wide range of potential administrative reforms, its most notable was *The Need for a National Budget* (1912).[19] The report proposed the adoption of a federal budget system as the most promising means for achieving governmental economy and efficiency and thus for increasing the federal government's ability to balance its budget. The commission believed that the ability to fine-tune the budget would make federal finances more responsive to changing macroeconomic circumstances. It would provide a means "whereby the Government may be kept in constant adjustment with the welfare needs of the people; a means also whereby the economy and efficiency of administration may be regularly brought to test."[20] Taft even prepared a federal budget for fiscal year 1914, along the lines recommended in the 1912 report, to demonstrate the efficacy of the plan.[21]

Although Taft's plan for a federal budget was ultimately defeated by a Congress that was not prepared to legislate that degree of institutional responsibility to the president, his attempt is nonetheless important. It provides an early example of how macroeconomic paradigms suggest institutional structures that give a specific form to institutional responsibility. This power, so defined, has particular implications for decision making; in Taft's case, presidential decisions in the American political economy were driven by the desire to move government finances into balance. The institutional structures defined by the balanced budget logic were designed to increase the likelihood of that goal being achieved.

Despite President Taft's loss to Woodrow Wilson in the general election of 1912, the latter also expressed a desire, like many of his contemporaries in the Progressive Era, for institutional reform that would separate partisanship from efficient and economical government.[22] The imperatives of World War I, however, pushed reform back to the end of the decade. By then, the balanced budget paradigm for decision making had gained wide acceptance, as had the need for institutional structures in the executive branch to implement it. In 1916 and in 1920, both the Democratic and Republican Party platforms called for a federal budget system.[23] House and Senate work on budget legislation during that period demonstrated that both sides of the aisle sought to reduce federal expenditures through a federal budget, thereby holding taxes (which were high during the war) in check.

Once again, changing macroeconomic conditions set the stage for institutional development, since the fiscal situation was markedly different after World War I. Federal expenditures had increased to a level of more than $3 billion annually, as compared to $700 million before the war. Interest payments alone exceeded total federal expenditures before the war, and income taxes were an especially heavy burden for the first time. In this context, movement toward a balanced budget, through economic and efficient government, had wide appeal.[24] As one scholar confirms, this sentiment entailed the first real acknowledgment that the president had a positive responsibility for conduct and control of the economy.[25]

President Wilson could have signed a budget measure in 1920 but instead vetoed it because the legislation created the office of Comptroller General to monitor federal expenditures. The president could appoint but not remove the comptroller general. Wilson claimed that, under the Constitution, the powers to appoint and to remove were inseparable. Congress failed to override his veto.[26] Instead, President Warren G. Harding signed a slightly modified Budget and Accounting Act in 1921. The budget act gave the president institutional responsibility for preparing and submitting an annual budget to Congress for consideration. To reinforce this new authority, executive agencies were prohibited from presenting their estimates directly to Congress, unless specifically requested to do so. The Bureau of the Budget was established in the Treasury to aid the president in fulfilling his new institutional responsibilities. Finally, the comptroller general in the General Accounting Office was established in order to allow congressional monitoring of executive actions.[27] Thus, a particular macroeconomic logic, in this case budget balancing, shaped the types of institutional structures for macroeconomic policy making that developed and dictated that control of those structures be located in presidential power. It was not a struggle for institutional control that led to the growth of the president's institutional responsibility but instead the acceptance of a macroeconomic paradigm, which by definition of its goals of economy and efficiency required that institutional responsibility rest with the president.

In keeping with this notion of institutional responsibility, the acceptance of a balanced budget logic and its related manifestations had profound implications for presidential decision making in the American political economy. Two historical examples illustrate these effects. First, as late as 1931, the balanced budget logic shaped President Herbert Hoover's decisions in confronting the Depression. In calling for a balanced budget, Hoover was constrained by a decade of policy making that employed institutional processes designed with budget balancing in mind. Believing that a balanced budget was a prerequisite for a revival of business confidence, President

Hoover recommended a substantial tax increase in 1931, despite extremely high unemployment, in order to counter a large budget deficit.[28] The result was a detrimental policy decision largely dictated both by a macroeconomic paradigm that held the balanced budget as a paramount macroeconomic goal and by a set of institutional structures designed to constrain policy in that direction.

A second example of how the development of institutional responsibility in this direction shaped decision making is found in the Bureau of the Budget during the 1920s. Its first several directors all functioned under the balanced budget paradigm, tailoring their institutional missions to its dictates. As a result, during the decade of the 1920s, the bureau strove to be both economical and efficient in its own administrative decisions to the point where staff, resources, and facilities were so depleted that the bureau was severely weakened in its operation as an institutional structure.[29] It will be shown below that just as the prevailing macroeconomic logic evolved in subsequent decades, so too did the institutional form of the Bureau of the Budget.

A New Paradigm and a New Deal

Much has been written about President Franklin Roosevelt's use of new institutional structures in policy making. Many scholars depict policy-making developments in the late 1930s as an attempt by FDR to institutionalize the emergency authority he wielded in the first few years of his administration. Other explanations focus on FDR's character or management style to explain these same developments. In keeping with the analysis presented for the Budget and Accounting Act of 1921, I offer an alternative interpretation of FDR's decision-making behavior. In building upon the interaction of logic and structure in the 1920s, the development of institutional responsibility in the 1930s was primarily determined by the requirements of the macroeconomic paradigms that shaped FDR's decision making at different moments during the Depression and World War II. As FDR functioned successively under the prevailing macroeconomic logics of budget balancing and macroeconomic stabilization (with a pump-priming interlude), so too were the institutional structures he proposed to translate macroeconomic logic into desired policy transformed.

The narrative below is divided into two parts. The first covers FDR's first term (1932–36), during which he wavered between traditional notions of the balanced budget and the spending dictates of pump priming. The second analyzes his second term (1936–40), a period in which ad hoc pump priming gradually gave way to at least partial acceptance of a new paradigm of macroeconomic stabilization and development of the institutional structures that went along with it. The continued growth of institutional responsibility in the 1930s therefore is a function of relatively discrete New Deal periods of interaction between macroeconomic logic and institutional structures. These interactions in turn produced specific types of presidential decision making in the American political economy. This interpretation stands in sharp contrast to the continuum of institutional development usually depicted for the New Deal.

Despite Hoover's disastrous attempts to balance the budget through tax increases in 1931, both the Democratic and Republican Parties continued to campaign for a balanced federal budget as the essential ingredient for recovery from the Depression and for prosperity in the future.[30] This circumstance is testimony to the strength of the balanced budget logic and to the growing focus on the federal budget as the prime institutional tool for remedying the country's economic woes. As a result, throughout his first term, FDR persisted in the belief that deficit spending was only a short-term measure to be ended as soon as the economy recovered. Even in 1933, he attempted to reduce projected federal spending by cutting veterans' benefits by $400 million and federal salaries by $100 million.[31] FDR believed that the deficit was due entirely to the Depression, and he thought that when regular business activity resumed the budget would regain its balance. Thus, his deficit spending strategy to reduce unemployment was to increase federal expenditures only long enough to prime the pump of the economy. Beyond this initial stimulus, FDR contemplated no departure from traditional budget policy.[32] Given that this pump priming was not really a bona fide macroeconomic paradigm, no new permanent institutional structures for macroeconomic policy making were promulgated. The budget apparatus was already in place, and FDR had the requisite emergency authority to prime the pump.

To this end, New Deal programs featured a number of action programs designed to quickly counteract the Depression in all sectors of the economy. FDR established no new statutory machinery to permanently integrate these institutional structures in the executive branch, for that was not a prerequisite of pump priming, and no new macroeconomic logic suggested alternatives.[33] As such, the policy makers viewed the resultant decisions as temporary measures. A stopgap, piecemeal approach to relief efforts was taken (an approach that some scholars view as a continuation of pre–New Deal practices, rather than as a style of organization unique to FDR).[34] FDR's decision making was designed to provide immediate relief to distressed sectors of the economy on a case-by-case basis rather than as part of a new coordinated fiscal program. The issue in terms of his decision making was "how much was needed to meet the relief rolls, or to sustain the price of cotton, or to satisfy other specific objectives, not how much was needed to produce recovery or reduce unemployment by some target amount."[35] These emergency agencies and piecemeal initiatives were loosely overseen by an executive council that underwent several administrative transformations during FDR's first term. Roosevelt abolished the council in his second term, however, when a new prevailing paradigm spawned the development of permanent institutional structures to oversee the use of the budget as a tool of fiscal recovery.[36] FDR's level of institutional responsibility for macroeconomic policy ultimately remained unchanged for most of the decade. He unsuccessfully pursued balanced budgets on a yearly basis, running deficits in spite of attempts to the contrary. FDR continued to view federal spending as a stopgap, pump-priming measure and was promising a balanced budget as late as 1938.[37]

The recession of 1937–38 initiated a new phase in the development of the president's institutional responsibility, a moment in which a new macroeconomic logic gained gradual acceptance as a replacement for the faltering pump-priming/budget-balancing hybrid. The new paradigm dictated development of a new set of institutional structures, rather than a consolidation of the old, and a new type of presidential decision making rooted in a very different macroeconomic logic. As a result of these changes between 1937 and 1939, the president's institutional responsibility for macroeconomic policy making underwent its most radical redefinition since 1921, a redefinition that brings one much closer to understanding the context for presidential decision making in the postwar world.

The new paradigm, developed by John Maynard Keynes in his 1936 work, *The General Theory of Employment, Interest, and Money,* represented a crucial transition in macroeconomic thinking from pump priming to a full-scale theory of countercyclical stabilization policy. The macroeconomic concepts presented in this work gained currency in the United States just as the recession of 1937 began. This recession put FDR at a loss to explain ongoing deficits, continued unemployment, and a general failure of the economy to respond to pump priming, while forcing the president to answer charges that the New Deal programs had scared off private investment.[38] Thus, a crisis-induced window of opportunity opened for a new macroeconomic logic to prevail. Keynes attacked the idea found in classical and neoclassical economic thought that the free market economy is a self-adjusting mechanism, one that tends to produce a condition of full employment and a maximum utilization of economic resources. Keynes argued that unemployment was not voluntary but was instead the result of insufficient demand in the economy. Rather than wait for the market to correct itself, the government could take action through the manipulation of fiscal policy to increase employment, thereby increasing demand. The government could increase national income by increasing consumption expenditures and/or investment expenditures. Applied to the American situation, the conclusion was that the New Dealers had actually not spent enough to boost employment.[39]

While most interpretations of this period claim that FDR never completely assimilated the Keynesian approach, its development nonetheless had a strong impact on the macroeconomic thinking of those around him. Keynesianism provided important reinforcement for Harvard economist Alvin Hansen and his colleagues on the National Resources Planning Board (NRPB), who were developing their own version of macroeconomic stabilization based upon the concept of secular stagnation. These "stagnationists" argued that the nation's economy had reached a state of maturity due to the territorial expansion, population growth, and technological innovation of the late nineteenth and early twentieth centuries. They claimed that the prospects for a continuation of this sort of growth were slim without ongoing and increasingly large investment by the federal government. The stagnationists envisioned a major program of public works and social spending that could be adjusted as needed, depending upon the condition of the economy.[40] During the recession of 1937–38, calls for this type of program grew, yet there was neither the institutional responsibility nor structure in the presidency sufficient to plan, implement, and monitor such an ongoing program of fiscal activity. It would take the acceptance of this ascendant macroeconomic paradigm, American Keynesianism, and the development of related policy-making tools to produce the institutional responsibility required for the president to make the fiscal policy decisions urged by these advisers.

This redefinition of institutional responsibility was aided in 1937 by the publication of the report of the President's Committee on Administrative Management, also known as the Brownlow Committee (after its chairman Louis Brownlow). The report represented a comprehensive review of the institutional apparatus of the presidency and had as its goal the adoption of administrative reforms that would equip the president with the personnel, planning tools, and fiscal control necessary to implement his social and economic programs.[41] The "financial control and accountability" section of the Brownlow Committee report was particularly important, for it suggested institutional reforms that were compatible with the macroeconomic logic favored by Hansen and the American Keynesians.[42] The section called for enhanced presidential responsibility for macroeconomic policy making, bolstered by a direct link to a revitalized and strengthened Bureau of the Budget to be placed under presidential control in a newly established Executive Office of the President (EOP). The proposed reorganization would rescue the bureau from its earlier status as a victim of the budget-balancing economy and efficiency that ironically had originally established it. The expanded bureau was assigned to fiscal policy and planning, execution and preparation of the budget, policy research and coordination, and legislative clearance.[43] *These were precisely the institutional responsibility and types of institutionalized structures (according to the American Keynesians) required for the president to take decision making in the American political economy to a new level of federal involvement.* These changes did not come easily to FDR; he suffered two legislative defeats with the Reorganization Acts of 1937 and 1938 before signing the Reorganization Act of 1939 into law.

Two historical examples are useful for illustrating that these changes in policy-making outlook actually occurred. First, during the congressional debates on reorganization, a number of amendments were introduced by Democrats and Republicans, all of which attempted to limit the president's institutional responsibility over fiscal policy in ways which hearkened back to the imperatives of budget balancing. None of these amendments was passed. It was clear to members of Congress that the focus of macroeconomic policy should change in favor of stabilization policy. Such a policy required that a variety of expenditure and revenue policies be coordinated by the president in conjunction with the Bureau of the Budget.[44]

Second, FDR established a Monetary and Fiscal Advisory Board consisting of, among others, the secretary of the Treasury, the chairman of the Federal Reserve Board, and the director of the Bureau of the Budget. The president charged the Fiscal Advisory Board with the mission of systematically studying the broader problems of fiscal and monetary policies in relation to national production and income. The board was to focus on developing policy approaches designed to avoid the peaks and valleys of the business cycle.[45] Its goal was to offer the president alternatives for stabilization policy. The assignment of such a task would have been unlikely during FDR's first term.

Both examples demonstrate how changes in thinking about macroeconomic paradigms and policy-making structures combine to strengthen a president's institutional responsibility, thereby facilitating new forms of presidential decision making. This development was institutionalized in June, 1939, when the Executive Office of the President was created with the Bureau of the Budget under its control. The National Resources Planning

Board, the very same agency where much of the early Keynesian thought first took hold, was also placed under the EOP's control. Thus, the acceptance of a particular macroeconomic logic by policy makers, be it budget balancing or stabilization policy, had significant implications for both the development of New Deal institutional structures in the presidency and for the types of policy decisions FDR implemented through them. By the close of the 1930s, the president was more than ever before charged with an ongoing responsibility for the nation's economic health. It was his sworn duty as president to use the institutional tools at his disposal to ensure economic prosperity.

Reconversion Policy and the Employment Act of 1946

The centralized economic planning and coordination required for the American effort in World War II augmented the president's institutional responsibility further along the path of the late 1930s. The massive growth of industrial production due to federal spending on the war temporarily alleviated the Roosevelt administration's unemployment troubles. Since federal spending accounted for more than one-half of the gross national product in 1944, however, concern arose (almost as soon as the war began) over what would happen to the economy when 30 million people (10 million in the armed forces and 20 million civilians in war-related industries) were demobilized.[46] Given the populace's recent memory of the Depression and the president's newly expanded role in the economy, a debate ensued over whether the federal government should act at the end of the war to ensure that there would be no return to high unemployment—in essence to head off the vicious cycle. In late 1944, a *Fortune* magazine poll found that 68 percent of respondents to a survey believed that "preventing unemployment after the war" was the issue "most important to America."[47] With basic institutional structures for ongoing presidential involvement in the economy already in place, movement toward a postwar full-employment paradigm once again expanded the president's institutional responsibility for macroeconomic policy making.

Both FDR and Congress were cognizant of the implications of postwar reconversion for the economy, and throughout World War II each remained at least partly focused on postwar policy. The manner in which they maintained this interest is instructive for understanding the institutional responsibility promulgated by the Employment Act of 1946. As early as 1940, FDR directed the National Resources Planning Board to undertake planning for significant public and private macroeconomic action in the postwar period. The result, given the macroeconomic logic of the late 1930s, was thoroughly

Keynesian in its macroeconomic assumptions and policy recommendations. In 1943, FDR transmitted the board's two massive reports to Congress, reports that proposed federal postwar macroeconomic intervention through a broad social security program, a national health and education program, a permanent policy of large-scale public works, comparatively heavy taxation (with an emphasis on individual income and inheritances), and federal action against monopoly.[48] Similarly, Congress established committees to take up reconversion legislation in 1943 and 1944. Legislators clearly recognized that new institutional tools would be needed to deal with the federal government's postwar responsibility for the economy. The result of the committees' work was the War Mobilization and Reconversion Act of 1944, which called upon the executive branch, through the Office of War Mobilization and Reconversion, to formulate plans for meeting the problems that might arise in the transition from war to peace.

In paradigmatic terms, many of the concepts formalized in the Employment Act of 1946 actually stemmed from drafts of the reconversion legislation. Ideas for central planning agencies and advisory bodies in the executive branch and for a joint congressional committee to monitor presidential decision making permeated the reconversion debate and appeared in draft legislation. Just as FDR's NRPB reports to Congress advocated ongoing federal involvement in the economy through stabilization policy, so too did a number of legislative proposals include the policy prescription that presidential responsibility should extend beyond the reconversion period and address more broadly the problems of maintaining employment and business prosperity in the future. As expressed in the reconversion debates and proposals, the idea was to establish new institutional structures in the presidency that would continuously review federal and private sector plans and monitor the necessity for additional programs or legislation "to promote peacetime full production and employment."[49]

That this macroeconomic logic was not legislated into law at the time signifies that policy makers in both parties were cognizant of the decision-making implications of partisan approaches to macroeconomic stabilization. Recall that the rational partisan models discussed in chapter 1 hypothesize that in the postwar period macroeconomic policy making is primarily partisan; Democratic and Republican administrations pursue consistently divergent approaches to stabilization policy over time, despite presidents commanding the same institutional responsibility. The reconversion debate should be viewed, therefore, as a harbinger of this postwar dichotomy. It signaled a partisan policy-making split that was eventually codified in the Employment Act of 1946.

Thus, the reconversion debate centered on which partisan version of stabilization policy would govern the functioning of those institutional structures in the presidency focused on macroeconomic decision making at a given moment. On this score, Republicans and Democrats had very different ideas, a conflict affirmed by the postwar debate over the partisan implications of reconversion policy. Given the evolution of macroeconomic thinking to this point, the debate was no longer an issue of whether to stimulate aggregate demand through increased federal spending (as it had been for FDR); it was instead about how best to use all the tools of fiscal and monetary policy to moderate fluctuations in the economy, including a consideration of the largely partisan tradeoffs in prioritizing inflation and unemployment as macroeconomic ills (i.e., Democrats favoring lower unemployment and Republicans favoring lower inflation).[50]

Partisan differences over how to exercise the president's institutional responsibility for stabilization policy were evident as early as the election of 1944, when both candidates called for full employment after the war yet presented very different conceptions of how that institutional responsibility should be manifested in policy decisions. The Democratic platform called for the federal government to "guarantee full employment and provide prosperity," while the Republican platform, in rejecting the approach of restoring prosperity through government spending and deficit financing, sought to "promote the fullest stable employment through private enterprise."[51] *Restated, the issue was no longer one of whether the president held the institutional responsibility to make these decisions, but one of which decisions should be made.*[52]

Movement toward the institutionalization of partisan differences is evident both in the Full Employment Bill of 1945 and in the version of that legislation finally adopted as the Employment Act of 1946. As initially introduced, the Full Employment Bill had four main goals. First, it sought to permanently establish the principle of the "right to work" and the federal government's obligation to ensure employment opportunities for all those "able to work and seeking work." Second, the bill placed responsibility on the president for regular monitoring of the economy, for informing Congress of any macroeconomic trends, and for presenting a macroeconomic program designed to deal with those trends. Third, the bill committed the federal government during difficult economic circumstances to a program of measures designed to forestall serious economic dislocation, the last resort being increased federal spending and investment to guarantee employment. Fourth, the bill established a mechanism in Congress to facilitate legislative consideration of executive branch policy actions.[53]

As finally adopted, the Employment Act placed partisan differences over policy approach within the context of expanded institutional responsibility for the president.[54] It embodied a macroeconomic policy-making logic that affirmed federal responsibility for fostering private enterprise, for promoting a high and stable level of employment, and for developing and consistently pursuing an appropriate economic program to those ends. The president was legislated the institutional responsibility to propose such a program; Congress would review it through consideration of the annual *Economic Report of the President* and other documents to be submitted on a regular basis.[55]

Partisan differences were institutionalized in section 2 of the act (refer back to the second quotation at the beginning of this chapter), which combined the liberal goal of "maximum employment, production, and purchasing power" with the conservative counterpart of obtaining these goals "in a manner calculated to foster and promote free competitive enterprise."[56] Both partisan interpretations were consistent with the broader paradigm of macroeconomic stabilization.[57] The new institutional structures promulgated by this act were the Council of Economic Advisers in the executive branch and the Joint Economic Committee in Congress. The Employment Act established the Council of Economic Advisers in the Executive Office of the President "to formulate and recommend national economic policy to promote employment, production, and purchasing power under free competitive enterprise."[58] The council's duties were described as "to develop and recommend to the president national economic policies to foster and promote free competitive enterprise, to avoid economic fluctuations or to diminish the effects thereof, and to maintain employment, production, and purchasing power."[59] The act also called for the Joint Economic Committee in Congress to consider presidential proposals and report its findings and concerns to members.

Conclusion

The Employment Act of 1946 represents the culmination of almost forty years of development of the president's institutional responsibility for macroeconomic policy making. As is true for each of the other periods considered, the interaction of a prevailing macroeconomic paradigm with new institutional structures shaped presidential decision making in the American political economy. Among the theories of institutional development discussed, only this explanation provides purchase on the actual policy content of presidential decisions made in the stable postwar institutional environment.

With the Employment Act, this interaction built upon the evolution that had preceded it and resulted in the institutionalization of partisan differences in stabilization policy; the postwar institutional context within which presidents of both parties grappled with the vicious cycle was thus established. We will see that their partisan use of a common set of institutional tools within a prevailing logic of macroeconomic stabilization led to very different political outcomes and ultimately changed the way each president viewed his role as our nation's most important decision maker in the American political economy.

An alternative explanation has thus been provided for how the presidency developed its institutional responsibility for macroeconomic policy making. In doing so, insight has been offered into why that responsibility has become institutionally stable, allowing administrations to pursue divergent partisan approaches to macroeconomic policy making. These phenomena have also been placed within the broader context of a theory of institutional development that depicts macroeconomic policy decisions as a function of the interaction between a prevailing macroeconomic paradigm and institutional structures for policy making. Instead of explaining these institutional developments in terms of the outcome of an interbranch struggle for control of the policy-making process, institutional responsibility relates the policy decisions of key political actors to the manner in which they conceptualize the macroeconomy. Those paradigms, once ascendant, shape the institutional structures designed to produce specific presidential policy decisions.

This study now turns to a consideration of how presidents make tradeoffs in partisan and electoral objectives when managing macroeconomic policy during the postwar period, given the political constraints of the institutional framework depicted above.

A Model of Partisanship, Institutional Responsibility, and Presidential Decision Making in the American Political Economy

Chapter 2 established the broad institutional framework within which presidents make decisions about management of the macroeconomy. It should now be evident from the preceding narrative that by the beginning of the postwar period presidents were able to make these decisions in a stable policy-making environment, one in which they were largely expected to enact their respective party's preferred vision of stabilization policy. The previous chapter underscores the nature of these partisan differences in the selection of policy-making instruments; these I refer to throughout the study as a party's preferred macroeconomic logic or calculus.

We have also seen that through the rise of new ideas about policy making, presidents now possess central institutional responsibility for implementing their party's macroeconomic policies. While augmentation of presidential authority gives the president powerful new tools with which to pursue partisan and electoral objectives, it also establishes a new imperative for sound management with which to approach these objectives. Presidents may still respond to political incentives in the policy-making environment, but the nature of the tradeoffs involved are now increasingly complex. It is this newly established conditionality in presidential behavior that is captured in some of the positive political economic models in chapter 1.

The present chapter starts from these premises—a stable partisan institutional framework, institutional responsibility, and the conditional nature of presidential decision making—in order to model in the aggregate precisely how and when institutional responsibility causes presidents to cycle between the various incentives for policy making discussed thus far. It is important to stress here that the model developed below is not a model of positive political economy in the sense of those discussed in chapter 1. It does, however, build upon their insights into partisan and electoral behavior in order to directly model the dynamics of shifts in presidential behavior over the course of a four-year term. It is in essence a decision-making model that captures the underlying principle of this study, *that both a president's partisan behavior and electoral accountability are fundamentally related to fulfillment of the institutional imperatives of sound macroeconomic management. The key difference here is that the president is accountable primarily as an institutional actor rather than as a partisan actor.*

After a discussion of the methodological issues involved in directly testing for presidential decision making, I first construct a partisan model of presidential behavior to serve as a baseline heuristic. By then adding in assumptions about institutional responsibility and variables designed to measure the construct, I highlight the dynamics of how and when presidents are willing to accept tradeoffs between the pursuit of partisan and electoral incentives and decisions about appropriate macroeconomic stabilization policy. The resultant institutional responsibility model provides useful insight into the contours of presidential decision making, insight that should provide a useful companion to the more complex models of the American political economy developed by the positive political economy scholars mentioned in chapter 1.

Testing for Presidential Decision Making

Econometric modeling of presidential decision making takes us into a somewhat different realm of estimation than the models of positive political economy do. Historically, econometric modeling of presidential behavior has been a very uneasy fit with other fields in American politics. Measurement issues are particularly thorny, as will be evident in the dependent variable discussion to come. If anything, my hope is that the discussion below will lessen the difficulty that presidency scholars often encounter when moving between the two worlds.

Econometric testing of rational partisan theory usually proceeds through the estimation of a single reaction function equation or through a system of simultaneous equations. This technique detects systematic relationships between changes in macroeconomic instruments and levels of macroeconomic indicators. Presidential selection of target is assumed a priori in the setting of macroeconomic instruments at particular levels. Patterns of movement (particularly cyclical ones) uncovered between instrument and indicator are interpreted as evidence of strategic decision-making behavior. These models generally take the functional form

$$x_{it} = a + b_{it}x_{it-1} + \left(\sum_{j=2}^{k} b_{ij}y_{ijt}\right)$$

In this reaction function, an adjustable macroeconomic instrument x_i at time t is a linear function of its own prior values x_{it-1} and current values of economic targets y_j. The remaining coefficients represent the decisions of the policy actors (such as the president) adjusting the macroeconomic instrument.[1] In modeling strategic rational behavior with this approach, one would theorize that when macroeconomic conditions differ from partisan or electoral preferences, the president manipulates instruments to move the macroeconomy in the desired direction. Presidential decisions about macroeconomic outcomes such as inflation and unemployment are therefore included in the vector of independent variables affecting instrument level x_i.

As Stephen Weatherford (1988) and George Edwards (1983) suggest, the drawback to this approach for modeling presidential decision making is that although instrument level and macroeconomic outcome are generally related, given the complexity of the decision-making process and the number of actors involved, the president does not always realize preferred macroeconomic outcomes. Weatherford notes that "the institutional complexity and fragmentation of the policy process opens the outcome to claims and amendments by strategically important legislators, interest groups, party elites, and others," so the resulting compromise outcomes may not directly represent the president's strategic decision-making intentions.[2] Movement in instrument levels and outcomes may or may not be a reflection of a specific presidential decision, so theorizing about strategic behavior from this movement is problematic for purposes of causal inference. In essence, instrument level here is the result of a multivariate process in which the presidential decision is only one variable. Thus, the reaction function approach, while extremely useful for studying the relationship between instruments and outcomes, provides only an indirect test of strategic presidential decision making.

John Woolley (1988) and Weatherford (1988) note the limitations of the reaction function approach and call for new ways of modeling presidential behavior in the macroeconomy. Following their suggestion, I argue that in order to model presidential decision making directly, one needs to shift the vector of policy decisions to the left-hand side of the equation. A discrete choice approach allows for precisely this sort of respecification. One can calculate the probability that a president will shift decision making from partisan preferences, given a vector of parameters measuring the policy-making environment. This approach enables me to directly capture the parameters of the tradeoffs made by presidents; the probabilities help underscore the conditional nature of that behavior. The logit models estimated in this chapter thus take the general functional form

$$P\left(Y_i = \frac{1}{X_i}\right) = \frac{exp(\hat{A}\,b_k X_{ik})}{[1 + exp(\hat{A}\,b_k X_{ik})]}$$

In this specification, the probability that an actor selects a particular alternative with $P(Y_i = 1)$ is a curvilinear function of X_{ik}, the vector of independent variables measuring the various attributes of the alternative selected (or decision made). Using the logistic cumulative distribution function, I will be able to measure how changes in the vector of characteristics describing the policy-making environment affect presidential decision making.[3]

Measuring the Dependent Variable

Since I am interested in explaining the conditions under which presidential decision making on the macroeconomy shifts between the various incentives for policy-making behavior, I employ the same dichotomous dependent variable, *decision,* for both of the binomial logit estimations presented below. Data for the dependent variable is taken from *Public Papers of the Presidents of the United States, Containing the Public Messages, Speeches, and Statements of the President.* In coding this data source as a vector of presidential decisions, I follow a theoretical precedent set by several scholars (Kiewe 1994; Light 1991; Shull 1983; Kessel 1974, 1975). Since I am attempting to isolate the dynamics of when and how presidential decisions shift from established partisan preferences (and thus from the expected partisan macroeconomic logic), *decision* is coded one for each presidential decision that deviates from expected partisan behavior, zero otherwise. Making these coding decisions, I adhere closely to the partisan typologies established by Douglas Hibbs (1977, 1986, 1987).

A few simple examples will help to concretize this coding algorithm. Jimmy Carter's April 15, 1977, message outlining actions to control and reduce inflation is coded one, because it deviates from the expectation that Democratic presidents focus on unemployment. The decision instead exhibits the expected Republican macroeconomic stabilization calculus. In contrast, Carter's January 31, 1977, message to Congress proposing a two-year economic stimulus package focusing on job creation is coded zero, since it conforms to our expectation that Democratic preferences are geared toward reducing unemployment. Similarly, Richard Nixon's July 21, 1971, statement on the Emergency Employment Act of 1971 is coded one, because it deviates from the expected partisan behavior that Republican presidents will focus on inflation. In contrast, Nixon's March 17, 1970, message on combating inflation is coded zero, because it conforms to expected Republican behavior. This coding scheme was applied to each of the 103 initiatives recorded for 1953–96, with an inter-coder reliability of 93 percent (96 out of 103). The seven decisions in disagreement were recoded after additional archival research to clarify presidential position. Appendix A provides complete information on each of the 103 presidential initiatives.

Thus, the dependent variable measures whether a particular presidential decision in the American political economy conforms to, or deviates from, expected partisan behavior. Empirically, it measures precisely those trade-offs in which presidents shift away from their expected partisan and electoral behavior. My contention is that the imperatives of institutional responsibility for sound macroeconomic management lead to those moments (as will be extensively documented in the case studies) when a president temporarily appropriates the stabilization logic of the opposition party in order to deal with the vicious cycle. Again, this model is not meant to replace (or even compete with) models of positive political economy, but it does unpack the black box of presidential behavior in ways that political economists should find quite useful.

Unpacking this behavior will help solve the interesting puzzle raised by the presidential decision data presented in table 1. Table 1 aggregates the number of macroeconomic decisions (n = 103) taken by each postwar president (1953–96), which have fighting inflation or unemployment as their macroeconomic target.[4]

Table 1. Presidential Decisions on the Macroeconomy, 1953–96

President (Party)	Number of Inflation Positions	Number of Unemployment Positions
Eisenhower (R)	6	8
Kennedy (D)	1	7
Johnson (D)	6	10
Nixon (R)	8	5
Ford (R)	1	4
Carter (D)	7	5
Reagan (R)	17	3
Bush (R)	5	5
Clinton (D)	0	5
Total	51	52
Total Decisions by Party		
Republicans	37 (60%)	25 (40%)
Democrats	14 (34%)	27 (66%)

Source: *Public Papers of the Presidents of the United States*, 1953–96.

As table 1 demonstrates, presidential shifts from expected partisan behavior are actually more common than one might expect. For Republican presidents, 40 percent of their macroeconomic decisions can be categorized as targeting unemployment rather than inflation. Similarly, 34 percent of Democratic presidential decisions deviate from partisanship by focusing on inflation rather than unemployment. It is evident from the data that virtually all postwar presidents have engaged in these sorts of decision-making tradeoffs with some regularity. Thus, understanding the dynamics of these tradeoffs should be of central concern to presidency scholars studying macroeconomic policy making. It will soon be clear from both the aggregate model of institutional responsibility and the case studies to follow that the underlying intuition for presidential decision making is that an institutional imperative for stabilizing the macroeconomy often interferes with presidential pursuit of partisan and electoral objectives.

The Rational Partisan Model

The rational partisan literature discussed in chapter 1 suggests several expectations for presidential decision making with which to begin constructing a baseline model of partisan decision making. If, as the literature assumes, American electoral politics is characterized by an ideologically polarized two-party system in which the executive of each party possesses divergent macroeconomic policy preferences, then Democratic presidents should make decisions that are responsive to rapid changes in unemployment and Republican presidents should make decisions that are sensitive to sharp spikes in inflation; these strategies would serve as the best means of addressing the interests of their core partisan constituencies. This suggests that for optimal partisan targets in macroeconomic outcomes to be sustained over time, presidents *should not* readily shift from their partisan objectives in order to respond to the macroeconomic preferences of the other party. In general, Republican presidents can be expected to make decisions that are *less* responsive to recessionary downturn and Democratic presidents should adopt positions that are *less* concerned with inflationary spiral. This is not to suggest that they will ignore serious problems in the macroeconomy, for that is the essence of the shifts in priorities implicit in the idea of institutional responsibility. Nevertheless, there should generally be clear partisan differences in how presidents position themselves in response to changes in unemployment and inflation.

Given the coding of the dependent variable, a model of partisan presidential decision making can readily test this implication for macroeconomic policy making. I measure recessionary downturns and inflationary spirals here as the difference between the current annual rate of an indicator and a weighted prior three-year average. Following Alesina and Rosenthal (1995) and Hibbs (1987), I employ deviation from a weighted moving average to capture those circumstances when status quo macroeconomic conditions take a substantial turn for the worse, either in terms of inflation or unemployment. The weighted three-year moving average for unemployment is calculated as follows:

$$U_{ma3} = \frac{(U_{t-1} + rU_{t-2} + r^2U_{t-3})}{3}$$

where the natural weight r is the coefficient of the bivariate OLS equation $U_t = rU_{t-1} + e_t$. The weighted average for inflation is calculated in similar fashion, where

$$I_{ma3} = \frac{(I_{t-1} + rI_{t-2} + r^2I_{t-3})}{3}$$

where the natural weight r is the coefficient of the bivariate OLS equation $I_t = rI_{t-1} + e_t$. Data are drawn from the *Economic Report of the President* (1953–97).

Annual, rather than monthly or quarterly, data are employed here for a very specific purpose. The decision to use annual data is based on the assumption that if presidential preferences are largely fixed at their partisan ideal points as the partisan literature suggests, then monthly or quarterly fluctuations in the macroeconomy are unlikely to have a significant effect on decision making. Only longer-term retrospective calculations of substantial macroeconomic deterioration would be likely to compel presidents to shift their decision-making calculus in meaningful ways. Thus, these weighted moving averages capture the intuition that presidents, like the voters they are trying to convince, most heavily weigh recent macroeconomic performance while discounting more distant years of their administrations.

Expressing each macroeconomic variable as the difference between the current value of the indicator and its weighted prior average models those instances in which a president encounters significantly deteriorating macroeconomic conditions. Under the assumptions of a pure rational partisan model, presidential decisions should only be responsive to deteriorating conditions that directly threaten the interests of core partisan constituencies. We understand that in reality, however, presidents may very well accept tradeoffs with other nonpartisan objectives in shifting away from their partisan ideal points. For purposes of this baseline model, however, presidents are constrained to performing in a strictly partisan manner.

In addition, if we accept the partisan business cycle's rational expectations argument that a combination of wage-setting economic agent behavior and swing voter moderation diminishes the president's strategic incentive for inducing partisan cycles after the midterm, then presidents should feel freer to make decisions that shift away from partisan preferences after the midterm. To test this expectation, the variable *midterm* is coded one for the years following a midterm election, zero otherwise. If the model's implications for presidential behavior are correct, then there should be an increase in the probability that presidential decisions shift away from pure partisanship after the midterm.

Finally, the partisan business cycle model suggests several testable implications for the impact of institutional control (particularly divided government) on presidential decision making. Much research has already been done on the impact of divided government on political behavior, and the results are still in dispute (Edwards, Barrett, and Peake 1997; Campbell 1993; Fiorina 1992; Cox and McCubbins 1991; Mayhew 1991; Sundquist 1988). The effects of divided government are variously hypothesized to decrease electoral accountability and increase partisan bickering, to moderate partisan behavior, or to have no effect at all (Campbell 1993; Fiorina 1992; Sunquist 1988; Alesina and Rosenthal 1995; Mayhew 1991). If we accept the partisan business cycle model's argument (following Chappell and Keech 1986a, 1986b) that voters (particularly swing voters) use midterm elections to counterbalance the president's partisan behavior by strengthening opposition in Congress, then divided government should increase the probability of presidents making decisions that shift away from partisan objectives. Swing voters act as a moderating influence, pulling presidential decision making away from the preferences of core partisan constituencies. To test this implication, the variable *divided* is coded one for years in which divided government exists, zero otherwise. Appendix B provides an overview of data on institutional control and the macroeconomy, and Appendix C provides data on the distribution of all variables used in this chapter's analysis.

One could also make the argument (as does Alesina and Rosenthal 1995), however, that a dichotomous variable for divided government is too crude a measurement for such a key theoretical construct. It is quite possible that the *intensity* of partisan or institutional conflict really drives tradeoffs in presidential decision making. To test for this possibility, two additional variables, *outecon* and *concur,* are included in the logit model to test for the impact of conflict intensity on presidential decision making. The variable *outecon* is calculated as the percentage of out-party support for the president on House roll call votes specifically dealing with issues of macroeconomic management. The variable *concur* measures the percentage of total House and Senate concurrence with the president. It is calculated as the number of congressional votes supporting the president divided by the total number of votes on which the president has taken a position. The data for both variables are take from Ragsdale 1996. All three of the institutional control variables, *divided, outecon,* and *concur,* were tested for multicollinearity and were found not to be problematic for estimation, as each measures a substantially different aspect of institutional control.

Given the partisan business cycle model's emphasis on institution balancing, one should expect partisan opposition to the president's economic program *(outecon)* to increase the probability that a president will move from partisan decision making. Similarly, strong institutional opposition (irrespective of partisanship) in Congress to the president (a low *concur* percentage) should also increase the probability that a president deviates from partisanship. In sum, if the partisan business cycle model's implications for presidential decision making are correct, then partisan and institutional conflict between presidents and the Congress should always lead the former to moderate their positions on macroeconomic outcomes, thereby increasing the probability that the president will need to accept a tradeoff and move away from the objectives of core partisan constituencies. A tradeoff in the stylized context of this pure partisan model would be represented by a switch in focus from unemployment to inflation for Democrats and the reverse for Republicans.

Having employed the assumptions and insights of rational partisan theory and the partisan business cycle model to specify the components of a baseline model of partisan presidential decision making, I estimate the following logit model:

$$P(decision = 1) = a_0 + b_1(U_t - U_{ma3}) + b_2(I_t - I_{ma3})$$
$$+ b_3 midterm_t + b_4 divided_t + b_5 outecon_t + b_6 concur_t + e_t$$

The results for the logit estimation of the rational partisan model are presented in table 2.[5]

Column one reports the independent variables included in the equation; column two, the estimation results with standard errors in parentheses; and column three, the marginal effect of each variable on the probability that a president makes a decision regarding the macroeconomy that deviates from the expectations of pure partisan behavior. The model's diagnostics suggest

Table 2. Presidential Decision Making and the Rational Partisan Model (Logit Estimates)

Variable	Coefficient (standard error)	Marginal Effect
$(U_t - U_{ma3})$	1.20*** (.32)	.27
$(I_t - I_{ma3})$	.27* (.13)	.06
midterm	1.17* (.55)	.26
divided	−3.60* (1.04)	.79
outecon	.06** (.02)	.01
concur	−.10*** (.03)	.02
(Constant)	3.77 (2.40)	
−2 Log Likelihood	95.58	
Chi-squared (df)	41.08*** (6)	
Percent Correctly Predicted	79.61	
n = 103		

*$p < .05$; **$p < .01$; ***$p < .001$.
Source: *Economic Report of the President, 1953–97; Public Papers of the Presidents of the United States, 1953–96;* Congressional Quarterly, *Members of Congress since 1789;* Ragsdale 1996.

a good fit of the data and a rejection of the joint null hypothesis that all coefficients except the intercept are equal to zero.

As shown in column two, each of the six independent variables in the equation is a statistically significant predictor of presidential decision making. The results demonstrate that a pure partisan logic does not fully capture presidential management of the macroeconomy. The economic variables show that presidents of both parties accept tradeoffs in macroeconomic objectives; Republican presidents are sensitive to recessionary downturns and Democratic presidents are responsive to inflationary spirals. The marginal effects of the unemployment (.27) and inflation (.06) variables reflect the relative importance of these deviating behaviors. The smaller marginal effect of the inflation variable, however, is in keeping with Alesina and Rosenthal's finding (1995) that Democratic presidents are somewhat more tolerant of inflationary spirals than Republican presidents are of recessionary downturns.

Thus, these results serve as a useful baseline confirmation that, although presidents are not easily moved from their partisan ideal points, they will accept tradeoffs with their partisan objectives if deemed necessary for responsible management of the macroeconomy. These findings underscore the conditional nature of presidential decision making suggested by positive political economy models. The difference is that the model tested here directly measures presidential decisions rather than inferring them from movement in macroeconomic indicators. So, at a minimum, we know that the findings can be extended to presidential behavior.

Also in keeping with the rational partisan model, *midterm* has a substantial marginal effect (.26) on the probability that a president shifts away from partisan behavior. This result fits with the partisan business cycle model's suggestion that presidents face a weaker incentive for partisan behavior after the midterm. Accordingly, the probability that presidents will act contrary to the preferences of their core partisan constituencies significantly increases after the midterm election. I will suggest later that the filter of institutional responsibility is strongest as presidents approach the end of a first term and as they become institutionalized in office.

Recall that the partisan business cycle model attributes this strategic behavior to a process of swing voter–induced balancing of institutional control between the president and Congress. A look at the performance of the three institutional control variables in table 2, however, makes this theoretical argument problematic for a direct test of presidential behavior. While all three variables, *divided, outecon,* and *concur,* are statistically significant, the sign on the *divided* coefficient and the marginal effects for *outecon* and *concur* raise important questions about the institutional control story told by the partisan business cycle model.

The variable *divided* clearly has a very strong marginal effect (.79) on the probability that a president deviates from partisanship.[6] The negative sign suggests, however, that divided government actually *reinforces* partisan behavior by the president rather than weakening it. Since the model was tested for multicollinearity, the incorrect sign cannot be attributed to an estimation problem. Instead, I will suggest a theoretical explanation for this result in the discussion of the institutional responsibility model below. Most importantly, although the signs on the *outecon* and *concur* variables are in the appropriate direction, the marginal effects (.01 and .02, respectively) of the two variables are so small as to suggest that neither partisan nor institutional conflict moderates the partisan nature of presidential decision making on the macroeconomy in any significant way.

One can conclude that rational partisan theory (and the partisan business cycle model in particular) provide some logical theoretical implications for presidential behavior. When one directly models presidential decision making using those insights, presidents are clearly seen to be engaging in partisan behavior yet are also willing to accept tradeoffs in partisanship with other objectives when sound macroeconomic management requires it, particularly after the midterm. Thus, we have some good baseline intuitions here about the relationship between presidential decision making and partisanship. In the next section, I factor into the model additional assumptions about how the imperatives of institutional responsibility constrain presidential decision making in the pursuit of partisan and electoral objectives. These additional considerations help to provide a more nuanced understanding of presidential shifts in focus from one set of political and macroeconomic objectives to another.

Factoring Institutional Responsibility into the Model

The concept of institutional responsibility argues that a president's strategic macroeconomic policy-making behavior is powerfully shaped by a conflicting desire to serve as party leader and win office, while still fulfilling the institutional mandate to be the nation's chief macroeconomic policy maker. Understanding how presidents resolve this inherent conflict between strategic incentives and institutional constraints should be central to any fruitful model of presidential decision making in the American political economy.

That institutional responsibility serves as a filter on presidential response to partisan and electoral incentives should be evident. Several scholars (Keech 1995; Frendreis and Tatalovich 1994; Anderson and Hazleton 1986; Edwards 1983) have suggested that, with the growth of media-center politics, the decline of political parties, and the breakdown of policy networks and institutionalized pluralism, public expectations of presidential responsibility are increasingly central to the president's strategic behavior. For the institutional responsibility model, presidential response to an electoral incentive for strategic decision making is closely tied to the response of the institution in dealing with the macroeconomy, more so than to the response of the president's party in dealing with the same. Presidents' strategic behaviors reflect their interest in the institutional position in addition to their partisan affiliation. Thus, the partisan accountability highlighted in the traditional responsible party model (Campbell 1993; Fiorina 1992; Sundquist 1988; Ranney 1962; Schattschneider 1942) is transformed into a notion of an institutional accountability (or constraint). The president, rather than the party, is held individually (and often unrealistically) accountable by the electorate for the performance of the macroeconomy.

The literature on institutionalization of the presidency notes that this transformation in presidential behavior, from party-centered to institution-centered politics, is not immediate but occurs gradually over the length of a particular president's time in office. This would be an explanation for the earlier finding that presidents are more willing to forgo partisan objectives after the midterm election. Several scholars have suggested the importance of time for understanding political behavior and institutional change (Skowronek 1993, 1995; Light 1991; Kessel 1975). In keeping with this idea, I agree that the incentive for partisan behavior should be strongest early in a president's time in office, when a president as party leader is most likely to reward core constituencies with favorable macroeconomic outcomes in exchange for their support during the recent election. Republican presidents target low inflation, and Democratic presidents focus on low unemployment. If a change in party control of the White House has occurred, suboptimal macroeconomic performance can be passed off as a lagged holdover from the prior administration's misguided policies. *Yet, as the president becomes acclimated to a new role as the nation's chief macroeconomic policy maker, institutional responsibility and the high public expectations that accompany it act as an increasingly strong institutional filter or constraint working against partisan decision making.*

The longer presidents occupy the office, the more likely they are to make decisions on the macroeconomy that target a Phillips curve tradeoff that *is not* in keeping with their party's interests, especially in response to the sort of inflationary spirals and recessionary downturns included in the first logit model. In these circumstances, public expectations exert pressure on presidential decision making, which reinforces presidents' need to be seen as institutionally responsible for the macroeconomy beyond the dictates of core partisan interests. Reelection to a second term should not truncate this institutional effect; if anything, it should magnify the effect. In a second term, presidents are much more concerned with how history, rather than their party, will hold them accountable for the office. Time should therefore have a monotonically increasing institutionalizing effect on strategic presidential behavior over the course of a two-term presidency.

As noted earlier, the notion of institutional responsibility suggests somewhat different implications for divided government than does rational partisan theory. Under the institutional responsibility model, I suggest that divided government actually decreases the likelihood that a president will shift away from party preferences rather than having a moderating effect on partisan presidential behavior. Under divided government, it is much more difficult for the electorate to hold presidents responsible for the condition of the macroeconomy, particularly if they are able to affix blame to the opposition in Congress. In contrast, unified government greatly increases the likelihood that a president will shift from a partisan objective, as unified control is particularly symbolic for raising the electorate's expectations of presidential responsibility for fighting inflationary spiral and recessionary downturn. With this type of institutional accountability argument, one can be less concerned with the partisan and institutional conflict variables that tested poorly in the first logit equation. This theoretical argument also explains the reversed sign on the *divided* coefficient. As noted above, this accountability argument is similar to that put forth in Campbell 1993, Fiorina 1992, and Sundquist 1988, with the crucial distinction that the president is being held accountable primarily as an institutional actor rather than as member of a political party.

In sum, the institutional responsibility model tested below argues that the probability that presidential decision making on the macroeconomy is partisan is highest early in the first term and decreases over time. The degree to which institutional constraints squeeze out partisan incentives in shaping presidential decisions is largely a function of the length of time that a president has been in office, the nature of the institutional balance between the president and Congress, and the type and magnitude of fluctuations in the macroeconomy with which the president must contend. As presidents accrue institutional responsibility for the condition of the macroeconomy with each additional year in office, and as they deal with the institutional accountability brought on by unified government, the probability dramatically increases that, even when faced with deteriorating macroeconomic conditions most threatening to the interests of the opposition party, presidents will shift their decision-making objectives away from partisan decision making.

To measure the condition of the macroeconomy for the institutional responsibility model, I employ the same unemployment and inflation variables used in the first logit model. Again, Republican presidents should respond to recessionary downturns, and Democratic presidents should be sensitive to inflationary spirals. To provide a clearer sense of how the institutional responsibility model relates to the condition of the macroeconomy, the calculated values for the inflation and unemployment variables are graphed in figure 1.

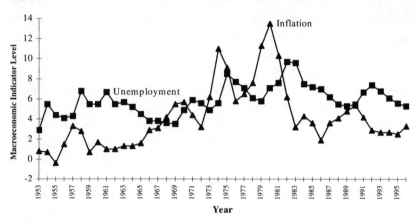

Fig. 1. Current Inflation and Unemployment, 1953–96

The model suggests, for example, that the probability of President Carter shifting away from partisan objectives to address the inflation spike in the fourth year of his term (1980) would be substantially greater than the probability of President Ronald Reagan moving from partisan targets on inflation to confront the unemployment spike in the second year of his term (1982). Carter had been president for two additional years and was serving under conditions of unified government. History confirms the model's intuition in these particular cases. Carter's decisions shifted from partisan objectives in 1980, but Reagan's did not in 1982. Similar probabilistic comparisons can be made between the other postwar presidents based on a consideration of temporal location in office, institutional control, and macroeconomic conditions.

Since the institutional responsibility model theorizes that the likelihood of a president abandoning rational partisan behavior *(decision = 1)* increases over the course of a president's time in office, *presyr* is coded one through eight for each year a president is in office. Shared terms such as Kennedy/ Johnson and Nixon/Ford are coded one, beginning with the first full year that each president serves in office. For example, Kennedy's time in office is coded one through three (1961–63), and Johnson's time is coded one through five (1964–68). This coding scheme best captures the manner in which each subsequent president experiences anew the interaction of partisan incentives and institutional responsibility. Lyn Ragsdale and Jerrold Rush (1999) use a similar counting variable to measure presidential time in office.

Since unified government is hypothesized to greatly magnify a president's institutional responsibility, the dichotomous variable *unified* is coded one for years in which unified control of the government exists, zero otherwise. As this is an accountability argument rather than a resource-based argument, the intensity of conflict is not of concern here. Thus, the two earlier variables, *outecon* and *concur,* would provide little additional explanatory power. Even if presidents barely achieve unified government (in terms of seats held by their party), voters will still hold the president more accountable for outcomes than under narrowly divided government, since in the former instance presidents would "control" Congress, whereas in the latter circumstance they would not. Accountability in an institutional context is the key issue for presidential decision making, not institution balancing per se.

Given the research into the relationship between the president and the macroeconomy discussed in chapter 1, two additional variables merit consideration for inclusion in the model. First, the impact of presidential popularity on behavior should be addressed. The level of popularity (or electoral security) enjoyed by a president may serve as a catalyst for strategic macroeconomic behavior (Schultz 1995). Research suggests that popular presidents would be less likely to feel constrained by institutional responsibility and may use the electoral breathing room to serve the interests of core partisan constituencies (Schultz 1995; Frey and Schneider 1978). Thus, variation in presidential popularity may affect the probability that a president will make a decision on the macroeconomy that deviates from the rational partisan norm. The variable *prespop* uses average annual presidential popularity data taken from Ragsdale 1996.

A second consideration relates to the president's indirect relationship with the Federal Reserve. As some research suggests, the Fed is often a key player in the politics of stabilization policy. Scholars look for a substantive connection between presidential behavior and Federal Reserve policy in their indirect relationship over monetary policy (Beck 1987; Woolley 1988; Grier 1989; Williams 1990; McGregor 1996). Policy signaling by the Federal Reserve, stemming from its own assessment of the macroeconomy, may have a significant independent impact on presidential behavior. Drawing from this literature, the model uses movement in short-term interest rates as a measure of potential signaling behavior. The variable *tbill* uses average annual rate data on three-month Treasury bills, drawn from the *Economic Report of the President* (1953–97). All three economic variables were again tested for multicollinearity and found not to be problematic for model estimation.

Annual data are again employed for these variables, based on the assumption that fluctuations in popularity and interest rates would have to be both substantial and prolonged over time in order to move the president from a fixed partisan ideal point; quarterly data would be less likely to clearly demonstrate this effect. In fact, early runs of the model employing either monthly or quarterly data were not statistically significant predictions of decision making.

Given the above considerations, I estimate the following binomial logit model of institutional responsibility:

$$P(decision = 1) = a_0 + b_1(U_t - U_{ma3}) + b_2(I_t - I_{ma3})$$
$$+ b_3 presyr_t + b_4 unified_t + b_5 prespop_t + b_6 tbill_t + e_t$$

This equation models the conditions under which presidents cannot satisfy their core partisan constituencies because institutional responsibility for deteriorating macroeconomic conditions is exerting pressure on decision making. It models the probability, under a given institutional configuration and political and economic environment, that the president will trade partisan objectives for the pursuit of other goals.

The results for the logit estimation of the institutional responsibility model are presented in table 3.

Column one reports the independent variables included in the equation; column two, the coefficient with standard errors in parentheses; and column three, the marginal effect of each variable on the probability that a president shifts from rational partisan behavior. The model's diagnostics suggest a good fit of the data and a rejection of the joint null hypothesis that all coefficients except the intercept are equal to zero. The inflation and unemployment variables are both again statistically significant predictors of presidential shifts away from partisanship. The institutional responsibility variables, *presyr* and *unified,* are also statistically significant predictors of presidential deviation.

The *presyr* variable, which arguably gives a finer measure of time over the course of a presidency than the *midterm* variable of the first logit model, clearly demonstrates the impact of institutionalization on behavior. The longer presidents are in office, the more likely they are to make decisions that accept tradeoffs with partisanship. The sign on the *unified* coefficient is correct, in keeping with the argument that presidential behavior responds to concerns over institutional accountability rather than conflict. Under divided government, institutional accountability for the condition of the macroeconomy is less easily assessed by voters than under unified government, so the president does not have an incentive to shift away from partisanship. Neither the *prespop* nor *tbill* variables, however, are statistically significant

Table 3. Presidential Decision Making and the Institutional Responsibility Model (Logit Estimates)

Variable	Coefficient (standard error)	Marginal Effect
$(U_t - U_{ma3})$	1.09*** (.32)	.25
$(I_t - I_{ma3})$	.26* (.13)	.06
presyr	.41* (.20)	.09
unified	1.87* (.78)	.42
prespop	−.04 (.03)	−.01
tbill	−.19 (.13)	−.04
(Constant)	.82 (2.55)	
−2 Log Likelihood	102.58	
Chi-squared (df)	34.07*** (6)	
Percent Correctly Predicted	78.64	
n = 103		

*$p < .05$; **$p < .01$; ***$p < .001$.
Source: *Economic Report of the President, 1953−97; Public Papers of the Presidents of the United States, 1953–96;* Congressional Quarterly, *Members of Congress since 1789;* Ragsdale 1996.

predictors. A decision does not appear to be driven by short-term considerations such as fluctuations in popularity or signaling by other institutional actors, such as the Federal Reserve. These results are directly in keeping with the notion of institutional responsibility.

Removal of the *prespop* and *tbill* variables from the equation allows for a more accurate estimate of the impact of institutional responsibility on presidential decision making. Table 4 presents the model reestimated with these two variables omitted from the equation.

As a result, the statistical significance of the core institutional and macroeconomic variables increases dramatically. Shifts in presidential decision making away from rational partisan behavior are strongly affected by institu-

Table 4. Presidential Decision Making and the Institutional Responsibility Model Re-estimated (Logit Estimates)

Variable	Coefficient (standard error)	Marginal Effect
$(U_t - U_{ma3})$	1.26*** (.31)	.29
$(I_t - I_{ma3})$	.32** (.12)	.07
presyr	.58*** (.18)	.13
unified	2.23** (.73)	.51
prespop		
tbill		
(Constant)	−3.26*** (.76)	
2-Log Likelihood	105.52	
Chi-squared (df)	31.12*** (6)	
Percent Correctly Predicted	73.78	

n = 103

*$p < .05$; **$p < .01$; ***$p < .001$.

Source: *Economic Report of the President, 1953–97; Public Papers of the Presidents of the United States, 1953–96;* Congressional Quarterly, *Members of Congress since 1789;* Ragsdale 1996.

tional accountability as it develops over time in office, under unified government, and by deteriorating macroeconomic conditions. The diagnostics for this model are similarly good, even with the removal of the popularity and interest rate variables.

The marginal effects of the four remaining variables underscore the impact of institutional responsibility on the conditional nature of presidential decision making. Recall that the coding of the dependent variable picks up those instances when Republican presidents shift away from partisanship in the face of a recessionary downturn, and Democratic presidents do the same when confronted with an inflationary spiral. In looking at the marginal effects in table 4, recessionary downturn does indeed have a significant probabilistic impact (.29) on Republican presidents. Similarly, an inflation-

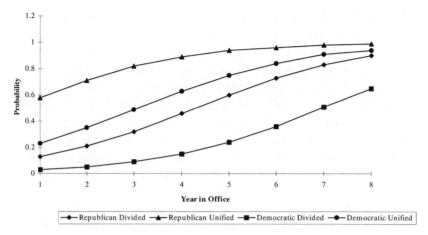

Fig. 2. Predicted Probability of Deviation from Partisanship in Simulated Two-Term Presidency

ary spiral has a measurable impact on the probability of Democratic deviation (.07), although not as strong an impact as that seen for unemployment
and Republican presidents. As is also evident in the marginal effects, a president's time in office has a significant impact on the probability of deviation
from partisanship (.13) with each additional year. Finally, unified government has a very strong marginal effect (.51) on presidential decision making,
greatly increasing the probability of a presidential shift in objectives. This
result fits with the theoretical idea that responsibility for stabilizing the macroeconomy and the resultant institutional accountability are central to understanding the dynamics of presidential decision making.

The marginal effects presented in table 4 provide a useful measure of the
impact of institutional responsibility on presidential behavior, but in order
to graphically illustrate the model's insights, figure 2 presents *predicted probabilities* that simulate the likelihood of a presidential shift away from partisan objectives, under several institutional and macroeconomic scenarios
encountered by Republican and Democratic presidents. The figure graphs
over time the probabilistic behavior of a hypothetical two-term Republican
president encountering a recession under conditions of unified and divided
government. The figure also graphs the same behavior for a Democratic
president encountering an inflation spiral under similar institutional con-
figurations. In substituting actual values into the table 4 logit model, for a
Republican president the variable unemployment is set at its third quartile
value to simulate a substantial unemployment spike while the inflation variable is set at its first quartile value. For the Democratic president, the infla-

tion variable is set at its third quartile value to simulate a substantial inflation spike while the unemployment variable is set at its first quartile value.[7] These specifications render a realistic simulation of the conditions encountered by postwar presidents and thus highlight the significant effects of institutional responsibility on presidential decision making.

The predicted probabilities illustrate the way in which partisanship in decision making is weakened in probabilistic fashion over the course of eight years in office due to the institutional constraints on the president. With each subsequent year in a presidential term, the probability of a presidential shift away from partisanship in the face of deteriorating macroeconomic conditions increases dramatically. Both Democratic and Republican presidents show a very low probability of abandoning their preferred partisan position early in their terms (with the exception of Republican unified government, to be discussed below). From the graphs, one sees that (in keeping with the marginal effects in table 4) Republican presidents are more likely to shift away from partisanship in response to recession than Democratic presidents are in response to inflation under the same institutional configuration. For both parties, however, unified government substantially increases the probability that a president will move away from partisan macroeconomic targets, even early in the term.

It is important to note, however, that the predicted probabilities line for the Republican president under unified government, while dramatic, simulates an institutional configuration (unified Republican government) that has been a rarity in the postwar period. The same can be said of the divided Democratic government line. Thus, the middle two lines of the graph, unified Democratic government and divided Republican government, most closely simulate the postwar U.S. experience with presidential decision making on the macroeconomy. Nonetheless, the predicted probabilities are intended to *simulate* what presidential behavior would look like under various political, institutional, and macroeconomic conditions. Perhaps the future will provide a useful test of the presidential behavior suggested by the two more speculative, yet provocative lines. *In general, the predicted probabilities provide graphic empirical evidence that the conditional nature of presidential decision making can be tested directly in order to demonstrate that it is affected by institutional responsibility and control and by macroeconomic conditions.*

Conclusion

The aggregate results provided by the models in this chapter confirm both the conditional nature of presidential behavior in the macroeconomic policy-making environment (as suggested by positive political economy models) and that this finding can be extended to a direct test of presidential decision making. The results provide important insight into the ways in which institutional constraints shape presidential acceptance of tradeoffs in macroeconomic objectives over the course of four years in office. Specifically, we can conclude that the longer presidents are in office, the more likely they are to move away from the pursuit of purely partisan objectives.

In addition, the condition of unified government greatly increases the likelihood that presidents will trade off on their macroeconomic objectives in order to be viewed as fiscally responsible by the broad heterogeneous reelection constituency. Under divided government, presidential responsibility for deleterious macroeconomic outcomes can more readily be obscured by deflecting blame onto the policies of the opposition party in Congress. Thus, divided government essentially buys the president additional time to more directly pursue partisan and electoral incentives for decision making.

Finally, the aggregate results suggest that any presidential shift in objectives is gradual, rather than volatile, as presidents are loath to give up the pursuit of political objectives unless forced to do so by the imperatives of institutional responsibility in the face of deteriorating macroeconomic conditions.

Part II
A Test of the Theory
with Four Presidential Case Studies

INTRODUCTION

Thus far we have seen that research on presidential decision making suggests that presidents are likely to pursue partisan and electoral incentives
when making decisions in the American political economy. Chapter 2 established that presidents make these decisions in a stable postwar policy-
making environment, one in which the focus is on competing partisan logics
for stabilization policy designed to favor core partisan constituencies. Republican presidents are generally expected to favor less inflation at the risk
of increased unemployment, while Democratic presidents usually prefer less
unemployment at the risk of increased inflation.

Chapter 3 also suggests, however, that presidents have primary institutional responsibility for the health of the economy. They are ultimately held
responsible by the electorate and by other policy makers for the success
or failure of stabilization policy, during both recessionary downturn and
inflationary spiral. I have argued that this institutional responsibility may
work at cross-purposes with exogenous political incentives for presidential
behavior. It is this tension between a president's institutional position and
political objectives that may lead to tradeoffs in the decision-making calculus. *Presidents may want to satisfy core constituencies or expand the economy
in an election year, but the imperatives of their institutional position may lead
them to make decisions that actually work against fulfillment of the incentives
modeled in the political economy literature.*

The case studies presented in chapters 4, 5, and 6 are developed to test
these expectations for presidential decision making. Chapter 4 presents the
first-term archival record on macroeconomic policy making for Democratic
presidents Johnson and Carter in order to determine if either president temporarily appropriates a Republican logic for stabilization policy in the face
of political opposition by members of their own party in Congress. I look
for evidence that both presidents filter their respective partisan concerns
through the decision-making lens of institutional responsibility. Similarly, in
chapter 5 I search for evidence in the archival record that Republican presi-

dents Eisenhower and Reagan make the same sort of decision-making trade-offs in reverse, temporarily accepting a Democratic logic for stabilization policy.

Chapter 6 presents a test of the relationship between the political business cycle hypothesis and institutional responsibility in order to suggest that for presidents from both parties, rapid expansion of the economy during an election year is the *last* decision-making strategy on their minds. In each of the case studies, the operative circumstance for a shift away from presidential pursuit of partisan and electoral incentives is an economic crisis that is not readily addressed by the tool kit associated with the presidential party's macroeconomic calculus. In contrast, if there is no vicious cycle to confront, a president has substantially more latitude to pursue party policy objectives.

What do these decision-making tradeoffs look like for macroeconomic policy? We know from the models of political economy discussed earlier that Democratic presidents generally expand the economy through increased discretionary spending and monetary ease while cutting spending and raising taxes to contract the economy. In contrast, Republican presidents generally prefer to expand the economy through tax cuts while contracting the economy through budget balancing and monetary restraint. With these partisan typologies in mind, it will be clear when a president from one party appropriates the stabilization logic of the other, as it is at those moments when presidential behavior most clearly diverges from the partisan decision-making calculus described in the political economy literature.

I will also test the expectation, suggested by the institutional responsibility model in chapter 3, that unified government actually magnifies this effect, as it deprives the president of any opportunity for hiding behind the guise of divided government gridlock. Ultimately, the surprise is not that presidents stabilize the macroeconomy but that they do so in ways that underscore the constraints that the president's institutional position places on decision making.

Democratic Presidents and the Republican Logic of Anti-Inflation Policy

Riding a landslide victory in the November, 1964, election and feeling the afterglow of the 1964 tax cut ($12 billion pumped into the economy), President Lyndon Johnson was poised to move the economy toward full productive utilization and the goal of full employment (defined as 4 percent unemployment) in 1965. In that year, the Keynesian "New Economics" paradigm that had supplied the demand-side macroeconomic rationale for the 1964 "Kennedy" tax cut called for LBJ to continue stimulation of consumer demand, thereby increasing plant capacity and output and creating new jobs.[1] This approach to macroeconomic policy making was in keeping with the postwar notion of a partisan Democratic macroeconomic logic; presidential decision making was designed to decrease unemployment through stimulation of demand.

This policy focus was precisely the one recommended by LBJ's key economic advisers in the wake of his 1964 electoral victory. During December, 1964, as the administration finalized its fiscal 1966 budget, LBJ's "troika," comprising the CEA chairman, the budget director, and the secretary of the Treasury, advised the president to pursue further macroeconomic stimulus along New Economics lines. Illustrating the Democratic administration's focus on a pro-employment agenda, a December 7, 1964, troika memo to the president urged that "to maintain progress toward the goal of full employment and to obtain adequate insurance against economic slowdown and recession, we need an additional fiscal stimulus of about $3 billion in the fiscal 1966 budget through a larger excise tax reduction and/or increased expenditure programs. As we see it, this must be realistically recognized as the near-term budgetary price-tag of a full employment program."[2] Basing its macroeconomic projections on a $100 billion budget, $2 billion in excise tax cuts, and a 7 percent retroactive Social Security benefit increase during 1965, the troika feared that without a sharp rise in nondefense spending and/or further excise tax cuts, administration policies would not continue to close the macroeconomic gap between potential and real growth (particularly after mid-1965, when there would be no further stimulus felt from the 1964 tax cut).[3] The troika concluded that without this additional stimulus, "the projected gains will not be large enough to achieve significant further progress toward full employment."[4]

CEA chairman Gardner Ackley emphasized the need for additional fiscal stimulus through the traditional Democratic means of increased expenditures (for Great Society programs) or through additional demand-side tax relief. In a memo dated December 13, 1964, Ackley tried to allay LBJ's concern that increasing the deficit through additional spending, or through a loss of tax revenues, might raise inflationary fears in the business community. Ackley noted that "especially after the demonstration provided by the tax cut, enlightened members of the business community understand the power of fiscal measures. . . . Fears that a more stimulating budget for 1965 would lead to a loss of confidence and a run on the dollar seem to us unfounded."[5] The CEA chairman argued that fiscal policy would continue to be expansionary throughout 1965, with the excise tax cut and Social Security liberalization taking place at midyear. The prospect of negative stimulus in fiscal year 1966 existed, however, due to a \$5.5 billion payroll tax increase scheduled for January 1, 1966, to finance Social Security and Medicare. This was despite the fact that the second stage of the 1964 tax cut was scheduled to kick in at the same time.[6]

Thus, as 1965 began, LBJ's advisers uniformly recommended a macroeconomic agenda that was consistent with the dictates of a partisan Democratic stabilization logic. The goal was to close the gap between potential and actual output, through demand-side policies of increased federal spending and tax relief (a combined additional \$3 billion), thereby perpetuating the economic expansion underway since the early 1960s. Little concern was evident at the time for inflation or for the enlarged federal deficit that might result from the president's decisions.

LBJ's response to the policy suggestions of his key economic advisers is instructive for understanding how the pull of institutional responsibility on presidential decision making acts as a filter on pursuing partisan and electoral objectives. Johnson's decision making in early 1965 marked the subtle beginning of a move away from Democratic concerns about full employment and toward an increasing Republican preoccupation with inflation caused by an overheating economy. As evidence of this institutional pull on LBJ, the president rejected the troika recommendation of an additional \$3 billion in fiscal stimulus for fiscal year 1966. Ackley recalls that LBJ, ever concerned with the political implications of his policy decisions, assembled an influential group of businessmen at the White House in order to solicit their opinion of the stimulus package. The White House Business Council was virtually unanimous in its belief that additional stimulus was a bad idea, for it would increase the deficit and the danger of inflation.[7] As Ackley noted, "It had no political appeal to anyone, so that was the end of it."[8]

In hindsight, Johnson's decision not to further expand the budget at the time appears wise, as the 1965 GNP ultimately hit $672 billion ($14 billion more than predicted by the administration), with a fourth-quarter GNP increase that was the largest in U.S. history. The result of this economic boom was an unemployment rate that dropped to 4 percent and a utilization of manufacturing that reached 90 percent of capacity with accelerated plans for future capital investments. This jump was in large part due to unexpected July increases in defense expenditures for U.S. military activities in Vietnam (a phenomenon that would plague LBJ's macroeconomic decision making) combined with ever-expanding Great Society programs. This combination pushed aggregate demand beyond the country's productive capabilities and toward an inflationary crisis.[9]

A Taxing Fight against Inflation

Throughout 1966, Johnson rejected the recommendation of his advisers for a tax increase to cool the overheated economy. With the escalating expenditures for both Vietnam and the Great Society, this decision has often been referred to as Johnson's attempt to fund both guns and butter without a tax increase. The increase recommended by his advisers was consistent with a partisan Democratic logic for fighting inflation. Increased taxes would pay for more programs while also siphoning money out of an overheated economy. Johnson instead responded to congressional and public concerns over a potential tax increase. During the midterm election year of 1966, he refused to raise taxes and instead relied on tight monetary policy by the Federal Reserve to cool the economy. *Not only did LBJ reject a Democratic focus on unemployment in order to deal with inflation but he did so in a way that suggests a decidedly Republican stabilization policy logic (even though a Democratic option was presented to him). Johnson clearly linked success in the midterm election as being contingent upon his ability to cool the economy in a responsible manner. His pursuit of Democratic electoral objectives was clearly filtered through the lens of institutional responsibility.*

The policy decision about-face by LBJ's advisers, from more stimulus to increased taxes, however, did not occur immediately after Johnson's rejection of the 1965 proposal for additional stimulus. As noted, spending for Vietnam did not take center stage until July. In June, 1965, the CEA was actually more concerned than ever that there was insufficient stimulus in the fiscal year 1967 budget. Advisers feared that the rate of economic growth would slow in the next four quarters, resulting in increased unemployment, their chief concern. To this end, the CEA assembled a group of top academic consultants, including Paul Samuelson and Robert Solow of MIT, John Lintner and James Duesenberry of Harvard, and Richard Musgrave of Princeton, in order to solicit their opinions on the need for additional fiscal stimulus. Ackley reported to LBJ that the group was unanimous in agreeing that "they would like to see more fiscal stimulus in early 1966. . . . [T]hey urged a strongly expansionary budget for fiscal 1967."[10] In the memo, Ackley downplayed the inflationary significance of recent small price increases and instead charted a path for LBJ toward the goal of full employment by 1968 (the next presidential election year).[11]

The options presented to LBJ by the CEA and its consultants in June were uniformly in keeping with a Democratic stabilization approach. The group called for $7 billion to $8 billion in combined stimulus, primarily through increased domestic spending and/or income tax reductions. *The tax reductions were also distinctly Democratic, geared to further stimulate consumer demand rather than increase capital investment.* To this end the group "endorsed raising the personal income tax exemption from $600 to $800 to pump in purchasing power where it will do the most good—in generating demand for consumer goods, and in helping those who need it most."[12]

By increasing spending for the escalating conflict in Vietnam in July, 1965, Johnson unintentionally provided the CEA with the desired stimulus. It was sufficient to get Chairman Ackley, in a memo on the economic implications of Vietnam, to back off from his recommendation of a tax cut to stimulate the economy in fiscal year 1966.[13] For the first time, Ackley conveyed concern to LBJ about the inflationary impact of Vietnam spending, noting that "we will need to intensify our concern about prices and wages."[14] He expressed concern that business might assume the administration was moving toward mandatory wage and price controls, as had been the case with previous administrations during World War II and the Korean War. Ackley urged LBJ to reaffirm his commitment to the voluntary guidelines first established during the Kennedy administration.[15] Still, Ackley (in true New Economic fashion) was not yet ready to jettison the Democratic focus on unemployment. He advised LBJ that "our economy has lots of room to absorb a defense step-up. There is still a $15–20 billion margin of idle industrial capacity and excessive unemployment. Our productive capacity is growing by $25–30 billion a year (apart from any price increases), making room for both more butter and, if needed, more guns."[16] Watchful of closing the gap between potential and actual growth, Ackley may have believed that both more guns and more butter were a possibility, but the Federal Reserve did not.

In fall 1965, the administration hoped to employ the "quadriad" (the troika plus Federal Reserve Board chairman William Martin) to reach agreement over possible restraint being planned by the Fed to fight inflation. In October, Ackley informed LBJ that this approach was fraught with some fundamental difficulties. He wrote,

> The fundamental issue is whether restraint is the right medicine to-day. And this is where we and Bill Martin reach opposite judgments. . . . In summary, monetary policy stands at the crossroads. If the economy needs to be slowed down—as Bill Martin believes—rises in the prime rate and the discount rate and still higher bond yields are in order. If, as we believe, the economy is not now moving ahead too rapidly, the level of interest rates should not and need not be permitted to jump upward. A clear signal of "no tightening" in the Fed's purchases of securities could hold the line.[17]

Ackley concluded that the best course for LBJ was to head off a Fed increase in interest rates while promising to take a careful second look at the need for restraint at the start of 1966, when the CEA could get a clearer picture of the budget, the price outlook, and key elements of private demand such as autos and business investment. Ackley reiterated this position in mid-November.[18]

Despite Ackley's use of the quadriad to gain support for a wait-and-see attitude by the Fed, by December, 1965, Fed chairman Martin was ready to act without the administration's consent to restrain the overheating economy through higher interest rates and a generally tighter monetary policy. The Fed raised interest rates from 4 percent in December, 1965, to 5.75 percent by August, 1966.[19] While this independent action initially angered LBJ, Ackley, and Treasury secretary Fowler, it had the side effect of lessening the political heat on LBJ for a tax increase. *It was LBJ's eventual acceptance of this tight monetary policy that ultimately symbolizes his movement away from the partisan Democratic alternatives presented to him, namely demand-side tax increases.*

With the Federal Reserve taking independent action to fight inflation, Johnson was forced to reconsider his own fiscal decision making, particularly in light of the continually escalating costs of Vietnam. Over the next several months, various advisers shifted LBJ's attention toward the inflationary implications of Vietnam and Great Society spending. In doing so, they aided Johnson's movement away from expansionary policies and toward fiscal restraint designed to take pressure off interest rates, particularly in the housing and auto markets slowly being squeezed by Fed policies.

Joseph Califano, the head of LBJ's domestic policy staff, was the first to suggest such a course to the president, largely in response to a memo by Ackley that set out the fiscal implications of increased spending for Vietnam. Califano informed LBJ that, regarding Ackley's memo, "it is indeed a gloomy report. I think you should give some pretty vigorous direction to Ackley, Schultze [the new budget director], and Fowler to come up with specific tax proposals on a most discreet basis. It may be desirable that you not order this directly. If so, I will be happy to talk to each of them, tell them to move this along rapidly and to be extremely discreet about it."[20]

LBJ returned the memo to Califano with a notation that he should speak to the others discreetly. The Ackley memo in question noted that with a projected budget of $110 billion to $115 billion for fiscal year 1967, there was little chance that a tax increase could be avoided. Ackley feared that the implication of such a budget would be a 1966 GNP growth rate of 7.5 percent, one that would put severe upward pressure on wages and prices.[21] With a budget of $115 billion for fiscal year 1967, Ackley concluded that "there is little question in my mind that a significant tax increase will be needed to prevent an intolerable degree of inflationary pressure."[22] Ackley provided LBJ with the following tight fiscal scenario: "If a $110 billion budget contained no more gimmicks than this year's, if FY 1966 could be held to $105 billion, and if we immediately introduced graduated withholding and a higher payroll tax rate for unemployment insurance, we might be able to take a chance and wait till later in the year before deciding on a tax increase. But it's a very close question."[23]

In reality, the "close question" had already been answered. Ackley (later in the 1970s) responded to Johnson's claim (made in LBJ's 1971 memoir, *The Vantage Point*) that the need for a tax increase was unclear at the time, given the projected $110 billion to $115 billion budget for fiscal year 1967.[24] Ackley sheds a different retrospective light on the memo quoted above and on the necessity of a tax increase for 1966:

> But the whole point of the exercise was that we knew damned well that neither of these figures [$110 billion or $115 billion] was in the least bit accurate, that the real figure they were talking about—the military program that had been approved—was represented by a substantially larger figure. Nobody knew precisely what that figure was, but it was surely above the $115 billion. So there was certainly no question about absence of sufficient information to reach a policy judgment,

and the policy judgment was very definite and clear that we needed a tax increase.[25]

Ackley was sure that the logical partisan decision at the time was a tax increase, although LBJ was unconvinced.

If LBJ needed additional confirmation of Ackley's December, 1965, diagnosis from outside of the CEA, he got it in a memo from the Office of Emergency Planning. Located in the Executive Office of the President, the OEP contained an Economic Surveillance Committee that met twice a week to measure the precise effect of the Vietnam War on the economy. Its January 21, 1966, report underscored the need for LBJ to begin to focus more directly on combating inflation. The report noted signs of growing shortages of labor, particularly in skilled worker groups. In addition, it saw production problems pressing in selected industries due to a shortage of materials, particularly defense-related metals such as copper, and also textiles.[26] The report concluded that the administration needed to be vigilant about the ever-increasing threat of an inflationary spiral caused by the demands that Vietnam was putting on manpower and production. The OEP warned,

> It is apparent from all the evidence that the major problem in the over-all economic picture is the threat of inflation. The quickening inflationary pace—at both retail and wholesale level—was the primary characteristic of general price trends in 1965. Prospects for 1966 are that prices and costs will continue to climb significantly, and at a faster rate than that experienced in 1965. . . . The situation in Vietnam obviously makes forecasting particularly difficult. It underscores the need for continued reliance on effective fiscal and monetary measures to mitigate inflationary pressures and to combat an inflationary psychology.[27]

All of the evidence presented to LBJ by the winter of 1966 suggested that he should switch his stabilization focus from unemployment to inflation if he intended to both escalate the war in Vietnam and fund the Great Society at a level he deemed acceptable. The question thus became one of what policy decision would implement this change. Would LBJ gravitate toward the Republican tool kit for stabilization or stick with Democratic prescriptives for the overheated macroeconomy? Would he accept recommendations for tax increases or follow the Federal Reserve? Given LBJ's institutional position, the decision was clearly his to make. *Ultimately, it is the notable absence of a Democratic logic for stabilization in Johnson's decision making that underscores the tension between his partisan and institutional positions.*

A stream of memos flowed to the president's desk in March, 1966, from the CEA, the domestic policy staff, and Cabinet members. Virtually all recommended an immediate tax increase to cool the overheating economy and to head off additional monetary tightening by the Federal Reserve. Fed actions were already crunching the mortgage market and making financial and commodity markets nervous. The CEA, which over the prior six months had been reticent to abandon the administration's expansionary, demand-side fiscal and monetary policies, now came out in favor of an immediate tax increase to slow the breakneck pace of capital investment. In several memos, the CEA noted that the nation's macroeconomic performance was exceeding all of the administration's predictions for 1966. With February's unemployment rate at only 3.7 percent and the administration's prediction of a $722 billion annual GNP likely surpassed and no longer credible to the private sector, the CEA believed that merely the announcement that LBJ would ask for a tax hike later in the spring would be sufficient to slow capital investment.[28]

In a joint March 12, 1966, memo to LBJ, all three members of the CEA argued that the longer the president waited, the larger the requisite tax increase needed to slow the economy.[29] They laid the logic of the argument out clearly for LBJ when they wrote, "The economy is breaking all reasonable speed limits today. . . . [S]ince September when the Vietnam era really took hold, we have been moving ahead at breakneck speed. . . . A continuation of the recent pace would mean general shortages by mid-year. . . . [I]nflationary psychology and inflationary symptoms are taking root. . . . Taxes are the main line of defense."[30]

The CEA offered LBJ a rationale, consistently Keynesian and Democratic in its logic, for why he would be justified in choosing a tax increase at that moment. The CEA stated,

> When demands were below our productive capacity, the 1964 Revenue Act yielded tremendous benefits by leaving more purchasing power in private hands and thus bringing demand up to balance supply. Now the situation is reversed. Siphoning off some purchasing power would help greatly to hold demand down in line with our productive capacity. It is generally recognized that the tax cut worked in 1964. A tax increase would generally be expected to work in 1966. Hence, if you announced soon a decision that you would ask for a tax increase later this spring, it would have some immediate stabilizing effect.[31]

The CEA's proposal was for an across-the-board personal and corporate tax rate increase and for a temporary suspension of the investment tax credit (which had been adopted during the Kennedy administration as a means of spurring capital investment while the country was still substantially below its productive capacity). The goal of the tax increase was to siphon an additional $4 billion to $7 billion out of the economy.[32]

There was some opposition to the CEA proposal within the administration, but it was primarily over the nature of the tax increase, not over whether one was necessary. Secretary of Defense Robert McNamara and budget director Charles Schultze joined the CEA in supporting the idea of an income tax increase and investment credit suspension. Treasury secretary Henry Fowler, however, was against suspension of the investment tax credit, for he feared that business would view the move as Fowler reneging on an earlier promise that the credit would be permanent.[33]

Labor secretary Willard Wirtz, likely representing the position of his agency's constituency, supported a corporate income tax increase and suspension of the investment credit but not an increase in individual income tax rates.[34] Ironically, Wirtz offered LBJ a rationale for at least partly ignoring the CEA's advice. He advised LBJ, "People in general are taxpayers more than they are economists. They won't understand or accept the economics of keeping the cost of living down by raising taxes up. Their acceptance of the tax cut in 1964 was not because they had learned their Keynesian economics; it was because it was a tax cut. An increase this year will be just as unpopular as in any other election year—or any year."[35] Wirtz also noted, however, that there was strong pressure on LBJ to remain consistently partisan in his decision making by following through with Keynesian tax increases to combat the inflationary spiral. The secretary of labor concluded that "the fact is that most economists, a good many newspapers, and now the Joint Economic Committee (in Congress), are making a tax increase a test of the administration's 'good faith.'"[36]

The Joint Economic Committee in Congress released its annual assessment of the *Economic Report of the President* on the same day that Wirtz's memo reached LBJ. The Democratic majority and Republican minority agreed that the economy was moving more rapidly than was earlier foreseen and that inflationary pressures had mounted since the president submitted his *Economic Report* on January 27, 1966.[37] Thus, there was no longer any issue over whether the president's agenda should be visibly pro-employment or anti-inflation. The majority on the committee recommended that, to deal with the inflation threat, Democrats propose immediate tax action through suspension of the 7 percent investment tax credit and a standby general tax program for increases that would take effect whenever Congress passed (and LBJ signed) a joint resolution. In contrast to the Republican minority, which called for cutbacks and delays in civilian expenditures, the majority did not support any cutbacks in Great Society programs.[38]

Even with the growing unanimity for a tax increase among advisers and Democratic partisans, LBJ kept his sentiments close to the vest, allowing the increasingly vocal debate to carry on into the spring and summer of 1966. The package of tax measures recommended to LBJ grew as the months passed and the macroeconomy continued to grow at an ever faster rate. Advisers pushed for a 10 percent tax increase on personal and corporate income, accompanied by suspension of the investment credit and of accelerated depreciation on nonresidential buildings. The troika was concerned that without a tax increase in 1966, GNP would reach nearly $800 billion by the second quarter of 1967. With real output growing at more than 4 percent per year and prices likely rising 5 percent a year, the country might end up facing a rate of inflation not seen since the Korean War.[39] The CEA chairman painted a gloomy future for the economic prosperity of the country without a tax increase to cool demand. He advised LBJ, "After 2 years of accelerating price increases, and with a very tight labor market—wage increases next year could average 6 to 7%—dooming the economy to a painful and prolonged spiral in prices, wages, and costs, even if employment and production slack off. We could even suffer a recession in 1968, accompanied by rapidly rising prices."[40]

Ackley was particularly concerned that a failure to raise taxes would mean that the Federal Reserve would be forced to tighten money a great deal more, putting further pressure on home building, threatening the solvency of many savings and loan associations, and penalizing small business, farmers, and moderate-income home buyers.[41] *From a partisan Democratic perspective, Ackley noted that the package he was proposing would protect the party's traditional electoral constituencies because it "puts a specially [sic] heavy bite on business."*[42]

Budget director Schultze, while agreeing with the scenario presented to the president by the troika, also attacked the argument that uncertainty over the future funding requirements for Vietnam was sufficient reason to postpone a tax increase. Some argued that perhaps a settlement in Vietnam might be sufficient to check inflation. Schultze countered that argument in a memo to LBJ: "On the best current forecast, serious inflation is almost certain unless taxes are raised. . . . In short, under almost every conceivable circumstance—except a Vietnam settlement between July and November [1966]—a decision to raise taxes at least for the remainder of this year and early 1967 is clearly warranted. And even under that circumstance, the risks of serious inflation, in my view, far outweigh the dangers of having a tax increase extend a few months past the date of a possible Vietnam settlement."[43]

Finally, former Kennedy CEA chairman Walter Heller, advising LBJ from his post in the Department of Economics at the University of Minnesota, tried to provide LBJ with a palatable political rationale for a tax increase. Heller wrote the president, "It's amazing how many people expect a tax increase and think it's only a matter of time. Even in the short run—in November—a position of fiscal responsibility in defending the little man against inflation (the Puritan ethic isn't dead in America) may even win more votes than the tax increase loses. History is going to say that in terms of domestic policy, the greatest president is not the one who floated the ship of expansion, but the one who guided it through the waters of full-employment without foundering on the rocks of inflation."[44]

In a letter to the *New York Times,* which Heller attached to the memo he sent to the president, he provided further confirmation that the tax increase was consistent with the Democratic version of Keynesianism. He stated that "Ackley and I agree that the 'New Economics' is a two-way street—that fiscal-monetary stimulus in periods of recession or slack must be matched by fiscal-monetary restraint in periods of overheating."[45]

So why did Johnson, in the face of largely unanimous advice from key advisers in the administration and Democrats in Congress, reject the partisan macroeconomic logic suggested to him? LBJ found himself with a budding inflationary spiral that forced him to shift his focus from a Democratic concern with unemployment to what had traditionally been a Republican preoccupation with inflation. Even after his advisers realized that some restraint was imperative, LBJ still rejected what was a logically consistent Democratic policy program for restraining inflation. As Ackley notes, "I don't know all of what went through LBJ's mind in reaching his decision *which was against the unanimous advice of his presumably principal advisers* in this area: the Treasury, Council [of Economic Advisers], and Budget Bureau."[46]

With clear institutional responsibility for taming the spiral, Johnson nonetheless feared that a request for a general tax increase would lead to Republican calls for cuts in the Great Society and would perhaps even increase opposition to his Vietnam policy (although this became more of an issue in 1967–68). This tradeoff allowed him to serve constituencies while pursuing other macroeconomic objectives. Republicans in Congress and the business community would not likely support a tax increase unless it was accompanied by a clear sign of nondefense fiscal austerity on the part of the administration. This argument was echoed by the *New York Times* and the *Washington Post,* two influential arbiters of public opinion.[47] So in an unusual way, LBJ rejected Democratic macroeconomic logic in 1966 in order to save those partisan policies he most wanted to preserve—an interesting political tradeoff that fits squarely within the parameters of presidential behavior defined in chapter 3. As he saw it, no other option was politically feasible, particularly during a midterm election year.

In retrospect, CEA chairman Ackley summed up LBJ's decision making in the American political economy during 1966, stating,

> The president was entirely convinced that he couldn't get it [a tax increase], that it would be a mistake to ask for it, and that it would boomerang in terms of substantial cuts in his social programs. He seemed obsessed with the conviction that he would be defeated if he insisted on a tax increase. As a political leader, he believed he couldn't afford to lose a major battle on a major issue of policy; his international stature and domestic ability to lead the country would be seriously weakened by a major defeat. I am convinced that from the fall of 1965 on he had no question in his mind that the failure to raise taxes would have very serious results. He never questioned that.[48]

Thus, LBJ moved away from a consistent Democratic set of macroeconomic policy decisions in the Keynesian, New Economics tradition. The political ramifications and institutional imperatives of the crisis he encountered forced him to accept a difficult political tradeoff in macroeconomic objectives. This strategy allowed him to address inflation (largely through Federal Reserve policy) while preserving some program benefits for core partisan constituencies. Yet, even this decision was not the end of the tax issue for LBJ.

Settling on the Surcharge

Although Johnson continued to reject the advice of his advisers, who favored an increase in personal and corporate income taxes as the centerpiece of an anti-inflation package, the president sensed in the summer of 1966 that a consensus was building on both sides of the congressional aisle for some sort of tax action to cool the overheating macroeconomy. The high interest rates caused by the Federal Reserve's tight monetary policy were of particular concern to members of both parties. That LBJ would likely ask for supplemental appropriations for Vietnam in the fall made action on the tax front more pressing.

For example, Democrats on the House Ways and Means Committee sought to directly influence the president's decision making on tax policy more strongly than they had during the winter and spring. Committee member Al Ullman (D-Oregon) wrote to LBJ, urging him to move back toward a Democratic macroeconomic logic and end reliance on the Federal Reserve to fight inflation. Ullman wrote,

As a member of the Ways and Means Committee I have strongly supported the "New Economics" of your administration, and in my public statements have been an outspoken advocate of policies to promote
sustained growth in the economy. *I regret very deeply that I now must
strongly differ with the administration on what I consider to be an
abandonment of the principles we have been following* [emphasis
added]. . . . I submit, Mr. President, that this administration cannot
afford either politically or economically to be swept along, compound-
ing the initial folly of the Federal Reserve. . . . Just as a mixed monetary and fiscal policy has proved successful in generating growth, the
same mixture is essential in restraining an overheating economy. High
interest rates will not do the job. They are inflationary in themselves.[49]

Ullman urged a revision of the investment tax credit, making it applicable
only to business and industry where expansion was vital to national defense.[50]

Similarly, the powerful House Ways and Means chairman, Wilbur Mills
(D-Arkansas), made it known through a conversation with CEA members
Ackley and Arthur Okun that he too favored immediate action on the investment tax credit. He informed the advisers that "you don't have to convince
me. . . . Just have the president tell me he wants it, and we'll go to work."[51]
In addition to having garnered support from the Federal Reserve, labor, the
Republican minority on the House Banking and Currency Committee, and
the JEC majority (the minority hedged), Mills informed the advisers that he
understood there would be a heavy majority in the Senate in favor of sus-
pending the investment tax credit.[52] This new consensus was further evidenced by the $6 billion tax increase urged by Sen. Jacob Javits (R-New
York) in July, a proposal, as Javits noted in a speech on the Senate floor, for
"improving the mix between fiscal and monetary policy" and for combating
inflation. Like many of his Republican and Democratic colleagues, Javits was
extremely concerned about the dangers of the Fed's tight monetary policy.[53]

To this end, LBJ requested a new round of tax proposals from his advisers (Califano, Fowler, McNamara, Ackley, John Connor, David Ginsburg,
Schultze, Nicholas Katzenbach, Laurence O'Brien, and Clark Clifford) in
August, 1966, in preparation for taking some action in September. Califano
summarized the group's consensus macroeconomic package in a September 1, 1966, memo. The recommendations included a statement of LBJ's
intention to ask, at an appropriate time in the future, for whatever tax measures were necessary to cover budget add-on for Vietnam; an announcement
that LBJ had taken steps to reduce federal programs in fiscal year 1967 by
$1.1 billion and highway contracts by $400 million; an announcement that

budget director Schultze was being directed to prepare proposals for further reducing fiscal 1967 expenditures by an additional $2 billion; suspension of the investment tax credit until January 1, 1969, or sooner upon an appropriate presidential determination; suspension of accelerated depreciation during the same time period; and a sharp reduction in the amount of federal "paper" put on the private market (using instead the trust fund).[54]

Given the changing political conditions in Congress and the recommendations of his advisers, Johnson finally took some tax action on September 8, 1966. He moved to relieve upward pressure on interest rates by calling for suspension of the investment tax credit and accelerated depreciation provisions and for additional cuts in nondefense spending of approximately 10 percent of the budget controlled by the president. He also urged the Federal Reserve and the nation's largest commercial banks to cooperate to lower interest rates and to ease the tight money situation. He did not, however, call for a surcharge on income taxes, an easy decision to make only two months before the midterm election. The proposed taxes were adopted in October. This package, coupled with a few piecemeal initiatives to rescind automobile and telephone excise reductions, speed up payment of corporate income taxes, and introduce graduated income tax withholding, marked the sum of Johnson's decision making designed to restrain inflation in 1966.[55]

After the severe credit crunch of August to September, 1966, and Johnson's September 8 tax proposals, the Federal Reserve responded by easing monetary restraint. Beginning in mid-October, the Fed relaxed open market operations. The Federal Open Market Committee voted to move toward easier money in mid-November, and at the end of December the Fed formally rescinded September restraints on bank lending.[56] In November and December, 1966, both the CEA and Federal Reserve forecast a substantial slowing in the rate of growth for the first half of 1967. Nonetheless, a number of LBJ's advisers believed that a small temporary surcharge on personal and corporate incomes would allow for a better mix of fiscal and monetary policy. The intention was to continue the move away from monetary restraint by the Fed, replacing it with an equal measure of fiscal restraint by the administration. The goal was to accomplish this shift without adversely affecting the growth of the economy in either an upward or downward direction.

Only weeks before the president was to issue his economic program for 1967, the administration was unsure as to whether to push the tax surcharge, with several of LBJ's key advisers unenthusiastically supporting it and others opposed. Those who favored the announcement of a small temporary surcharge in January, such as Schultze, Ackley, Califano, and Heller (again weighing in from the University of Minnesota), nonetheless uniformly favored an effective date of July 1, 1967. They believed that a surcharge with this effective date would give the president sufficient time to withdraw the proposal if the economy remained soft beyond mid-1967. Alternatively, it would provide the administration with ready restraint if the Vietnam War should require additional funding.[57]

Understanding the nature of LBJ's political calculations, Walter Heller, who narrowly favored the surcharge, managed to again cast it in an appealing political light. He advised LBJ that "raising taxes now will appeal to a wide spectrum of voters on grounds that . . . it will enable us to finance Vietnam without taking it out of the hides of the poor through program cutbacks. With an eye on November 1968, the higher-tax-easier-money program concentrates the economic risks of timing and turbulence in 1967; offers the stimulus of a tax cutback in 1968 (by letting the surtax lapse); will put housing and small business in a healthier condition by 1968 than they would be without this program."[58] A temporary surcharge effective at midyear was just the sort of flexible fiscal tool favored by New Economists such as Heller, Ackley, and the others. Given their previous experience of trying to get LBJ to raise taxes, they presented the proposal to LBJ as such.

Those who opposed the idea of a tax increase at midyear did so for two primary reasons. First, some advisers were not convinced that the move made political sense. They believed that LBJ should not depend on the Fed for increased monetary ease to balance out a tax increase, given the Fed's behavior in 1966. Also, they did not buy into Heller's take on how politically useful the tax increase would be for the 1968 election. One of LBJ's advisers, Francis Bator, noted, "[A]n appreciable tax-rate increase this spring seems to me to be not only bad economics but exceedingly dangerous 1968 politics. . . . That, I fear would be a prescription for slack unemployment, and possibly a serious recession in '67–'68."[59] Another adviser, Robert Kintner, underscored concerns about the electorate's perception of the administration when he wrote, "I believe the average citizen is having difficulty understanding the really remarkably large cuts of authorizations and appropriations you have enacted and understanding why new taxes are needed."[60] Second, as Bator's memo hinted, some advisers, such as Secretary Fowler and the governors and staff at the Federal Reserve in particular, were sufficiently bearish about the economy to fear that a recession was more imminent than another bout of inflation.[61] Fiscal restraint would only exacerbate a potentially sluggish economy in 1967. Nonetheless, in January, 1967, President Johnson ended his year-long flirtation with Republican stabilization logic by recommending the 6 percent surcharge on personal and corporate income taxes. In addition to the 6 percent surcharge (effective July 1), Johnson's 1967 fiscal program called for federal expenditures to rise $12 billion, largely due to the cost of Vietnam, increases in Medicare transfer payments, an (already scheduled) payroll tax increase on January 1, 1967, and a further speedup in corporate tax collections.[62]

The Republican response to Johnson's surcharge proposal clearly demonstrates that the administration had returned full circle to a partisan Democratic conception of macroeconomic stabilization. Senate Republican leader Everett Dirksen responded that Congress would want to take a much closer look at possible economies in the Johnson budget before agreeing to a tax increase. Similarly, House Republican leader Gerald Ford commented that Johnson had not made a case for the tax increase. Nor were all congressional Democrats in favor of the tax surcharge. An informal poll of members of Congress showed almost solid opposition to a tax increase, although members of Congress acknowledged that the July 1 effective date allowed for another six months of watching the economy.[63] Nonetheless, the administration had returned to a state of partisan disagreement with Republicans in Congress, preferring to raise additional tax revenues to pay for Vietnam costs and Great Society programs rather than make further cuts in discretionary domestic spending.

In contrast, the Republicans continued to call for cuts in spending before any tax increase would be considered in Congress. The economy did soften substantially in the first half of 1967, but even more so than predicted by the CEA and Federal Reserve. As a result, the CEA recommended that Johnson request early termination of the investment tax credit and accelerated depreciation suspensions. LBJ made such a request in March, and Congress enacted it in June, 1967.[64] In such an economic environment, the idea of a tax increase, even at midyear, did not hold much appeal for either party in Congress. Even the Democratic majority on the Joint Economic Committee, in releasing its report on Johnson's 1967 economic program, did not believe that the case for a tax increase had been sufficiently made.[65] Due to the "mini-recession" and resultant lack of congressional enthusiasm for the surcharge proposal, the troika determined that a July 1 tax increase was neither politically viable nor economically desirable. The troika forecast also noted that the macroeconomy was showing preliminary signs of a possible acceleration during the summer. It therefore recommended keeping the proposal around for possible implementation later in the year.[66] Ackley noted in a memo to LBJ, "[N]early all economic forecasters are reaching the objective technical verdict that we are building up steam for a new surge. Still the surge has not started. . . . Thus, we could not make an airtight case today to the Congress that fiscal restraint will be needed."[67] The CEA chairman did advise LBJ little more than a week later that "we are more confident now than we were in January that a tax increase will be sound economic policy by the end of this year."[68] Ackley was particularly concerned that if defense spending could not be slowed, a 6 percent surcharge on incomes might be too small to contain inflationary pressures and result in a return to a tight monetary policy by the Federal Reserve.[69]

Walter Heller expressed similar sentiments to LBJ the following month when he noted, "As I said at lunch today, stepping on the fiscal and monetary gas has been good—in fact, excellent—policy so far this year. . . . But unless a lot of us are wrong on our GNP forecasts for next winter, we should soon ease up on the accelerator. A 6 to 10% surtax . . . to take effect by January 1 ought to be just about right." Heller also worried about the possibility of a new round of inflation and the concomitant brutally high interest rates that would likely accompany it. He noted that the surtax would have the added benefit of reducing the deficit in a time when "the economy no longer needs such a big budgetary booster shot."[70]

On the recommendation of his advisers and Fed chairman Martin, LBJ finally sent a larger tax package to Congress on August 3, 1967, than he had recommended in his January, 1967, economic program. The president called for a 10 percent income tax surcharge to be effective on personal income as of October 1, 1967, and on corporate income retroactive to July 1, 1967. In addition, he asked for a speedup of corporate tax payments, continuation of excise taxes on telephones and automobiles, congressional restraint on appropriations, and a tough review of where the executive branch could cut expenditures.[71] In his message, LBJ noted the dangers posed by the large deficit that would result from congressional failure to pass a tax increase, including a serious inflationary spiral, higher interest rates and tight money, an unequal and unjust distribution of the costs of Vietnam, and deterioration in the balance of payments.[72]

The larger surcharge proposal was no more well received than the 6 percent proposal had been back in January. The tax package became immediately embroiled in a debate over its necessity that dragged on into the fall, particularly in the House Ways and Means Committee.[73] Even in October, with the Federal Reserve threatening substantially higher interest rates in lieu of a tax increase and the CEA predicting a 4 to 5 percent rate of inflation without one, Congress was still at an impasse over the proposal.[74] The sticking point was a general belief in Congress and the public that the administration had shown insufficient good faith in proposing expenditure cuts before recommending a tax increase. An October 16, 1967, Harris Poll showed that, while 78 percent of Americans opposed the 10 percent surcharge, 73 percent preferred a reduction in federal spending.[75]

As further evidence that LBJ's policy was now back to a Democratic decision-making calculus, the poll data caused one adviser to comment, "Apparently the public has learned only half the lesson of the 'new economics'—the part about cutting taxes and increasing federal spending to stimulate the economy. They don't buy lesson number two—the steps necessary to control inflation."[76]

Ackley also expressed concern over the expenditure cuts versus tax increase issue. He noted that, while the administration could blame Republicans for the failure to enact the surcharge, "we don't have a specific expenditure offer which we can later say was irresponsibly rejected by the Republicans."[77] Even a November attempt at pushing the package with an additional $6 billion in cuts in fiscal 1968 expenditures was not sufficient to get the tax bill through Congress.[78] The debate over the 10 percent surcharge continued along these lines for another seven months. The dispute was over the form of a tax increase, whether spending cuts should be coupled with the tax increase, how much spending should be cut, and which branch should do the cutting. The surcharge was finally signed into law on June 28, 1968.[79]

Thus, the narrative of LBJ's decision making in the American political economy highlights several key aspects of the notions of institutional responsibility and presidential decision making developed in this book. The stable postwar policy-making environment allowed LBJ to fluctuate between Democratic and Republican stabilization logics, within the constraints of his institutional position. His willingness to accept tradeoffs in partisan policy objectives, even in the face of unanimous advice to the contrary by key advisers, allowed LBJ to salvage some funding for Great Society programs; his decision to utilize instruments from the Republican macroeconomic tool kit in the fight against inflation also allowed him to continue his escalation of an increasingly costly Vietnam War. It is clear from his decision-making calculus at the time that unified government substantially magnified the need for LBJ to be seen as behaving responsibly with regard to inflation. As Gardner Ackley noted years later, "Lyndon Johnson accepted the advice of the 'New Economics' only when he wanted to."[80]

Jimmy Carter Moves from New Economics to Fiscal Conservatism

The macroeconomic policy decisions made by President Jimmy Carter during the years 1977–79 offer examples of bold partisan continuity and contrast. Like LBJ, Carter ranged freely between Democratic and Republican conceptions of stabilization policy. Unlike LBJ, however, Carter's movement from a Democratic calculus actually brought him closer to his own brand of fiscal conservatism. While LBJ shifted his focus to inflation in 1966, he did so out of political and institutional necessity and quickly returned to the New Economics fold in 1967 and 1968 for the fight over the tax surcharge. Ironically, Carter's consistent Democratic partisanship in 1977 was a function of political and institutional necessity; as the new kid in town, he sought to work successfully with Congress. His strong shift in 1979 and 1980, from a Democratic focus on unemployment to one on inflation, represented a return to a more comfortable fiscal logic, despite the fact that it caused him tremendous political problems with his own party in Congress. Also, while Johnson's policy shift was a function of his rejecting the advice of his White House staff and Cabinet, Carter's change resulted from his taking the advice of his staff, both in their recommending a stimulus package in 1977 (when he was personally more concerned about inflation) and in shifting the focus of the administration's macroeconomic policy to inflation during the last two years of his term.

Jimmy Carter faced a difficult set of macroeconomic conditions upon taking office in January, 1977. Unemployment was close to 8 percent, yet inflation was also running at an annual rate of almost 6 percent. The president inherited a $66 billion budget deficit due primarily to a recession that had begun after the first oil price shock in 1973. Upon Carter's taking office, the economy was in the early stages of a recovery, although his advisers ultimately misjudged just how rapidly that recovery would proceed.[81] As a result of this miscalculation, Carter took his advisers' recommendation and submitted a partisan Democratic economic stimulus package to Congress in January, 1977. Charles Schultze, LBJ's former budget director and now Carter's newly appointed chairman of the CEA, was the chief architect of the stimulus package. The intention of the package was to give a quick stimulus to the macroeconomy in order to speed the recovery already taking shape. The $30 billion package included public works, youth employment and training, and increased public employment. It also gave a $50 tax rebate to each taxpayer (to the tune of $11 billion in lost revenue) and investment tax incentives for business. As the recovery accelerated in April, Carter removed the rebate and investment tax credit proposals from the package, leaving the stimulus package closer to $20 billion.[82] Carter's own fiscal conservatism made him somewhat skeptical of the need for a Democratic stimulus package. Yet he did not move away from a partisan Democratic logic during his first year as president, for his advisers and the congressional leadership strongly supported a Democratic approach to policy making, with its focus on unemployment rather than inflation.

Carter's director of the Office of Management and Budget, James McIntyre (he replaced Bert Lance in the first year of the administration) brought Van Ooms into OMB as its economic adviser. Ooms has noted the influence of traditional Democratic macroeconomic thinking on Carter's 1977 partisan decision making. He has stated, "At the beginning of the administration back in '76–'77 the economic policymakers in the administration came in very much with a rather conventional 1950's–1960's view of the way the economy worked and of the way in which inflation worked. Only that kind of view could have given rise to a relatively conventional stimulus package of a tax rebate and some jobs programs."[83] McIntyre notes that the result of that macroeconomic logic, and the stimulus package associated with it, was a program whose impact "was to generate inflation which became double-digit, and [which] became the basis of our real economic problems in the last two and a half years of the administration."[84]

Interestingly, Carter was somewhat of a prisoner to this partisanship, as was made clear by CEA chairman Schultze. He noted regarding the stimulus package that "it was clear that the traditional idea, particularly on the part of the Congress (Jim Wright, Tip O'Neill and the like) that we have to spend our way out of this led to some substantial pressure for putting in some accelerated public works as part of this."[85] Schultze offered further insight into why Carter did not reject Democratic macroeconomic influences on his decision making during 1977. He comments, "My impression was he [Carter] realized that he was the leader of the Democratic Party, and they all told him he had to do these things which meant a bigger deficit. He wasn't sure he liked that. He would go along with it . . . So on a more general basis, Carter, in his first two years was a fiscal conservative who (in the first year particularly) was going along with deliberately beefing up the deficit because he guessed he had to."[86] Thus, the policy-making environment in which Carter initially found himself acted as a substantial constraint, favoring a partisan Democratic influence on macroeconomic decision making.

Realizing that the recovery was beginning to accelerate rapidly in the spring of 1977, the administration, in addition to rescinding the fifty-dollar rebate and investment tax credit proposals from the stimulus package (to lessen its impact on growth), announced an anti-inflation initiative on April 15. Along with pledging fiscal discipline as the economy returned to normal and a balanced budget by fiscal 1981, the initiative established a framework for consultation between business and labor to aid in voluntary adherence to wage and price guidelines suggested by the administration. The initiative also sought to restrain spiraling hospital costs and to moderate the sharp fluctuations in commodities, such as sugar and grain, and raw materials that had triggered bouts of inflation in recent years. The administration's Council on Wage and Price Stability was empowered to oversee coordination of the various programs under the initiative.[87]

This particular anti-inflation initiative, however, did not represent a substantial shift in macroeconomic thinking by President Carter. The rationale for the initiative was explicitly tied to a pro-employment Democratic policy outlook. To begin with, the initiative was considered weak within the administration. Carter's advisers believed that he would be best served by announcing explicit wage and price increase targets (7 and 5 percent, respectively) and by pledging to foster public pressure on business and labor to obtain voluntary compliance with them.[88] As two of Carter's advisers noted, "This is not a tough anti-inflation program. There is little, if anything, here which the public will perceive as being new or forceful."[89] The two concluded that, "without some quantifiable targets, our strategy will have no focus and will not be understandable to the public."[90]

In addition, if Carter had intended the initiative as a signal of his changing focus, other members of the administration were there to remind him that it was not. The executive committee of the Economic Policy Group, chaired by Treasury secretary Michael Blumenthal, reminded Carter one week before the announcement of the anti-inflation initiative that "the stimulus package is the centerpiece of our economic strategy."[91] Blumenthal himself, in testimony before Congress, sought to dispel the idea that the initiative was a shift from Democratic decision making. He stated, "It is important to note that the administration's actions on the anti-inflation front in recent weeks do not represent new departures or changes in policy objectives. The decision to rescind the request for the tax rebate and the investment tax credit, for example, does not imply any reduction in our economic objectives."[92] The idea was not that the administration was backing away from stimulating the growth of new jobs, only that it did not need quite as much stimulus to achieve the same rate of real growth (approximately 6 percent).[93]

Finally, President Carter's own statements on the initiative made it clear that, even as a fiscal conservative, he was nonetheless operating from a distinctly partisan Democratic viewpoint in proposing the measures. He saw the employment and manpower programs of the stimulus package as a key means of fighting inflation, for they were measures "which improve job skills, increas[ing] the efficiency of the labor market."[94] He also argued that if Congress passed the Republican alternative to the stimulus package, a permanent tax cut that he called "irresponsible," he would veto it.[95]

In his press conference following the announcement of the anti-inflation initiative, Carter drew a sharp distinction in the partisan differences separating Republicans and Democrats on macroeconomic policy. In response to a question about how his approach toward macroeconomic problems differed from that of the Ford administration, Carter stated,

> I think their [Nixon and Ford's] basic approach to controlling inflation was to deliberately dampen the economy and to accept in the process, again deliberately in my opinion, a very high permanent unemployment rate. We have tried to address this in a completely different fashion by deliberately stimulating the economy with the $20 billion or $23 billion package still intact and also addressing directly the unemployment rate . . . and at the same time attacking the direct causes of inflation. I refuse to connect the two. I think that if you deliberately accept unemployment as a means to control inflation, that is wrong. That is the basic distinction.[96]

Carter's statement underscores the distinction between Republican and Democratic preferences for relative levels of inflation and unemployment that are at the heart of partisan differences in postwar stabilization policy. At least in 1977, President Carter was able to say that "high unemployment is a morally unacceptable—and ineffective—way of combating inflation, and I totally reject that approach. Inflation must not be attacked by causing additional human misery."[97] As will be seen below, he broke with this partisan Democratic logic in little more than a year.[98] The pull of institutional responsibility for the nation's macroeconomic health would provide the impetus for the shift.

A Return to Fiscal Conservatism

In late 1977 and early 1978, the threat of recession reappeared, with the administration forecasting a slowdown for the second half of 1978. Consistent with Keynesian dictates, the administration pushed for an expansionary budget in January, 1978. In keeping with partisan Democratic decision making, the fiscal 1979 budget (January, 1978) contained a new stimulus package designed to provide the economy with demand-side stimulus through tax reform and tax cuts.[99] This was the last time that Carter would put forth this sort of expansionary budget proposal. The president would soon initiate a series of Republican-style anti-inflation initiatives over the next two and a half years, measures designed to decelerate the rate of inflation through wage-price actions and tight fiscal policy.

As early as March, 1978, the administration realized that despite rising farm prices, 1978 was going to be a boom year for the economy.[100] Carter's advisers began to assess whether the anti-inflation measures taken by the president during the first year and a half of his administration would be sufficient to combat a rate of inflation estimated to approach 7.5 percent in 1978. In particular, the administration feared a national acceleration in wage increases exacerbated by large labor settlements in the coal and railroad industries.[101] Barry Bosworth, the head of Carter's Council on Wage and Price Stability, summed up the status of the president's anti-inflation program in March, 1978:

> Recent economic developments reinforce my own concern that the anti-inflation program is floundering. Unless the administration acts, with a substantially increased involvement of the president, the program will fail. A low key program had been anticipated; but, particularly after the coal developments, such an approach does not seem feasible. The program remains almost invisible. . . . Most of the administration initiatives affecting inflation are stalled or have fallen by the wayside. . . . Without a major increase in presidential backing this program is going nowhere.[102]

Advisers argued that the administration's existing 7 percent wage guideline was arbitrary and likely 1 to 2 percent below the current rate of inflation. The price guideline was so vague and generalized that it was impossible for the public and government to determine compliance. Finally, even if the government could determine compliance, it lacked adequate staff to enforce any sanctions.[103] Several of Carter's advisers, particularly CEA chairman Schultze and Treasury secretary Blumenthal, sought to bring inflation to the forefront as a macroeconomic issue by devising a new and stronger anti-inflation initiative. *This initiative, unlike prior ones, marked the onset of Carter's shift from a consistent Democratic calculus, a transition clearly recognized by several of his advisers. Not only did the initiative switch Carter's focus from unemployment to inflation, but it did so in a manner that threatened to alienate some of the president's core Democratic constituencies.*

Those opposed to Carter's shift from prior policy were particularly concerned about the Blumenthal/Schultze proposal to cap federal pay raises at 5.5 percent for the following year. The two also advised the president to urge state and local governments to follow suit.[104] The president's Congressional Liaison Office was particularly concerned about alienating support in Congress and the public. The deputy liaison, Les Francis, commented on the two pay cap proposals in a memo to Frank Moore, Carter's congressional liaison:

> From what I've seen and heard during the past few days, I am convinced that Secretary Blumenthal and Chairman Schultze are about to

recommend to the president some anti-inflation measures which are
sure to cause serious political and legislative problems. . . . Aside
from the fact that to change our public focus from stimulus (tax reductions and jobs) to anti-inflation is bound to confuse the public and the
Congress ("$50 rebate reversal revisited"), two of the specific recom-
mendations are political dynamite. . . . I urge you to consider these
points seriously and to do whatever you can to resist their economic
recommendations which are bound to cause us severe political and
legislative problems.[105]

Francis did not buy the argument that wage action by the president in
the public sector would act as leverage on the private sector, thereby holding
down wage pressures there as well. Considering that the administration had
assured labor that it would not undertake this sort of action without prior
consultation, the deputy liaison feared that the initiative would alienate the
American Federation of Government Employees and AFL-CIO at the federal level, and American Federation of State, County, and Municipal Employees and the National Education Association at the state and local levels.
These unions had strongly supported Carter in the 1976 election.[106] *It was
clear to those opposed to the proposal that such an action would be viewed by
Democrats in Congress and labor as an unwelcome change in decision making, one that would likely have adverse consequences for Carter's legislative
agenda and electoral support.*

Carter's domestic policy chief, Stu Eizenstat, brought the potential
breakdown into sharper focus when he commented on another aspect of the
Blumenthal/Schultze plan, in particular the proposal that Carter should
state that he would veto any bills that went above his $500 billion budget
and that he would not ask for any additional expenditures. Eizenstat argued,
"Such an arbitrary statement is unrealistic, fails to recognize the real world
of Congressional action and compromise, gives the impression that you have
adopted GOP economic thinking regarding the relation between federal
spending and inflation in a high unemployment economy, and may lead to
the appearance of backing down when congressional compromises are necessary."[107]

Eizenstat's fear that Carter might give the impression of having adopted
GOP thinking is clearly indicative of the president's movements, under the
weight of his institutional responsibility for dealing with inflation, away from
partisan consistency in his thinking on macroeconomic decisions.

Despite the concerns of some of his advisers, President Carter announced the new anti-inflation initiative on April 11, 1978. In his address,

he signaled the administration's switch from a focus on unemployment to inflation, noting that "our nation's economic health can be protected only if we can cope with the two developments that now threaten it most seriously—the high level of oil imports and the increasing rate of inflation."[108] Carter went ahead with the proposal for a cap on federal, state, and local employee wages. In addition, he called for regulatory reform directed at containing airline and hospital costs and for a general review of price escalation clauses in all federal contracts, in order to ensure that they reflected the administration's new deceleration policies.[109]

Most importantly, the president employed precisely the Republican logic over which some of his advisers had shown concern; he put forth the idea that wage and price action in the public sector would serve as sufficient leverage to bring the private sector in line. To this end, he appointed his special trade representative, Robert Strauss, to serve in the role of special counselor on inflation. Strauss, along with the Council on Wage and Price Stability, would seek, through voluntary consultation, to have industry and labor keep price, wage, and salary increases significantly below the average rate of the previous two years.[110]

As predicted, labor was quite unhappy with the new anti-inflation initiative, in particular the cap on federal pay and the call for the same at the state and local level. The AFL-CIO Executive Council urged the president to reconsider the pay cap, noting that "President[s] Nixon and Ford sought to make federal workers the scapegoats, and neither was able to defeat inflation by further widening the gap between pay in the federal and private sector."[111] The union's grouping of Carter with Nixon and Ford makes clear that it viewed the policy as a significant departure from what the union considered acceptable partisan behavior. The AFL-CIO concluded, much to Carter's chagrin, "that we will not deceive the president by committing the labor movement to any kind of fixed figure or predetermined percentage increase. Such a figure would stultify the give-and-take process of collective bargaining and exacerbate existing inequities."[112]

Despite the April, 1978, initiative, inflation continued to accelerate, forcing the administration to consider more stringent fiscal measures. By May, the CEA, OMB, and Treasury were all advising the president "that the likely course of the economy requires a tighter fiscal policy and a reduced deficit."[113] Carter signaled his willingness to move in this direction by making public his intention to reduce the size of the tax cut requested in the fiscal 1979 budget proposal and his preference for a very tight fiscal 1980 budget (being planned in the fall of 1978). His advisers were particularly concerned that Carter be prepared to wield the veto, as Democrats in Congress were already making expansionary changes in the fiscal 1979 budget. His advisers believed that this circumstance would make it particularly difficult for the president to appear to be the strong leader of a unified party.[114]

This decision-making moment represents a crucial juncture for understanding Carter's shift. Going back to Carter's statements in announcing the administration's anti-inflation initiative in April of 1977, *the president explicitly rejected the idea that inflation should be controlled through strict fiscal policy. He had refused to equate less inflation with more unemployment. Now the president was moving toward accepting precisely this tradeoff, one that had been anathema to Democrats for so long.*

This partisan transformation was not lost on the president's advisers. One noted that "the economic policies themselves will be controversial with some Democratic Party constituencies."[115] Another was concerned that making the budget deficit a major preoccupation of the administration entailed the danger of having inflation become too closely equated with federal government actions.[116] That same adviser, Al Stern, captured the essence of what this new approach to macroeconomic policy making could mean politically for President Carter. He stated, "The results of trying to respond to concern for inflation by fiscal constriction is to eliminate our ability to deliver programs and services. A direct result of this restriction is on our ability to deliver new initiatives. I need not spell out the consequences for a Democratic administration. If we continue to behave in an overly cautious manner, we will have little to point to in 1980."[117]

It is clear from the above quote that Carter's behavior had the potential to alienate those Democratic constituencies most crucial to his own reelection. The very nature of a program of fiscal restraint would prevent him from delivering the partisan programs and services most desired by those traditional constituencies—the central motivation for the pursuit of partisan objectives.

Despite the April, 1978, initiative, wages and prices continued to accelerate throughout the summer. By the beginning of September, consumer prices were rising at an annual rate of 10 percent, and the administration feared independent action by the Fed to cool the economy, particularly through higher interest rates.[118] Recent polls showed that the public was evaluating the relative success of the administration based upon its ability to fight inflation.[119] Gerald Rafshoon, assistant to the president for communications, informed Carter that "a failure to demonstrate some control over inflation will make it very difficult for most Americans to be enthusiastic about your presidency."[120] Rafshoon called for the toughest anti-inflation program that the administration could devise short of mandatory wage and price controls, including specific guidelines for wages and prices, procurement penalties, strict regulatory review, an early announcement of a low 1980 budget ceiling, a federal hiring freeze, and, in the next session of Congress, consideration of a tax incentive program, Social Security postponement, minimum wage postponement, and trucking deregulation. In short, Rafshoon concluded, "It would be difficult to err on the side of too tough a program."[121]

The Economic Policy Group also weighed in with a similar assessment of the political and economic climate and urged Carter to consider a strengthened anti-inflation program. The EPG suggested an explicit numerical standard of 7 percent for wage increases and a strengthening of the price deceleration standard at 5.75 percent. In addition, the EPG called for specific government sanctions that would be triggered when the standards were exceeded by business or labor.[122] The EPG also informed Carter, however, that he "should realize that this program is the last step short of a commitment to high unemployment. . . . [T]he announcement and implementation of this program will severely strain relations with major political interest groups."[123]

CEA chairman Schultze also supported the EPG proposals, despite the political danger involved.[124] He was particularly concerned with what the proposals would mean for labor, because "where labor is, in effect, striking against the [wage] standard, we will necessarily be in the public position of siding with management against labor." He concluded, however, that "after reviewing all of the options, I believe it is necessary to take these risks. If we do nothing, inflation will continue to poison the economic and political climate of our country. We cannot lick inflation solely by tight money and highly restrictive budgets, except at huge cost in high unemployment and low investment. Wage and price controls cannot be obtained from the Congress, or if so only after a bitter and protracted struggle."[125]

Given this advice from both the EPG and the CEA, Carter again prepared for the launch of a new and improved anti-inflation initiative, despite the clear political dangers that it could hold for his presidency.

In spite of the general consensus for a stronger anti-inflation initiative, as the October 24 date for the announcement of the initiative drew near, several advisers expressed concern about the political implications of the administration's new firmer stance on deficit reduction. Stu Eizenstat was concerned that the language on fiscal restraint to be included in the inflation speech, which called for no real growth except in programs vital to national security, would place the Democratic president in a politically unsustainable position. Such language would entail a 2 to 3 percent real increase in defense

spending while achieving budget reduction exclusively through cuts in domestic programs. Eizenstat advised Carter that "such an imbalance will
make this look exactly like a Republican speech and will lock you into making decisions in the budget process which will be extraordinarily damaging
to your Democratic constituency."[126] Several weeks earlier, Health, Education, and Welfare secretary Califano had weighed in with similar concerns
over the administration's move toward fiscal restraint. He advised Carter that
"not only are the chances for Congressional success relatively small, but we
will be in the wholly unenviable position of making—and quite possibly
losing—proposals that cut directly against the grain of the interests held by
the traditional constituents of the Democratic Party. In HEW, for example,
we will be hurting the poor, the aged, minorities, labor—to name a few
obvious groups. Not only will we invite serious defeats in the Congress, but
we may manage to alienate important supportive constituencies in the
process."[127]

Carter ultimately accepted Eizenstat's advice to eschew the planned no-
program-growth fiscal restraint language in favor of a promise to reduce the
deficit to $30 billion or less during 1979 (about one-half of the $66 billion
deficit existing when Carter took office).[128] It was believed that this was a
more flexible and credible (for a Democratic president) way of moving further toward fiscal restraint.[129] Given the advisers' comments on how close
the president was coming to exhibiting Republican preferences for relatively
more unemployment and less inflation, Carter, in his speech, also moder-
ated his anti-inflation rhetoric a bit. He informed the nation "that fighting
inflation will be a central preoccupation of mine during the months ahead,"
but he rejected the idea that a deliberate recession (and thus higher unemployment) would be a useful fiscal tool for cooling the economy.[130]

In addition to the deficit reduction promise, the October 24 anti-inflation
initiative called for annual wage increases not to exceed 7 percent; for individual firms to limit their price increases to one-half of 1 percent below their
average annual rate of price increase during 1976–77; a partial freeze in federal hiring; formation of a new Regulatory Council in the executive branch
to coordinate and reduce duplicative and overlapping regulations; a delay
of further tax cuts; real wage insurance to offer rebates to workers who meet
the pay standard if the rate of inflation in the next year exceeds 7 percent;
federal channeling of procurement to firms whose price and wage decisions
meet the standards; and an expanded (one hundred additional staff) Council on Wage and Price Stability (CWPS) to monitor wage and price activity
in the private sector more closely.[131]

*Thus, during the midterm election year of 1978, Carter attempted to strike
an uneasy tradeoff between his preference for fiscal restraint on the one hand*

and the political dictates of his own party in Congress and Democratic constituencies throughout the country on the other. Both the April and October anti-
inflation initiatives represented initial, yet substantial, shifts away from a
partisan Democratic logic in macroeconomic decision making. The president's
advisers recognized them as such and sought to minimize damage to Democratic constituencies.

Carter's OMB economist, Van Ooms, has retrospectively noted his own
belief that Carter was prepared to move even further from Democratic preferences on deficit reduction by October, 1978, but was held back by the lack
of support for such a change from some members of his own administration
and from Democrats in Congress. Ooms stated in reference to the $30 bil-
lion deficit reduction target, "[T]o really have achieved budgetary balance,
we would have somehow had to have had an administration that was prepared to launch the kind of massive attack on the budget that the current
[Reagan] administration launched. You couldn't do that around the edges.
You had to have an ideological commitment that went throughout the administration. We needed an agreement that would not only have put the
president wholeheartedly behind it, but would make him feel politically secure by being wholeheartedly behind it. That was never in the cards."[132]

OMB director James McIntyre has also noted the important influence of
election-year politics on Carter's decision to forgo a no-growth fiscal policy
in October, 1978. He has commented retrospectively that "you have to remember that Democrats have traditionally been more concerned about the
unemployment rate than Republicans. There was a tremendous concern on
the part of people in the administration about a rising unemployment rate
in an election year. If you're going to slow growth, you're naturally going to
have some rise in unemployment."[133]

The administration noted that "further progress in reducing unemployment will depend on our success in reducing the rate of inflation. The budget that will be submitted in January will give top priority to moderating
inflation."[134] *In October, 1978, Carter had therefore accepted the very same
Republican macroeconomic logic that he had deemed "morally unacceptable"
when announcing his first anti-inflation initiative in April of 1977. This new
policy of fiscal austerity would increasingly preoccupy the administration in
1979 and 1980 and bore the full weight of Carter's institutional responsibility
for stabilizing the economy.*

The Politics of Fiscal Austerity

Following through on his October, 1978, pledge of a new level of fiscal restraint to fight inflation, President Carter introduced on January 22, 1979,
a fiscal 1980 budget deemed "lean and austere" by the administration. In

submitting the budget, Carter noted the emphasis on restraint of federal spending, which would decrease as a share of GNP from 22.1 to 21.2 percent in 1980. The budget also met the $30 billion deficit pledge.[135] The president concluded that the action was "imperative if we are to overcome the threat of accelerating inflation."[136] With the fiscal 1980 budget, Carter became increasingly preoccupied with the idea of fiscal austerity and the need to fight inflation through deficit reduction. As the administration continued to experience difficulties in its attempts to obtain private sector voluntary compliance with its wage and price standards, Carter put more political stock in cooling the overheating economy through budgetary action.

In actuality, economic indicators signaled a stronger first half for 1979 than predicted, with resultant sharp price increases, especially for food and oil (costs that are often passed on down the manufacturing line). In particular, the CEA was concerned that the acceleration of price increases might lead to a general business scramble to build inventories. The resultant productive imbalances in the market could then potentially lead to a recession in late 1979 or early 1980, as orders for capital goods dropped off once inventories were filled.[137] CEA chairman Schultze noted the importance of these developments when he commented to the president that "the anti-inflation program is likely to collapse if some price deceleration is not achieved soon."[138]

Given the possibility of double-digit inflation and continuing problems with food, energy, and housing prices, Carter's advisers recommended new action on inflation. They recommended increased monetary restraint, possibly through higher short-term interest rates; selective controls over consumer credit; increased budgetary restraint, if it could be accomplished readily; and intensified monitoring of prices by CWPS.[139] On fiscal austerity, Carter was advised to veto spending programs that would prejudice a balanced budget and aggravate inflation; defer new liberal spending programs until the productive base of the economy was rebuilt to support the programs; defer environmental and other regulations that would heighten inflation or blunt productivity; and reject large tax cuts for individuals but offer smaller cuts to encourage savings and investment and to boost productivity.[140] *One could easily mistake such a list of macroeconomic decisions for a Republican tool kit for fighting inflation.*

Treasury secretary Blumenthal summed up the implications of this policy approach for partisan politics when he commented,

> In theory there are several economic strategies open to the president for the remainder of his first term. In practice, I believe there is only

one viable course: continuation of tough and austere macroeconomic policies, requiring sacrifices by many—and hence causing political dissatisfaction among a broad array of interest groups whose support the president needs for re-election. . . . This approach would put him on the offensive—as a responsible visionary—against those in the Congress and the party who think it is the highest duty of a Democratic President to meet the short run demands of every special interest group."[141]

Carter's advisers believed that a restrictive fiscal policy would take some of the pressure off of monetary policy that, due to the unexpected strength of the economy, was becoming increasingly tight, with high interest rates pressing the mortgage market much as it had in 1966, when President Johnson was confronted with his inflation crisis.[142]

Some advisers believed that Carter should go so far as to announce a revised 1980 budget that was balanced, as a means of sharply altering public expectations. The administration realized that, regardless of whether the current inflation was actually due to the deficit, the public believed that that was the case. Such a budgetary strategy would reduce the public's inflationary expectations, thereby having a beneficial impact on wages and prices and making government requests for adherence to the wage and price standards more credible in the eyes of the public.[143] The strategic problem with the administration's emphasis on adjustments to the fiscal/monetary mix as a means of controlling inflation was that neither instrument could be used rapidly, as both acted on the economy with some lag. Thus, the administration was ultimately forced to continue to emphasize its monitoring activities through the wage and price guidelines, although the deficit was increasingly seen by many as the true obstacle to cooling the economy. The administration also attempted to develop a legislative strategy that recognized the political implications of Carter's decisions. Frank Moore, the congressional liaison, understood that for Carter and the Democrats, "Inflation threatens Democratic majorities in the Congress, particularly in the Senate, as seriously as it threatens your [Carter's] prospects for reelection."[144]

The idea was to head off Democratic criticism of any new fiscal restraint measures (of the sort noted by Blumenthal above) by bringing members of Congress into the policy formation process. Moore noted that "the Democrats in Congress have not joined you [the president] in the war on inflation"[145] The congressional liaison emphasized that "we are suggesting that Congressional Democrats be co-authors of a revised inflation program, rather than after-the-fact consultants."[146] Moore also realized, however, that

Carter's shift to a Republican macroeconomic logic had implications for where he could best draw legislative support for his anti-inflation fiscal measures. He concluded,

> Without the support of all major factions of the Congressional Democratic party, no inflation program can pass without Republican help. This is especially true in the Senate. Consequently, the process should not be presented initially as the development of a "Democratic inflation program." Instead, it could be styled as a process of intensive consultation—first with Democrats, then with Republicans. If working group deliberations reveal Democratic consensus is impossible and produce major defections, consultation with Republicans will have to be extensive.[147]

Thus, despite unified Democratic government, the administration was willing to exercise its preference for fiscal measures designed to curb inflation, even if, legislatively, that action required close work with Republicans in Congress.

Ultimately, this debate over fiscal restraint and the need for a balanced budget to fight inflation carried over into preparation of the fiscal 1981 budget. Summer 1979 saw the administration derailed by a big oil price shock, long gas lines, a very rapid acceleration of inflation, rising interest rates, and political fallout from Carter's "malaise speech" and subsequent dismissal of his Cabinet. The result of all this turmoil in budgetary terms was actually an upward reestimation of domestic outlays of tens of billions of dollars. From this, as Van Ooms has noted, "came the perception of fiscal irresponsibility."[148]

In response, the fiscal 1981 budget (January, 1980) was Carter's most austere, as he tried desperately to cool inflation through fiscal policy. Unfortunately, 1980 also proved a tumultuous year for the president, as he pushed a conservative program of fiscal austerity during a recession. For the remainder of 1979, the administration made some (perhaps symbolic) gains on the wage and price standards front. On September 28, 1979, the administration and labor leaders signed a "National Accord" that established agreement that anti-inflation policies must be both effective and equitable and stated that the administration would not abandon its efforts to pursue full employment and balanced growth. As a result of the accord, Pay Advisory and Price Advisory Committees were established to provide labor and industry with greater input into federal implementation of the standards.[149] Given labor's general lack of support for the various Carter anti-inflation initiatives and the administration's commitment to fiscal and monetary restraint, the usefulness of labor's attempt to bring Carter back into the Democratic macroeconomic fold with the accord's "full employment" language is doubtful.

As was true for President Johnson in 1966, the Federal Reserve continued to do the heavy lifting on inflation throughout the remainder of 1979. On October 6, 1979, the Fed underwent what is often referred to as the Volcker Revolution. The Fed abandoned its technique of controlling the expansion of monetary aggregates by setting a target for the interest rate on federal funds. It instead began to conduct open market operations by supplying the volume of bank reserves that was consistent with desired rates of monetary growth and allowing interest rates to fluctuate in a wider range. The result of this shift in policy was a marked decrease in the growth of money and credit. The discount rate was raised to 12 percent, and overall interest rates rose to record postwar levels in the last quarter of 1979. One result of this policy shift, which the administration had hoped to avoid, was a severe disruption in local housing markets reminiscent of LBJ's housing crunch.[150]

Thus, President Carter entered his reelection year with the hopes of his administration tied to a macroeconomic policy of fiscal austerity and monetary restraint. In particular, the administration's adoption of the Republican logic that deficit reduction was the primary tool in the battle against inflation represents a striking change from the stimulus-oriented administration of only three years earlier. While Carter saw much good in Democratic social policies directed at the poor, elderly, and minorities, he was increasingly willing to work with Republicans to pursue macroeconomic policy (in a time of crisis) that was clearly outside the bounds of Democratic stabilization logic. In fact, the administration was convinced by 1980 that the president's reelection depended largely on his ability to successfully win the battle against inflation.

Conclusion

In both of the cases considered here, Democratic presidents adopted the notion that contraction of the macroeconomy was the most appropriate means of satisfying their respective policy-making objectives. *In doing so, both presidents temporarily appropriated a Republican conceptualization of the functioning of the macroeconomy and its associated tools in order to deal with the unemployment-inflation tradeoff in a fashion not normally associated with their party and in direct opposition to the preferences of their majorities in government.* In fact, unified government in both cases appears to have been a liberating rather than constraining factor on their decision making in the American political economy. Both presidents were able to temporarily repudiate the preferences of their partisans in Congress without the fear of legislative gridlock usually associated with divided government. Most importantly, it is clear from the evidence that the presidents' institutional mandate to stabilize the macroeconomy worked at cross-purposes with a partisan Democratic incentive to adopt expansive fiscal policy (a partisan objective that was a policy-making option for both presidents at the time). As will be shown in the next chapter, Republican presidents are sometimes willing to make these same kinds of decisions in reverse, during recessionary macroeconomic crises, in order to pursue a policy of full employment at the risk of increased inflation.

Republican Presidents and the Democratic Logic of Unemployment Policy

President Eisenhower entered office in January, 1953, exhibiting the expected macroeconomic concerns of a Republican president. He intended to reduce federal spending, balance the budget as a prerequisite for cutting taxes, and reduce the overall role of the federal government in economic activity. His primary concern, in keeping with a postwar Republican stabilization logic, was the danger posed to private enterprise by inflation and excessive government intervention in the economy. In particular, with the Korean War coming to a close, the administration moved quickly (by spring, 1953) to remove the wage and price controls originally put in place by President Truman.[1] As was often the case when wage and price controls are removed, the president feared that pent-up demand could lead to a new postwar inflationary spiral. As a result, Eisenhower spent the first half of 1953 trying to move toward a balanced budget, hoping to thereby avoid an inflationary spiral that might be exacerbated by tax cuts proposed by some Republicans in Congress.

At least during 1953, Eisenhower was in agreement with the conservative Senate majority leader, Robert Taft (R-Ohio), on the desirability of a balanced budget, the dangers of deficits, and the need to avoid inflationary tax cuts. Both men expressed their agreement on these issues early in February, 1953, at a Legislative Leadership Meeting. Eisenhower stated his belief that the anticipated value of any tax reduction would be illusory, since the reduction could lead to inflation and create a requirement for additional taxes. Senator Taft similarly noted that to reduce taxes in 1953 would only serve to produce a big deficit that would have an adverse effect on the 1954 midterm elections.[2] Eisenhower would repeat this argument throughout the first half of 1953, noting to his Cabinet on May 1 that he had never promised a tax reduction until the budget could be balanced; he saw any earlier tax reduction as bringing additional inflation and, thus, as a self-defeating proposition.[3]

The fiscal reality in 1953 was that there was little hope of Eisenhower actually balancing the fiscal 1954 budget. For Eisenhower, communism in China and the Soviet Union posed security concerns and incurred obligations for the United States in Europe, Korea, Southeast Asia, and the Middle East. As Eisenhower's budget director, Joseph Dodge, noted at a Legislative Leadership Meeting on April 30, 67 percent of the budget was devoted to security programs and another $16 billion was for interest and other untouchables, leaving only about $10 billion available. Since the greatest increase in the budget after 1950 had been for national security expenditures, the result was that the administration rapidly approached a $50 billion defense commitment. Many of the Republicans to the ideological right of Eisenhower saw $35 billion as a more reasonable figure and feared that the administration would attempt to raise taxes to make up the difference.[4]

Republicans were particularly concerned with differentiating themselves fiscally from the performance of the Truman administration. Several key Republican leaders expressed their dismay at the administration's budget proposals. Senate majority leader Taft, speaking at the April 30 Legislative Leadership Meeting, claimed that the net result of the Eisenhower program would be to spend as much as the Truman administration. The senator argued that Congress would either have to raise taxes or accept a large deficit. He further stated that it would be impossible to elect a Republican Congress in 1954 if the administration were to stick with its budget estimates. Finally, he informed Eisenhower that two-thirds of Republicans in Congress would vote for further budget reductions, a decision at odds with the administration's position.[5] Sen. William Knowland (R-California), who would serve as majority leader after Taft's death in July, 1953, similarly noted the danger of the administration's program for partisan unity, arguing that Democrats would hit hard if the Republican Congress cut military appropriations below the level in the president's program; the likely result would be a split in the Republican Party.[6]

Given the budgetary demands of Eisenhower's security program, the administration responded to Republican complaints by proposing tax policy designed to reduce the deficit. At a subsequent Legislative Leadership Meeting, Treasury secretary George Humphrey, a fiscal conservative, noted that previously legislated postwar tax changes (expiration of the excess profits tax and reduction of corporate and individual income taxes) scheduled to take effect January 1, 1954, would cause a revenue loss of $2.1 billion in fiscal 1954 and of $8 billion in each ensuing full year.[7] In addition to the $4.5 billion in budget cuts proposed by the administration, Secretary Humphrey, with Eisenhower's approval, proposed a tax program that would extend the excess profits tax to December 31, 1954; rescind the scheduled 4 percent reduction in corporate incomes (52 to 48 percent); not lower individual income tax rates prior to January 1, 1954; rescind the scheduled reduction in certain excise taxes; and postpone for two years the scheduled increase in the Social Security wage tax (OASI).[8]

Although Eisenhower's 1953 fiscal program did not satisfy all members of his party, it did stay within the bounds of the postwar Republican macroeconomic agenda. As promised, the president was ultimately successful in making progress against the deficit. As a result of his spending and tax proposals, the estimated deficit for fiscal 1954 was lowered from $9.9 billion to $3.9 billion.[9] Since Eisenhower had already stated that achieving a balanced budget was a multiyear undertaking and that he would not reduce taxes further until that goal had been accomplished, the president was ultimately consistent in his macroeconomic decision making.

That Eisenhower was consistent in his decision making on inflation is evident in his own writing at the time. Yet his statements also reveal that he saw the Republican process of fighting inflation as striking a delicate balance between the need to balance the budget and the desire to cut taxes to spur economic growth. He wrote confidentially to Gen. Alfred M. Gruenther, who served as Supreme Allied Commander of NATO in Europe (1953–56), that "if we should proceed recklessly and habitually to create budget deficits year after year, we have with us an inflationary influence that can scarcely be successfully combated. . . . Money is the normal incentive in our kind of society; this means that taxes must not take so much away as to destroy incentive, nor must inflation be allowed to destroy money. . . . So a growing number of people believe that we must remove all possible inflationary tendencies, and one of these is obviously the deficit."[10]

In prioritizing the twin Republican macroeconomic goals by placing budget balancing over tax reduction in the fight against inflation, Eisenhower viewed his decisions as nothing less than an issue of national security. He wrote in his personal diary on June 1, 1953, that "I believe that the American public wants security ahead of tax reduction and that while we can save prodigious sums in the Defense Department without hurting our security, we cannot safely, this year, knock out enough to warrant an immediate tax reduction. To do it . . . would, of course, produce another deficit of extraordinary size, force us to seek an increase in the legal debt limit, and would be most inflationary in its effect."[11]

Eisenhower disagreed with those in his party, including Senator Taft, who argued that a tax cut was essential if the Republicans were to retain unified control of the government after the 1954 election. Those Republicans believed that a cut of about $10 billion to the Defense Department's budget would allow for such an election-year tax cut.[12] Eisenhower clearly did not view such a cut as feasible in the existing international climate. Given the political climate in Congress, Eisenhower wrote to a friend that "I spend my life trying to cut expenditures, balance the budget, and then get at the popular business of lowering taxes."[13]

Eisenhower Confronts the Vicious Cycle

Eisenhower's brand of balanced budget fiscal conservatism, even in the face of all the new security commitments taken on by the United States since World War II, might lead one to question how his response to a recession might differ, if at all, from Hoover's balanced-budget-at-all-costs macroeconomic performance at the beginning of the Great Depression. Eisenhower's close adviser, Secretary of the Treasury George Humphrey, was a fiscal conservative with views on monetary and tax policy that only reinforced the likelihood that Eisenhower would stay to the right in macroeconomic matters.

Yet the reality was that Eisenhower had no intention of returning to the budgetary politics of the Hoover era. Eisenhower's choice of personnel to revitalize the moribund Council of Economic Advisers, Arthur Burns, was a foremost authority on business cycle behavior who was intent on using the CEA to develop flexible fiscal and monetary programs designed to prevent major downturns in the economy. Unlike Humphrey and other conservative advisers in the administration, Burns saw the usefulness in some macroeconomic conditions of employing Keynesian tools such as deficit spending, public works, and easy credit. Despite the reticence of Humphrey and others, Burns was able to push Eisenhower into accepting a more active role for the federal government in macroeconomic policy making.[14]

Burns was significantly aided by Eisenhower's administrative assistant for economic affairs, Gabriel Hauge, who also took a more activist view of the federal government's role in macroeconomic stabilization. Hauge was perhaps the first adviser to suggest that the administration would likely need to shift away from partisanship to deal with the specter of recession. While Arthur Burns was busy reorganizing the CEA in early 1953, Hauge told George Humphrey to be prepared for a presidential switch in macroeconomic policy-making emphasis. He informed Humphrey in a memo that "we are going to have to shift our mental gears on this preoccupation with inflation sometime before too long."[15] As for the balanced budget logic, Hauge had this to say to Humphrey: "We may have to defer balancing the budget a year or two longer. But a moderate unbalance need not in itself be inflationary if wise debt and monetary policies are employed. I do not believe an immediate balanced budget is the summum bonum of our administration."[16] Clearly, these are not the words of a fiscally conservative Republican. Due in large part to Hauge and Burns, Eisenhower did not reverse the New Deal but instead accepted institutional responsibility for the macroeconomy, particularly during the recession of 1954 when many Republicans feared a replay of 1929.[17]

These influences came into play beginning in September, 1953, when macroeconomic indicators signaled the onset of a downturn. At a September 25 Cabinet meeting, Eisenhower reemphasized his pledge to use the full power of government to prevent "another 1929."[18] Yet the tone of the policy discussion at the Cabinet meeting remained consistently partisan. Burns emphasized that the CEA was still thinking in Republican terms about precautionary measures, including easier monetary policy and private business action, tax reductions rather than increased government expenditures, and practical government programs with preference given to loans and loan guarantees rather than direct government construction. Secretary Humphrey noted that on the monetary front, the Fed agreed to continue to ease monetary restraint for the next several months.[19]

Yet only several weeks later, Burns, in a memo to Eisenhower, broached the idea of using military spending in countercyclical fashion. He argued that some defense programs, "which might now appear to be of marginal significance, may deserve the very highest priority in any expansion of governmental spending in the future to relieve unemployment." Burns further advised Eisenhower that, "In view of the recent turn in economic conditions with which you are familiar, this may be a good time to consider how military requirements may be fitted into a broad program of anti-depression planning."[20]

More generally, Burns believed that the administration should have a shelf of public works plans to be quickly activated as needed to counter rising unemployment. He informed Eisenhower that "our objective here is to make sure that if substantial additions to public construction should be desired to stave off depression, the new construction can be gotten under way promptly and on the desired scale."[21] While Burns had not played up this aspect of countercyclical policy at the September Cabinet meeting, perhaps because he felt conditions did not warrant it or because of concern over the reaction of Humphrey and others, it is clear that he saw this sort of New Deal public works policy as an important contingency plan in case of a sharp downturn in the macroeconomy. *Thus, the groundwork was being set for Eisenhower's 1954 movement away from the partisan macroeconomic logic of his own party, the same sort of decision-making shift (in reverse) engaged in by both Johnson and Carter.*

If Burns's planning at the CEA was not sufficient to turn Eisenhower's thoughts to unemployment rather than inflation, then information coming from outside sources tipped the balance. For example, Eisenhower himself forwarded a memo to Treasury secretary Humphrey in December, 1953, from Congressman William Ayres (R-Ohio), giving the congressman's opinion on the macroeconomic direction of the administration. Eisenhower referred to Ayres as "one of the finest and keenest observers in Congress."[22] Ayres commented that, "regardless of the good things you have done and will continue to do, Mr. President, any appreciable amount of unemployment in 1954 will add considerably to the burden of electing Republican Congressional candidates in marginal districts."[23] Ayres forcefully concluded that "it is impossible to over-emphasize the fear of depression. . . . Fear of a so-called 'Hoover' depression under a Republican administration, is in my opinion the largest single obstacle which confronts General Eisenhower. This is the biggest silent issue on which a defense must be made to the independent voter. I say it is silent because those people who are most likely to be influenced by this feeling of uncertainty, don't talk about it. Percentage-wise, it is as prevalent in the country club and the office as it is in the union hall and the shop."[24]

Ayres's position received a very important seconding from Eisenhower's close friend and adviser Henry Cabot Lodge. Lodge had served as manager of the Eisenhower campaign in 1952 and was then serving as the United States' ambassador to the United Nations. In a confidential memo, Lodge, who despite his position at the U.N. still regularly counseled the president on political strategy, advised Eisenhower that

> the greatest single danger appearing on the horizon now, insofar as public confidence in your administration is concerned, is the possibility of serious unemployment. . . . It is, of course, vital to have all the preliminary work completed which will enable you to put the full resources of the Federal Government to work to help maintain maximum employment, as you have said you would do. I assume that this is being done. But, from a public relations standpoint, this is not enough. The public must see with its own eyes that you are constantly at work and perpetually preoccupied with the question.[25]

Thus, advisers such as Burns and Lodge, and congressmen such as Ayres, helped acclimate Eisenhower to a traditionally Democratic mindset for countercyclical decision making.

That they were successful in persuading Eisenhower is clear from the president's statements and actions over the first six months of 1954. During this period, Eisenhower moved aggressively to stimulate the macroeconomy, using an eclectic and pragmatic mix of countercyclical instruments before returning to his preoccupation with budget balancing and inflation toward the end of the year. *That his decision making cycled between Republican and Democratic logics for stabilization, just as LBJ's and Carter's decision making did, testifies to the manner in which institutional responsibility often works at cross-purposes with the pursuit of partisan and electoral goals.*

Eisenhower had accepted the idea of countercyclical macroeconomic policy making by the beginning of 1954. In a personal and confidential letter to his brother, Milton Eisenhower (president of Penn State University), the president expressed his thoughts on the issue: "Maintenance of prosperity is one field of governmental concern that interests me mightily and one on which I have talked incessantly to associates, advisers, and assistants ever since January. . . . In these days I am sure that the government has to be the principal coordinator and, in many cases, the actual operator for the many things that the approach to depression would demand."[26] That Eisenhower saw the federal government's role in the macroeconomy as a substantial one is obvious from the list of possible macroeconomic decisions he offered to his brother:

> In one way or another, practically every department and agency of gov-
> ernment is involved. Means available to the government include revi-
> sion of tax laws to promote consumption; extension of credit and
> assuring of low interest rates; vigorous liberalization of all social secu-
> rity measures; extension of all kinds of reinsurance plans, as well as di-
> rect loans and grants; acceleration in construction programs involving
> everything from multiple purpose dams, irrigation projects, military
> equipment and public buildings on the one hand, to increased expen-
> ditures for soil conservation, upstream water storage and public hous-
> ing on the other.[27]

The president saw the undertaking as so vast and complex that he even wondered to Milton "whether we should not have an office in government that in the economic field would parallel the Office of Defense Mobilization in the military field [he did not view the CEA as the equivalent]."[28]

Similarly, adoption of the above decision-making outlook required Eisen-hower to be more flexible regarding his preference for a balanced budget. That he became more flexible is evident in a letter he sent to R. C. Leffin-gwell, vice chairman of the board for J. P. Morgan & Co. Leffingwell wrote Eisenhower to express his anxiety over the recession and his sentiment that, based upon experience under Presidents Wilson, Harding, Hoover, and

Roosevelt, relief from the federal government was usually too little and/or too late. Not surprisingly, Leffingwell requested additional corporate income tax relief to stimulate the economy.[29] Eisenhower, while not committing to tax reduction, responded that "there can now be no disagreement among responsible citizens about the proper role of the Federal Government as a preventive agent in times of economic stress."[30] The president commented with respect to his fiscal priorities that "I want to say, however, that budget balancing is not in my mind the single or governing criterion of our economic and financial policy. Economic stability and growth is another and one of compelling importance at certain times. If conditions require, we shall not hesitate to subordinate the first of these criteria to the second."[31] *So, in institutional terms, Eisenhower saw a substantial and flexible role for the federal government in combating the 1954 recession. This was a significant change from his prioritizing of a balanced budget above all else in 1953.*

Translating these ideas into decision making, the administration began the year by transmitting to Congress (January 28, 1954) the annual *Economic Report of the President.* In addressing concerns over the recession and unemployment, the report not only emphasized the role of built-in stabilizers, such as Social Security payments and farm price supports in cushioning the downturn, but it also set out a strong countercyclical program liberalizing housing credit, easing lending rules, broadening old age and unemployment benefits, extending tax incentives to investors, and expanding the highway construction program.[32] Treasury secretary Humphrey, in particular, adamantly opposed the countercyclical program, arguing that fiscal restraint was still essential in order to maintain economic stability. With a previously legislated (pre-Eisenhower) postwar income tax cut scheduled to take effect on January 1, 1954, Humphrey feared that the loss of revenue, compounded by the countercyclical program during a recession, would lead to greater deficits and inflation. The administration did note that the tax cut would have an additional stimulative effect on the macroeconomy.[33]

For the next six months, a very Democratic-looking version of fiscal stimulation was the centerpiece of the Eisenhower macroeconomic agenda. This development represented a particularly startling partisan shift for a Republican president, given that the last member of that party in office was Herbert Hoover. Under conditions of macroeconomic crisis (recession), Eisenhower did not push a version of macroeconomic stabilization that was firmly situated in a Republican calculus. He instead chose Democratic countercyclical measures designed to rapidly stimulate the macroeconomy.

As early as February, 1954, several months before the recession bottomed out, Eisenhower informed his Cabinet that he was ready to request supplemental appropriations from Congress should any Cabinet members see the necessity of initiating new federal spending projects for countercyclical purposes. For confirmation that this behavior was viewed within the administration as a shift in stabilization logic, one need look no further than Ambassador Lodge's comment at the meeting that the president's approach to the recession demonstrated effectiveness in defeating charges that Republicans were devoted to the "trickle down" theory of economics.[34]

As the situation worsened over the next several months, Eisenhower became increasingly concerned with the need to fight rising unemployment. He noted at a Cabinet meeting on March 26 that action had been taken a year previously to check inflation and that now seemed to be the time for "liberal action to stimulate the economy."[35] Less than two weeks later, Eisenhower wrote in his personal diary of the necessity for decisive action to fight the recession. He stated,

> During the last Cabinet meeting, Dr. Burns reported on the economic situation and reflected much more emphatically than ever before that we should begin to "do something." . . . I have the feeling that we are about at that place which the aviator would call the "point of no return." From here on I believe it will become clear that we are going one way or the other and I am convinced that the dangers of doing nothing are far greater than those of doing too much. By which I mean that everything the government can now do to increase the spending power of the country, both by the individual and the government, will, at least until there is a decided upturn in economic activity, be a good thing. Only the future will determine whether or not this is a fairly accurate estimate or merely the expression of ignorance.[36]

Over the next several months, the president made a host of macroeconomic decisions designed to stimulate the macroeconomy, primarily through executive administrative action. Initially, Arthur Burns suggested a list of administrative actions to be taken by the president. Eisenhower ordered liberalization of VA and FHA mortgage and modernization regulations, short-term funding by the Treasury, a quickening of domestic procurement, immediate repayment by the IRS of over-assessment claims prior to adjudication, early decisions on proposed public utility expansion cases, and consultation with state governors on acceleration of public works projects.[37] At this time, Eisenhower also personally directed Treasury secretary Humphrey to contact Federal Reserve chairman William McChesney Martin "in order to develop real pressure on the Federal Reserve Board for loosening credit still further."[38]

By May, 1954, Eisenhower called for a further intensification of the administration's countercyclical efforts. He ordered that every effort be made to initiate public works in critical unemployment areas. Arthur Burns recalled the particular day that Eisenhower completely committed to a program of countercyclical spending. Remembering May 25, 1954, he commented, "[T]he order went out on that day to the defense department to no longer cut back on military spending, in fact to start increasing it by a substantial amount. Other agencies were also instructed to speed up their spending."[39]

Overall, Eisenhower approved expedited federal expenditures totaling approximately $600 million and involving almost $2.5 billion in contracts and other obligations likewise expedited. About two-thirds of the expenditures and 80 percent of the obligations related to the Department of Defense, following the lines already suggested by CEA chairman Burns in the early stages of the downturn.[40]

In June, 1954, Burns informed the president that the recovery was underway, but fears that it might abort led him to recommend, and Eisenhower to approve, additional administrative action designed to further liberalize VA and FHA loan programs, more rapidly let federal procurement contracts, pressure private banks to liberalize loan requirements, and continue the acceleration of public works projects.[41] Although the administration was initially resistant to the Republican logic of tax cuts to stimulate the economy (for fear of running budget deficits even larger than that already being predicted for the recession), Eisenhower did eventually propose some tax relief. The proposals focused on excise tax reduction and accelerated depreciation. These tax proposals, however, were criticized as too pro-business, too late, and too moderate. Nonetheless, the fact that they were proposed demonstrates that the administration was willing to abandon the fiscal conservatism of Cabinet members such as George Humphrey in time of recession, even if doing so required an increased budget deficit as a countercyclical measure.[42]

That Eisenhower did not focus on tax reduction as the key countercyclical technique is not surprising, given the political context in which he operated as the first Republican president since the New Deal. Although his tax proposals were consistent with Republican stabilization logic and he was operating under unified government, Eisenhower still preferred to rapidly expand the economy through the administrative means at his disposal. In general, tax policy is lagged as a countercyclical measure by the need to navigate the proposals through Congress. Unified government did not accelerate the consideration of tax measures, nor did it act as a general deterrent to shifts in partisan decision making. Eisenhower actually found himself to the ideological left of many members of his own party who found his deficit-increasing countercyclical spending and tax proposals to be irresponsible fiscal policy.

Correspondence at the time makes it clear that the president did not necessarily view unified Republican government as a policy-making blessing. Writing to Indiana governor George Craig, Eisenhower spelled out his feelings on the Republican Party:

> The Republican party has got for once and for all to make up its mind whether to follow the ludicrous partnership of the Old Guarders and the McCarthyites (one of my friends has called it a "marriage of convenience"), or whether it is going to stand behind the program of the administration and the middle-of-the-road philosophy in which we firmly believe. I have done, and continue to do, everything in my power, both as president and as titular leader of the Republican party, to urge adherence to that middle-of-the-road philosophy and to the program we have advanced.[43]

In another letter to a friend, Eisenhower mused about the need of the Republican Party "to get itself squared away in the public mind," and concerning the right wing of the party, he commented that "I, for one, have always thought that we cannot afford to appear to be in the same camp with them."[44] Eisenhower wanted the post–New Deal, postwar Republican Party to be seen as taking responsibility for stabilizing the macroeconomy during a recession; the president realized that, politically, there was no returning to the Republican macroeconomic policy making of the 1920s.

In response to a letter from key economic adviser Gabriel Hauge, in which Hauge jokingly suggested euthanasia for the "Neanderthal Wing" of the party, Eisenhower laid out the electoral implications of the party's split. The president stated that "if the right wing really recaptures the Republican party, there simply isn't going to be any Republican influence in this country within a matter of a few brief years."[45]

The irony that unified Republican government could actually be a policy-making hindrance to a Republican president was driven home by Eisenhower's close friend and adviser Henry Cabot Lodge when he wrote to the president that

> your fate is not tied to the Republican party today anymore than it was tied in 1952. You pulled the Republican party through in '52. You must not become the tin can tied onto the Republican tail this year— which is precisely what some individuals, many of them well-meaning,

would have you become. . . . As far back as 1951 I thought that you could be just as successful a president with a Democrat as with a Republican Congress and I still think so. . . . In fact two years under Democratic organization of Congress might be easier for you than the last two years—which may be why some Democrats in their hearts don't want victory in 1954. They believe it will impair their chances in 1956.[46]

The above is not to suggest that Eisenhower was actually a Democrat in disguise, *but it does underscore the theoretical notion that presidents will move away from the perceived excesses of their own party during unified government, if that choice is viewed to be in keeping with the imperatives of the institutional position.* Eisenhower realized that his countercyclical policies would be more amenable to Democrats than to the right wing of the Republican Party.

A Return to Balanced Budget Orthodoxy

Eisenhower's flirtation with a Democratic stabilization logic ended as soon as Arthur Burns informed the Cabinet on July 23, 1954, that the decline in economic activity had definitely come to an end.[47] As the administration started planning its fiscal 1956 budget in the fall of 1954, the president warned that government revenues would be declining even as the recovery got underway. The result would be greater pressure for keeping the budget under control. Whereas during the recession the administration had been willing to consider tax cuts, Eisenhower, now returning his focus to balanced budgets and inflation, indicated that the administration would have to postpone the scheduled reduction of the corporate income tax and also oppose other tax proposals that might crop up in Congress.[48]

Eisenhower did not change his position in early 1955, when conservative members of the Cabinet led by George Humphrey pushed for tax relief in light of the expanding economy. At a Cabinet-legislative conference in January, 1955, Eisenhower questioned the advisability of even mentioning the possibility that the administration would propose tax reduction in 1955 or 1956. At the meeting, the president commented to Secretary Humphrey that while the secretary regularly stressed the need to balance the budget, when it came to tax reduction Humphrey seemed eager to anticipate possible fiscal savings that had yet to develop.[49]

The Republican leadership was also split. Senate majority leader Knowland cautioned that the promise of tax reduction that might not be delivered would open the party to criticism from Democrats during the 1956 election campaign. In contrast, House majority leader Charles Halleck (R-Indiana) argued that tax reduction would be a necessity for the party in 1956, regardless of the budgetary situation at the time.[50] Eisenhower was back in the realm of Republican decision making with his desire to tighten the budget and forgo tax reduction. In fact, as the split in congressional leadership demonstrates, Eisenhower was now more fiscally conservative than some members of his party who (as is often the case with Republicans) wanted tax relief, rather than additional federal spending, to accompany the expanding macroeconomy.

The president's decision-making position did not change during 1955. In fact, Eisenhower became increasingly adamant about the need to cut spending while maintaining federal revenues at their present levels. Upon hearing from budget director Rowland Hughes that a small budget surplus might be realized in fiscal 1957, Eisenhower reemphasized to his Cabinet that balancing the budget was the primary goal of the administration.[51] The president informed the Cabinet that a balanced budget was now his great objective, and that if he succeeded in achieving it he would have largely accomplished his job. Ike further noted that he would fight a tax cut in 1956 (his reelection year) if it were proposed at the expense of a balanced budget. He even stated his preference for a small budgetary surplus that could be applied toward reduction of the debt.[52] Secretary Humphrey, however, continued to push the supply-side line, arguing that a tax cut was the surest way to expand the economy and generate a budgetary surplus.[53]

Eisenhower was unpersuaded by Humphrey's argument. He preferred the policy suggestions of CEA chairman Burns, who argued that "we must take care that progress is not endangered by overconfidence, speculation, or price inflation. . . . Many things must be done by different agencies of government and by private citizens to restrain somewhat the excessive exuberance that now appears to be taking hold of commercial markets."[54] To counter the threat of a resurgence of inflation, Burns recommended several restrictive policy steps to the president and Cabinet. These included cutting federal expenditures immediately, rather than letting government agencies take six months or more to do so; applying the brakes to the expansion of federal credit, particularly in VA and FHA mortgage programs; and being prepared to move rapidly (yet flexibly) toward restrictive monetary policy at the Federal Reserve.[55] In fact, during the prior two weeks Eisenhower had already ordered movement in the policy direction suggested by Burns. After being informed by the budget director that the estimated deficit for fiscal 1956 was only 3 percent of anticipated government spending, Eisenhower ordered that this 3 percent be deducted from each federal agency's estimated expenditures. The president also acted administratively to tighten the terms of VA and FHA mortgage credit programs.[56]

Thus, Eisenhower entered the fall 1955 fiscal planning season for fiscal 1957 with the same Republican macroeconomic preferences he exhibited throughout 1953. He was firm that no tax relief would be proposed before a balanced budget was achieved and that any small surplus would go toward retiring the national debt rather than toward Republican tax cuts. *Eisenhower's shift away from a Republican stabilization logic during the 1954 recession and the political difficulties it engendered within his own party under unified government graphically illustrate the ways in which a president's institutional position may shape presidential response to other partisan and electoral incentives present in the policy-making environment.*

Neil Jacoby, a member of the CEA during the period, put this temporary blurring of partisan logics into historical perspective years later, when he commented that "now, if you read the writings of [Walter] Heller and other fiscal historians of the period, you get the impression that it was only with President Kennedy and the Democratic administration that Keynesian economic thinking began to influence public policy. This, I say, is false. Keynesian economic thinking played a key role in the recession of 1954 under Eisenhower."[57] Thus, Eisenhower accepted his institutional responsibility for macroeconomic stabilization. Just like Johnson and Carter, however, the decisions made by Eisenhower in the American political economy of 1954 flowed from attempts to use his institutional rather than partisan or electoral position to confront the vicious cycle.

Ronald Reagan and the Supply-Side Revolution

For the years 1981–83, Ronald Reagan exhibited what (at least on the surface) appeared to be a consistently Republican macroeconomic calculus in his decision making. Despite scathing fiscal rhetoric to the contrary, however, the administration also presided over the largest budget deficits in U.S. history. So why, one might ask, were partisan Republican policies designed to fight those deficits so unsuccessful in realizing their intended outcome? Members of the Reagan administration would answer that congressional Democrats reneged on promises to enact cuts in federal spending agreed upon with the administration. Democrats, in contrast, would respond that the huge revenue loss stemming from the administration's tax cuts combined with a substantial increase in defense spending to cause the expanding deficits. The reality appears to have been somewhere in between these two partisan macroeconomic policy-making scenarios. Understanding partisan differences for the Reagan administration, therefore, is a question not only of determining whether the president focused primarily on anti-inflation or on unemployment policy but also of assessing whether the consistent partisan rhetoric of the Reagan administration actually matched the decisions made by the president from 1981 to 1983.

Ronald Reagan defeated incumbent Jimmy Carter for the presidency in an election year that experienced recession, including a 7.5 percent rate of unemployment during the critical pre-election months of September to November, 1980. Despite this recessionary economy, however, 1980 also experienced an annual rate of inflation of 13.5 percent, with interest rates reaching unprecedented levels, including a prime rate set at a whopping 21.5 percent.[58] Into this macroeconomic environment, President Reagan brought a consistently partisan Republican logic to his decision making, a calculus that combined elements of monetarism, supply-side economics, and traditional balanced budget orthodoxy. The mix embraced several macroeconomic goals, including lower inflation, a balanced budget, and less government. Realization of these goals would lead, in turn, to rapid growth and increased employment.[59] The macroeconomic instruments initially chosen to implement this agenda included individual and corporate income tax cuts; additional incentives for capital investment; deep cuts in nondefense federal spending, welfare, and subsidies; and monetary restraint.[60] The administration also made it clear, however, that it would reject macroeconomic approaches to the recession that included any industrial policy or national economic planning, short-term monetary expansion, or massive public works and other jobs programs, all of which could be utilized to temporarily ease unemployment.[61]

As one scholar has noted, these distinctions embodied in the Reagan macroeconomic agenda had "a very considerable influence on the range of economic policies that were considered respectable."[62] To this end, the Reagan administration shifted the focus of countercyclical stabilization policy away from increased federal spending and monetary ease during a recession. It instead combined instruments from the conservative macroeconomic approaches mentioned above, all of which had been around in various forms for decades, into a full-scale assault on inflation, despite the presence of substantial unemployment. *A partisan Republican rationale for this initiative was clearly present in the administration's approach: reduce inflation first, and economic growth and increased employment would naturally follow.*

As a result, President Reagan made a set of macroeconomic decisions during 1981 that were consistent with Republican stabilization logic. These decisions comprised the administration's "Program for Economic Recovery," which the president announced on February 18, 1981.[63] The program proposed a three-pronged strategy of tax cuts, reductions in the rate of federal spending, and monetary restraint. The tax cuts were embodied in what came to be known as the Economic Recovery Tax Act of 1981 (ERTA). The ERTA provisions followed closely along the lines of substantial tax cuts proposed in Congress, known as the Kemp-Roth plan. ERTA proposed to reduce individual income tax rates 30 percent during 1981–84, at 10 percent intervals per year. In addition, the top tax rate on capital gains would drop from 70 to 50 percent during this period. The rules governing Individual Retirement Accounts (IRAs) would be liberalized, and the marriage penalty for couples filing jointly would be alleviated through a new set of deductions. To promote investment, ERTA proposed an Accelerated Cost Recovery System (ACRS). The ACRS would increase business investment through a shortening of the period over which assets could be depreciated and by allowing firms to claim more of the depreciation up front. In addition, ERTA proposed an increase of the investment tax credit for some types of equipment.[64]

The administration's spending cut proposals were contained in a revised fiscal 1982 budget, submitted as a replacement for the one offered by President Carter before he left office. The revised fiscal 1982 budget emphasized reduction in the rate of federal spending growth and reallocation of budgetary priorities toward defense (ironically, a change in direction that Carter had initiated near the end of his term). Carter's fiscal 1982 budget had proposed outlays of $739 billion, receipts of $712 billion, and a deficit of $27 billion.[65] In contrast, Reagan's revised fiscal 1982 budget called for an increase of $6 billion for defense with nondefense reductions of $48.6 billion. Total outlays were estimated at $695 billion. Because of revenue loss due to the ERTA proposals, however, the revised budget projected only $650 billion in receipts and a $45 billion deficit.

Since actual fiscal 1981 outlays and receipts were $657 billion and $599 billion, respectively, the Reagan budget represented a 5.8 percent increase in outlays and an 8.3 percent increase in receipts. In contrast, Carter's budget proposed a 12.5 percent increase in outlays and a 17.8 percent increase in receipts over fiscal 1981 levels.[66] Reagan's revised fiscal 1982 budget represented a cut of approximately 50 percent in the rate of increase for both proposed federal outlays and receipts over the Carter budget. The administration argued that the budget deficit would be closed (and the budget balanced) once the economic growth and increased productivity spurred by ERTA increased federal revenues in subsequent years. This was the essence of the supply-side theory guiding the administration's decision making throughout 1981.

Monetary policy also played a key role in the administration's 1981 attempt at spurring noninflationary economic growth. While the administration obviously could not unilaterally set monetary policy, it was extremely supportive of Federal Reserve chairman Paul Volcker's attempts to use monetary policy to wring inflation out of the economy. The goal of monetary policy in 1981 was to significantly reduce the growth of the money supply relative to the record high rate of growth experienced during late 1980. In addition, the Fed attempted to reduce the within-year variability of money growth, thereby supporting a more stable and predictable monetary policy geared toward promoting business confidence. The administration agreed with the Fed that these two components, reduced growth and reduced fluctuation, would lower inflation and short-term interest rates. Ironically, it is Fed policy, more than any other decision made by the administration in 1981, which is usually held responsible for the recession that hit the macroeconomy in late 1981 and 1982.[67]

The administration focused on fighting inflation, even with the existence of relatively high unemployment (it would go even higher in 1982) and utilized a variety of decidedly Republican policy instruments (e.g., supply-side tax cuts, reductions in federal spending, monetary restraint) to implement its macroeconomic policy goals. Of interest to note is that Congress accepted ERTA and the fiscal 1982 budget revisions with only minor modifications. The primary change in the version that Reagan signed in August, 1981, was that the reduction in individual tax rates was revised to 23 percent (from 30 percent) over three years, as a means of incurring a smaller federal deficit. Similarly, the Omnibus Budget Reconciliation Act of 1981 cut spending by $35 billion for fiscal 1982 and $130 billion over three years.[68]

Although the 1980 election saw the Senate move into Republican hands for the first time since the Eisenhower administration (1953–55), Reagan still had to deal with a substantial Democratic majority in the House led by Speaker Thomas "Tip" O'Neill (D-Massachusetts), whom Reagan official Edwin Meese has described as "a welfare state of the old-fashioned type."[69] The hope was that with twelve new Republicans in the Senate and forty to fifty conservative "boll weevil" Democrats in the House (which would easily give Republicans a working majority), the president would be able to get his partisan macroeconomic agenda through Congress reasonably intact.[70]

Some Republicans were quite skeptical of the logic underlying ERTA. Most notably, both Senate Finance Committee chairman Bob Dole (R-Kansas) and Senate Budget Committee chairman Pete Domenici (R-New Mexico) had doubts about the efficacy of the tax cuts.[71] Ed Meese has noted that the party in Congress was not uniformly behind Reagan's tax cut proposals at the outset. He wrote, "At the time [1981] misgivings about cutting back taxes extended into the Republican party and the administration itself. Repeated efforts from within the GOP and the administration were made to undercut the Reagan program and to force the president to back off from his pledges."[72] Simultaneously, Democrats were labeling the proposals as a "Republican tax plan" and claiming that the cuts were a disastrous prescription for huge deficits and runaway inflation, the very symptoms they were intended to alleviate.[73]

With partisan lines drawn, OMB director David Stockman sought to bridge the gap that was developing between supply-siders who favored the cuts and orthodox conservatives in both the GOP and southern Democratic ranks who feared that the cuts would lead to larger budget deficits rather than to budgetary balance. Enlisting the aid of Congressman Phil Gramm of Texas (still a conservative House Democrat at the time), Stockman reworked the budget cut/tax cut tradeoff to show both a balanced budget and a large tax cut. In essence, there would be something for everyone, supply-side Republicans and orthodox fiscal conservatives of both parties. As has been often noted, Stockman developed strong reservations about whether sufficiently deep spending cuts could ever be made to balance out the loss of revenue from the tax cuts. In retrospect, he firmly indicted the Republican supply-side principles underlying Reaganomics: "The irony was that the supply-side idea was properly suspect by the GOP politicians from the very beginning: they knew in their bones they couldn't live with massive tax and spending reductions. Given the breadth of their skepticism, supply-side by rights should never have been the centerpiece of the 1980 GOP platform, the 1980 presidential campaign, or the new Reagan administration's economic policy."[74] As noted above, however, the administration prevailed in realizing its macroeconomic agenda during 1981; divided government did not have a political impact sufficient to affect presidential decision making. *The question was whether the vicious cycle brought on by the recession, which began in August, 1981, would be of sufficient scope to cause President Reagan to shift partisan logic in the fashion of Eisenhower, Johnson, and Carter, leading him to switch his focus from inflation to countercyclical unemployment policy.*

In short, the answer to this question is a qualified no. Reagan's decision making remained consistently Republican throughout 1982 and 1983. Even in the face of the 1982 recession, in which the U.S. economy contracted by 1.5 percent (rather than growing by the 5.2 percent forecast by the administration), Reagan continued to emphasize deficit reduction and the fight against inflation.[75] Deficit reduction became particularly important to the administration in 1982, as the recession automatically increased outlays by $30 billion and decreased revenues by an additional $23 billion. These changes drove the administration's $45 billion deficit projection to $98 billion for fiscal 1982.[76]

In addition, criticism from some members of Congress suggested that the nation's primary fiscal problem was that the initial ERTA cuts had been too large. Thus, some members called on Reagan to increase taxes in order to cut the deficit. Reagan rejected this approach, however, in his January 26, 1982, State of the Union address:

> The doubters would have us turn back the clock with tax increases that would offset the personal tax-rate reductions already passed by this Congress. Raise present taxes to cut future deficits, they tell us. Well, I do not believe we should buy their argument. Higher taxes won't balance the budget. It will encourage more government spending and less private investment. . . . So I will not ask you [Congress] to try to balance the budget on the backs of American taxpayers. . . . I will seek no tax increases this year, and I have no intention of retreating from our basic program of tax relief. . . . I will stand by my word.[77]

This revenue stance by Reagan made the expenditure side of the fiscal 1983 budget (January, 1982) even more critical. As one scholar has noted, "The FY 1983 budget proposals reflected both the new concern about deficits and faithfulness to the original Reagan program."[78] The budget offered a $239 billion deficit reduction plan that included cuts in non–Social Security entitlements of $12 billion the following year and $52 billion over three years; domestic discretionary cuts of $14 billion initially and $76 billion over three years (a 20 percent decrease in real terms for fiscal 1983 alone); and a further reduction in federal credit programs (a $20.3 billion decrease in new federal loan guarantees was already in place for fiscal 1982). The budget continued the administration's reallocation of spending toward defense with funding scheduled to increase at a rate of 8 percent annual real growth. Finally, the timetable for achieving a balanced budget was pushed back from fiscal 1984 to fiscal 1987.[79]

Reagan attempted to put the best possible spin on the administration's increased emphasis on deficit reduction and simultaneous postponement of a balanced budget. He commented in his annual economic message,

> We must redouble our efforts to control the growth in spending. We face high, continuing, and troublesome deficits. Although these defi-

cits are undesirably high, they will not jeopardize the economic recovery. We must understand the reasons behind the deficits now facing us: recession, lower inflation, and higher interest rates than anticipated. Although my original timetable for a balanced budget is no longer achievable, the factors which have postponed it do not mean we are abandoning the goal of living within our means. The appropriate ways to reduce the deficit will be working in our favor in 1982 and beyond: economic growth, lower interest rates, and spending control.[80]

Except for increases in some user fees and the closing of a few tax loopholes, however, the fiscal 1983 budget did not make any changes to the administration's tax policy. As a result, numerous members of Congress, still concerned about large projected budget deficits, began to call for an increase in taxes in spring 1982.

In particular, Senator Dole responded to the fiscal 1983 budget by proposing a $105 billion, three-year package that would repeal the third year of ERTA cuts. In addition, Democrats countered with a proposal for $165 billion in new taxes over three years, also repealing the third year of tax cuts.[81] Given Reagan's strong January, 1982, refusal to give back any of the 1981 tax cuts, one might be surprised that the president ultimately accepted a compromise spending reduction/tax increase package.

Reagan signed the Tax Equity and Fiscal Responsibility Act (TEFRA) into law in September, 1982. The bill was a compromise agreement designed to raise $98.3 billion in taxes over three years in return for spending cuts of $280 billion during the same period.[82] Treasury secretary James Baker and OMB director Stockman pitched the compromise to Reagan as three dollars of budget reductions for every one dollar of tax increases.[83] TEFRA accomplished this tradeoff through a number of means. It increased tax enforcement and eliminated some loopholes. While it left the individual income tax cuts passed in 1981 and many of the corporate tax provisions of ERTA intact, TEFRA repealed the accelerated depreciation scheduled for 1985–86. Overall, TEFRA recovered approximately 25 percent of the tax cuts originally passed in ERTA.[84]

Despite this change on taxes, the administration still initially viewed TEFRA as a continuation of its partisan focus on inflation and deficit reduction. Spending cuts outweighed tax increases by three to one, and even the tax increases were conceived of as a means of moving the budget closer to balance. In practice, however, TEFRA did not realize its goals. While the tax increases were promptly enacted, the budget reductions did not materialize as planned. In actuality, spending for fiscal 1983 ended up $48 billion higher than the budget targets and no progress was made toward lowering the deficit. In addition, tax receipts actually decreased due to the lingering recession, a circumstance that the TEFRA taxes did not redress.[85]

In addition to Reagan's partisan focus on spending and taxes, the president remained firm in his support of the Fed's monetary restraint throughout the 1981–82 recession. The policy was ultimately successful in bringing inflation all the way down to a rate of 4.4 percent for the year.[86] In contrast, recall that Eisenhower moved away from a Republican stabilization logic during the 1954 recession, aggressively pushing for monetary ease as a way of spurring economic growth and employment. Ed Meese noted that Reagan remained consistent despite intense political pressure to shift on the issue for the duration of the recession. Meese wrote, "During the grim recession days of 1981–82, before the Reagan economic program had had a chance to take effect, the president was under obvious pressure to 'bash' the Fed and seek easy money. But he steadfastly refused. On the contrary, he often conveyed to Fed Chairman Volcker (through myself and others) that the administration stood by the Fed in following a path of prudent money growth, even though the president was under great criticism because of the recession."[87] Thus, Reagan exhibits a somewhat different notion of institutional responsibility during a recession, signifying the magnitude of his Republican preference for relatively less inflation and more unemployment.

If the above is not sufficient evidence of Reagan's decision-ordering of anti-inflation policy over unemployment policy, even during a recession, then the following quote from his January, 1983, economic address provides the requisite proof:

> I am deeply troubled by the current level of unemployment [10.8 percent in December, 1982] in the United States and by the suffering and anxiety that it entails for millions of Americans. The unemployment that many of our citizens are experiencing is a consequence of the disinflation that must necessarily follow the accelerating inflation of the last decade. Allowing the upward trend of inflation to continue would have risked even greater increases in unemployment in the future. In spite of the present high unemployment rate and the accompanying hardships, it is essential that we maintain the gains against inflation that we have recently achieved at substantial cost. Continuing success in restraining inflation will provide a stronger foundation for economic recovery in 1983 and beyond.[88]

Even with a whopping 10.8 percent unemployment rate in December, 1982, Reagan nonetheless clung to the traditional Republican macroeconomic logic that inflation must be wrung from the economy before substantial gains in employment could be made. That the dictates of recession did not move Reagan toward a Democratic-looking countercyclical employment policy of increased federal spending of the sort used by Eisenhower in 1954 is further underscored by Reagan's statement that "it is understandable that many well-meaning members of the Congress have responded to the current high unemployment rate by proposing various public works and employment programs. However, I am convinced that such programs would only shift unemployment from one industry to another at the cost of increasing the Federal budget deficit."[89]

The president clearly rejected the type of policy decisions that would have signified a shift from a partisan stabilization calculus. Reagan's negative stance on countercyclical policy was likely influenced by the $208 billion budget deficit projected for fiscal 1983. The administration attributed the astronomical figure to a loss of tax revenue and concomitant automatic increase in federal outlays for unemployment benefits during the recession.[90] As a result, the president was forced into an extremely tight fiscal policy in the fiscal 1984 budget (January, 1983).

Overall, the fiscal 1984 budget had the partisan Republican look of the two previous Reagan budgets. The key issues addressed were the current and projected huge deficits, the traditional Reagan themes of defense preparedness, caps on social spending, and resistance to individual income tax increases. The proposed $43 billion increase in outlays for fiscal 1984 actually represented only a 5 percent nominal increase in spending and virtually no real increase over fiscal 1983. With only a 5 percent real increase in receipts scheduled, the deficit for fiscal 1984 was projected to be $189 billion.[91]

Specifically, the administration proposed a four-point plan for increased economic growth and deficit reduction that included a recommendation for a federal spending freeze; a request for Congress to adopt specific measures to control the growth of so-called "uncontrollable" spending programs; an adjustment in defense spending that would save $55 billion over five years; and most interestingly, a contingency tax program, beginning in fiscal 1986 and lasting no more than three years, that would kick in if the federal deficit surpassed 2.5 percent of GNP. The potential contingency taxes included a tax surcharge (similar to LBJ's) of 5 percent on all individual and corporate tax liabilities, and a $5 per barrel ($0.12 per gallon) excise tax on gasoline. The taxes could raise as much as $49 billion in revenues during fiscal 1986–88 but could only be levied if Congress had first approved the spending freeze and budget control portions of the program. Several new Social Security taxes were added for an additional $23 billion increase in revenue.[92] Thus, the fiscal 1984 budget represented another attempt by the administration to trade tax increases for spending cuts.

Thus, one is left with the question for 1981–83 of whether President Reagan's decision making actually lived up to the logic of the consistently partisan rhetoric for which he is best remembered. Given the above treatment of the period, the answer must be a qualified "yes." Reagan clearly established inflation as his primary macroeconomic concern for 1981–83. At no time, even during the recession in 1982, did he substantially shift his focus to countercyclical spending to alleviate unemployment. The primary instruments he employed to implement his anti-inflation agenda (supply-side tax cuts, spending reductions, and monetary restraint) all fall within the realm of Republican stabilization policy.

It is also true, however, that Reagan did not even remotely approach the balanced budget promised throughout his first term. The distinct partisanship inherent in divided government, however, makes it particularly difficult to assign him blame for that result. Democrats (and Republicans too) in Congress clearly reneged on some of their budget-cutting promises. The revenue loss from the ERTA tax cuts and defense buildup (sometimes referred to as Reagan's most effective countercyclical spending program) were also partially responsible for the large deficits.[93] Ed Meese admitted retrospectively that "we were not nearly so successful in reducing spending as we were in cutting tax rates."[94]

Despite the mixed track record of the Reagan administration's macroeconomic behavior for 1981–83, the decisions actually made by the president during this period clearly fit within a Republican stabilization framework. Reagan's consistent focus on inflation during the 1981–82 recession offers one of the few examples that defies the notion that institutional responsibility drives presidents to temporarily adopt macroeconomic logics not suited to pursuit of the typical partisan and electoral incentives that are so central to partisan theories of presidential behavior. Reagan's consistency is either a tribute to his partisan fortitude or a sign of the manner in which divided government lessens the ability of the public to assign blame to just the president and political party in power. If the latter case is true, then presidents need not shift from the partisan fold to confront the vicious cycle; they may simply attribute the macroeconomic ills of the nation to the counterproductive policies of the opposition party.

Conclusion

The above Republican case studies demonstrate, albeit not as conclusively as the Democratic cases (due to Reagan's partisan consistency during the recession), that Republican presidents will respond to a recessionary crisis by adjusting their decision-making tradeoffs to favor relatively less unemployment and more inflation. In essence, they will behave in Democratic fashion to bring the country out of recession through expansionary fiscal policy. The historical record shows that Eisenhower, in accepting institutional responsibility to stabilize the macroeconomy, adopted both a Democratic conception of the macroeconomy and the attendant Democratic policy instruments in dealing with the 1954 recession. He quickly abandoned this approach once the economy rebounded.

Reagan is a more problematic case study than Eisenhower, for he suggests that Republican presidents need not move from partisanship in a recession, if a Democratic Congress is willing to increase federal spending. *Thus, Reagan reaped the same countercyclical macroeconomic benefits as Eisenhower, without having to abruptly change policy direction to ameliorate the vicious cycle.* This result again casts an interesting light on the relationship between partisanship, institutional control, and macroeconomic conditions.

Presidents, Electoral Politics, and the Logic of the Political Business Cycle

We have seen in the last two chapters that institutional responsibility may require tradeoffs in decision making on the macroeconomy, as presidents are constrained in their ability to pursue partisan political objectives. The resultant behavior suggests that in accepting these tradeoffs, presidents fluctuate between Republican and Democratic logics for stabilization policy. Now we turn specifically to the relationship between institutional responsibility and presidential pursuit of the electoral incentive for decision making. In contrast to the findings of the political business cycle literature, all four presidential election-year case studies presented in this chapter demonstrate that presidents do not necessarily view rapid expansion of the macroeconomy as a strategic means of winning reelection. In keeping with the ideas presented in chapter 1, the cases suggest that the electoral incentive is also mediated by a president's institutional responsibility for sound macroeconomic management. Sometimes that may entitle presidents to rapidly stimulate the economy, but other times it may force them to actually prefer contraction, a notion of presidential decision making that is clearly at odds with business cycle depictions of presidential behavior.

Eisenhower in 1956

As discussed in chapter 5, by late 1955, the administration had shifted its macroeconomic focus back to fighting inflation by implementing policies designed to balance the budget and to encourage monetary restraint. That 1956 was Eisenhower's reelection year did not seem to have a substantial impact on the consistently conservative decision making of the president that year. Whereas tax cuts in an election year would be a likely Republican macroeconomic instrument to be utilized to stimulate the economy, by November, 1955, the administration had decided against proposing any tax cuts for the next fiscal year. The president and Cabinet approved a continuation of excise taxes (originally set to expire April 1, 1956) for another year and also recommended that corporate tax reductions (originally effective April

1, 1956) be postponed for another year. This position was reaffirmed in the president's January, 1956, *Economic Report*.[1] Agreement was also reached in the administration that tax cuts would only be considered if the budget was balanced for fiscal 1956 *and* showed a surplus in fiscal 1957, otherwise, "any attempt to reduce taxes is to be resisted in every possible manner."[2]

Given that the administration had experienced ongoing difficulty in reducing defense spending during its first term, it was particularly concerned that any loss of revenue to tax cuts would jeopardize Eisenhower's prized goal of a budget surplus for fiscal 1957. As noted in the earlier discussion of Eisenhower's decision making for 1953 and 1955, the president preferred to use any small budgetary surplus to reduce the national debt, rather than kick it back to the public as tax cuts. He made this preference clear in a message sent to a key White House assistant, Sherman Adams, in January, 1956. The president wrote, "It is essential, in the sound management of the government's finances, that we be mindful of our enormous national debt and of the obligation we have toward future Americans to reduce that debt whenever we can appropriately do so. Under conditions of high peacetime prosperity, such as now exist, we can never justify going further into debt to give ourselves a tax cut at the expense of our children."[3] Eisenhower reemphasized his preference for debt reduction over an election year tax cut at a Cabinet meeting two weeks later. The secretary of the Cabinet, in his minutes of the meeting, noted that "the president said that he just could not see any desirability in talking about tax cuts at this time, and that he did not want this administration to be the one to be cutting taxes constantly for the sake of politics when there is so great [a] need for debt reduction."[4]

This "no tax cut" position was formalized in the president's *Economic Report* on January 24, 1956. The report stated, "To add further to our public debt in order to win for ourselves reduction in taxes, which in the current state of high prosperity might chiefly serve to raise prices, would be irresponsible. In times like these we should bend our thoughts to the desirability of debt reduction, and not concentrate exclusively on the desirability of tax reduction. . . . Such an act of fiscal integrity would signify with unmistakable clarity that our democracy is capable of self-discipline."[5] *These are not the words of an administration intent on rapidly stimulating the economy in an election year, regardless of the inflation that might follow. In fact, the quote makes it clear that the administration actually considered tax cuts in the existing macroeconomic environment a prescription for inflation (and irresponsible), the very same macroeconomic ill it was attempting to ward off through fiscal discipline.* Nor is there any strong evidence on the expenditure side of the 1956 fiscal program of a deliberate attempt by Eisenhower to spend his way to electoral victory. A budgetary surplus was the president's fiscal priority, and most of his energy was spent on trying to control the growth of the defense budget in order to facilitate the realization of that surplus.

As further evidence that Eisenhower explicitly rejected rapid expansion in an election year, one can look at his position on accelerated public works planning. During 1956, the president's public works coordinator, Gen. John Bragdon (who worked under CEA guidance), drafted legislation for standby presidential authority to accelerate public works during a recession, much as the administration had done on a more ad hoc basis in 1954. In the record of a May 19, 1956, meeting in which Bragdon presented the proposed legislation to Eisenhower, the president noted the political temptation inherent in such presidential authority. The record of the meeting stated that "the president observed that, irrespective of the political affiliation of the administration at the time, the opposition party might consider such carte blanche authority as subject to improper use in an election year. The president said that the draft bill should provide a minimum unemployment level or similar criterion which must exist before the president may invoke the acceleration plan."[6] Thus, Eisenhower exhibited neither the requisite intentions nor the decisions to stimulate the economy in the fourth year of his term. *The above quote demonstrates that the president understood the political ramifications of federal spending in an election year and attempted to circumscribe presidential authority that might lend itself to that sort of macroeconomic behavior.*

The one macroeconomic area in which the administration sought some liberalization during 1956 was in monetary policy. There is some evidence, beginning in spring 1956 and running virtually up until the November election, that the administration was concerned that the Fed's policy of monetary restraint was beginning to unduly squeeze consumer credit, mortgages, and construction. The administration moved to encourage Fed chairman Martin to take steps toward monetary ease and a relaxation of credit. Initially, Treasury secretary Humphrey conveyed the administration's position to the Fed chairman.[7] Then, several weeks later, after a long conversation with Martin, CEA chairman Burns informed the president that the Fed would take steps in that direction.[8] At a June Cabinet meeting, Burns expressed his belief that, despite Fed action, some dramatic step was needed to ease credit, such as a reduction of the discount rate or a reduction of reserve requirements. Burns suggested that perhaps the president himself should confer with Martin on easing monetary policy, but the minutes state that, after warning against any infringement of the prerogatives of the Fed, "the president recalled how his beliefs were already clearly known and stated he would not want to be in the position of seeming to pressure the Federal Reserve Board."[9]

Eisenhower did act in the fall to ease the terms of federal credit programs for home buyers and builders through the usual government outlets, including the VA, FHA, Federal National Mortgage Association (FNMA), and Federal Home Loan Bank Board (FHLBB). The Small Business Administration also substantially increased its number of loans.[10] The administration did not, however, increase pressure on the Fed any further. Eisenhower clearly understood the importance of communication with the Fed chairman but did not view monetary policy as an instrument that he could directly fine-tune. In this sense, it was limited as a macroeconomic instrument for political business cycle (PBC) behavior.

Thus, Eisenhower did not engage in PBC behavior during 1956. That year he consistently pushed a conservative, balanced budget approach to fiscal policy making that was designed to moderate inflation. The president clearly believed in the efficacy of using any budgetary surplus (which the administration claimed to have achieved in summer 1956) to retire debt rather than to stimulate the macroeconomy through tax cuts. *If anything, the pull of institutional responsibility on Eisenhower's decision making in the American political economy further constrained his desire to strategically stimulate the economy.*

Lyndon Johnson in 1964

A consideration of political business cycle behavior for the Johnson administration must consider the special political circumstances surrounding his reelection year of 1964. Of most obvious importance is the fact that LBJ came to power in the wake of President Kennedy's assassination. This allowed him to serve as president for barely a year before he faced reelection. The year 1968 would have been a more suitable year for a test of PBC theory, given that by then there existed a track record of macroeconomic decision making that would allow for comparison and contrast of LBJ's agenda over time. Since LBJ did not seek reelection, however, 1964 must necessarily serve as the PBC test year. In addition, Johnson's macroeconomic agenda in 1964 was, in large measure, an extension of the Kennedy agenda, and as such, Johnson perhaps received some legislative goodwill in his reelection year that would not likely have been forthcoming had he run in 1968. Since LBJ was Kennedy's vice president, there is nonetheless sufficient continuity in macroeconomic decision making between administrations to proceed.

Given these considerations, one can say that there is some evidence in the record that LBJ's decision-making focus in 1964 was macroeconomic stimulation. What must be determined, however, is whether LBJ's behavior was of the strategic PBC type or merely represented a faithful continuation of the New Economics agenda of the Kennedy administration. Before his assassination, President Kennedy was a big proponent of a Keynesian tax cut to stimulate demand, thereby increasing productivity and GNP. As early as November, 1963, Kennedy's CEA chairman Walter Heller (who stayed on with LBJ until after the 1964 election) warned President Johnson that without the tax cut the second half of 1964 would likely experience a slowdown. He informed LBJ that with the tax cut 1964 GNP would be $12 billion higher than without the cut and that, when fully in effect, the boost to GNP would be $30 billion or more per year.[11]

As the 1964 fiscal program began to take its final shape in January, Heller further underscored the scope of the stimulus being provided by LBJ's proposals: "Under your tax and budget program, the Federal Government's net fiscal stimulus to the economy in 1964—to jobs, production, income and profits—will be greater than in any other peacetime year in history. . . . The stimulus will be three times as great as in any of the years 1961, 1962, and 1963. The 1964 stimulus to the economy from the Federal budget will be more than $3 billion greater than in any other peacetime year. . . . But by 1965, I take it, added initiatives could be taken as needed to keep us moving toward a $700 billion GNP."[12] Such a large fiscal stimulus during an election year, especially in comparison to prior years, seems like quintessential PBC behavior. Yet Heller's comment about keeping the economy moving toward a $700 billion GNP causes one to place LBJ's election-year decision making in the broader context of the whole New Economics enterprise begun under Kennedy. One must keep in mind that Kennedy moved to aggressively stimulate demand through increased federal expenditures during 1961–63 (a 17 percent increase over the period).[13] The underlying New Economics rationale for this program of federal spending was that an increase in consumer demand would stimulate output and investment, thereby moving the economy closer to full productive capacity and full employment (4 percent unemployment).

As LBJ's *Economic Report* made clear, at the start of 1964 unemployment was still at 5.5 percent, 13 percent of factory capacity was idle, manufacturing rates were at 87 percent of capacity, and inflation was not yet the burning issue it would become in 1966.[14] The report noted that Johnson was merely carrying on the New Economics enterprise by shifting the demand stimulus focus to tax cuts in order to continue closing the gap between actual and potential output and to realize full employment.[15] In this sense, LBJ's choice of stimulus in 1964 is consistent with the partisan Democratic decisions that preceded him. He set out the logic of the tax cut in his 1964 economic report: "Far too long, our economy has labored under the handicap of Federal income tax rates born of war and inflation: Those rates were designed to curb demand in our economy bursting at the seams. But now, when demand and incentives are not strong enough to make full use of our manpower and machines, the tax brake is set far too tight. We need to release that brake quickly to put billions of dollars of new consuming and investing funds into the hands of the private economy."[16] *Cast in this light, Johnson's 1964 fiscal program appears to have been, from a partisan differences perspective, the logical macroeconomic decision for him to make, irrespective of any electoral incentive.* To this end, the administration proposed $8.8 billion in individual income tax cuts and $1.5 billion in corporate income tax rate reductions for 1964.[17]

In fact, this argument is precisely the one that LBJ employed only weeks before the November election to refute suggestions by opponent Barry Goldwater that the administration's economic performance in 1964 was an "artificial prosperity."[18] Goldwater argued that there had been a massive tax cut concentrated in a single year; there had been an extremely rapid expansion of money and credit; and that the granting of contracts for government purchases had accelerated.[19] Goldwater essentially accused LBJ of PBC-style behavior. Campaign briefing materials urged LBJ and his campaign staff to respond that the fiscal and monetary program needed to be viewed within the broader context of the solid forty-four-month expansion that had begun back in 1961 under President Kennedy. Johnson was simply acting *responsibly* to expand that growth streak. In addition, the campaign materials offered the following response to be used as necessary to combat charges of "artificial prosperity" and electorally motivated manipulation of the economy: "In four years of this Democratic administration, our great prosperity is boosting total output more than the preceding 8 Republican years. This is real output, after all price changes have been eliminated. There is nothing artificial about this 2-to-1 ratio of economic performance. . . . The dollars that are raising living standards, adding to savings, filling corporate treasuries, and financing business expansion are real dollars—not artificial ones."[20] Note that no distinction in the briefing material is even made between the Johnson and Kennedy administrations. The only distinction made is between Democratic and Republican macroeconomic performance.

While this Democratic continuity does not in any way lessen the stimulative nature of LBJ's election-year fiscal decision making, it does make it more difficult for one to assume that his policy would have been any different had 1964 not been an election year. In fact, by October, 1964, with unemployment down to 5 percent, the troika was already focused primarily on the need for fiscal stimulus in mid-1965. One memo from Walter Heller to the president noted that "too much slack remains in labor markets. Too much plant and equipment are still idle. At 4% unemployment the economy could produce $20 to $25 billion more a year. . . . Stability in prices to date also points to further room for expansion."[21] Yet another argued that "to sustain prosperity after mid-1965, it now appears that we will almost surely need: a fairly sharp rise in nondefense spending; or further tax cuts; or some combination of the two."[22] Heller concluded with the New Economics mantra that had been voiced many times before during the Kennedy administration, "If we don't provide new stimulus [in 1965], more and more of our potential output will never get produced, more and more plant capacity will become idle, and more and more of our potential jobs won't open up. These growing 'gaps' could soon produce a recession."[23] CEA chairman Heller clearly applied the same macroeconomic logic to the nonelection year of 1965 as he did in 1964. This consistency makes it more difficult for one to assess strategic electoral behavior in the president's election-year decision making.

Thus, it is difficult to isolate and measure the impact of an electoral incentive on LBJ; his macroeconomic decision making for 1964 was largely consistent with expected Democratic behavior. In contrast, remember from the previous discussion of LBJ's 1965 policy making that he rejected additional fiscal stimulus in January, 1965. This sort of fiscal restraint immediately after electoral victory is usually considered the end point of PBC behavior. *LBJ's behavior appears to have the structural attributes of PBC behavior, but not the strategic, manipulative intent usually assigned to the models.* The election-year decision making of Jimmy Carter offers a striking contrast to the partisan Democratic unemployment focus of the Johnson administration.

Jimmy Carter in 1980

Recall from chapter 4 that during the second half of 1978 and throughout 1979, Jimmy Carter shifted away from a partisan Democratic logic in his decision making, instead employing fiscal austerity and monetary restraint to fight double-digit inflation. If Carter then engaged in election-year PBC behavior during 1980, the abrupt change in direction should be readily visible in the president's decision making. Despite Carter's track record of fiscal austerity for the preceding year and a half, some administration members were cognizant of the political value of PBC-style behavior, particularly for situating Carter as the party's nominee. One adviser, Philip Bobbitt, warned in March, 1980,

> It is my opinion that the only political step the president could take that would revive the chances of Senator Kennedy would be a set of drastic budget cuts. As things now stand, the administration is almost invulnerable to charges from [Sen. Edward] Kennedy that we are not sufficiently sensitive to inflation. Everyone realizes that big spending is part of the Kennedy program. . . . But if the president were to frighten voters by threatening their economic well-being through various inflation cures—to say nothing of alienating the many interest groups whose very survival often depends on the federal budget—Kennedy could suddenly become a plausible alternative. No one thinks Kennedy can deliver lower inflation; but a great many people believe he can deliver good times.[24]

Individuals in the administration were aware of the appeal that an election-year expansion of the economy might have to voters and to important Democratic constituencies in particular.

For most of 1980, however, Jimmy Carter pursued a macroeconomic policy focus that was diametrically opposed to PBC behavior. When, several months before the election, he finally proposed some fiscal relief that was in keeping with PBC behavior, it was too little, too late. His proposals to expand the macroeconomy were not even scheduled to be considered by Congress until January, 1981, let alone actually provide stimulus to the macroeconomy in 1980. Thus, if Carter was really looking to engage in PBC behavior before the election, he showed poor timing. More likely, the administration hoped that the promise of easier fiscal and monetary policy sometime in the future would be sufficient to secure electoral success. History proved Carter wrong on this count as well.

In January, 1980, President Carter submitted a fiscal 1981 budget that called for $616 billion in outlays and $600 billion in receipts with a resultant budget deficit of $16 billion.[25] Despite Carter's austere budget, inflation continued to run at a whopping 18 percent for the first several months of 1981. In a remarkable attempt to further assert fiscal discipline and cool the overheated macroeconomy, Carter actually recalled his fiscal 1981 budget and issued a revised one in March, 1980, that showed a balance for fiscal 1981. Unfortunately, no sooner had Carter submitted the revised and balanced fiscal 1981 budget than a sharp recession set in, invalidating all of his budget projections. The president was forced to issue a second revised fiscal 1981 budget.[26] These ongoing fiscal problems and persistent inflation led Stu Eizenstat to inform Carter, "I believe we truly are on the verge of an economic crisis which is as severe for the country as the foreign policy crises you have been dealing with over the last several months. There is a growing national sense that things are out of control–a feeling exacerbated by the continuing escalation in interest rates at every level."[27] Eizenstat was a prime mover in urging Carter to revise the fiscal 1981 budget to show a balance. He noted "the need, the politics and the feasibility of budget cuts so deep that we can claim to have achieved a balance."[28] He advised the president to remove the $16 billion budget deficit in the original fiscal 1981 budget through a combination of 3 percent across-the-board spending cuts (including defense) and tax increases.[29]

Citing the need for "discipline and restraint" and "sacrifice and shared responsibility," President Carter announced the revised fiscal 1981 budget on March 14, 1980, as part of yet another new anti-inflation initiative.[30] In addition to the revised fiscal 1981 budget, the program called for additional monetary restraint by the Federal Reserve, new restraints on federal credit programs, and a redoubling of wage and price activity by the Council on Wage and Price Stability.[31] The revised fiscal 1981 budget called for outlays of $611.5 billion and receipts of $628 billion, resulting in a budget surplus of $16.5 billion. The budget recommended $15 billion in spending reductions ($4 billion in defense) above the January, 1980, version, leading the administration to boast that the budget was balanced through cuts alone. Additional receipts were to be raised through a $10.6 billion oil import fee and $3 billion from withholding of interest and dividends, resulting in the $16.5 billion surplus.[32]

As mentioned above, the estimates in the revised fiscal 1981 budget were quickly proven wrong as the economy slipped rapidly into recession in April, 1980. A steep employment drop in April was followed by almost 8 percent unemployment in May.[33] One would think that conditions (a recession in an election year) were ripe for PBC behavior by Carter. Materials distributed to the Cabinet and senior staff, however, noted that the administration's line on the macroeconomy was still that "quick fixes, in the shape of large, new government spending programs, are not the way to get lasting recovery and lower inflation."[34] In addition, the administration ridiculed the Kemp-Roth tax cut proposal of candidate Reagan as "a blatant act of political gimmickry that is obviously designed for election year dramatics. . . . No concrete suggestions have been offered as to which federal programs would be eliminated or slashed to pay for this massive tax reduction."[35]

It was not until after the mid-session review, in which the Congressional

Budget Act required the administration to provide revised estimates for fiscal years 1980 and 1981, that Carter moved to liberalize fiscal and monetary policy. The review painted a bleak macroeconomic picture for the administration only four months before the election. The fiscal 1980 deficit was revised upward from $35 billion to $61 billion, and the prized fiscal 1981 surplus of $16.5 billion was revised all the way down to a $30 billion deficit. In addition, the unemployment rate was projected to average 8.5 percent and inflation, 12 percent, during the fourth quarter.[36] These were not encouraging statistics for the president to take to the polls in November.

Backed into a macroeconomic corner, Carter finally unveiled a new program on August 28, 1980, designed to stimulate the macroeconomy along traditional Democratic lines. The proposals called for an 8 percent tax credit for individuals and business on Social Security taxes paid; liberalization of the earned income credit; liberalization of income tax deductions for married couples; accelerated depreciation and a liberalized investment tax credit; a $1 billion countercyclical revenue sharing program to assist communities undergoing economic difficulties; an extension and expansion of unemployment benefits; $300 million to expand Comprehensive Employment and Training Act programs; and $1 billion in funds for public works construction.[37]

The big drawback to labeling this expansionary countercyclical program as PBC behavior is that President Carter also announced that the measures would not actually be introduced into Congress until 1981.[38] *Thus, unless one accepts the idea that the promise of rapid expansion is sufficient to cause a PBC response from voters, the bleak economic reality surely mitigated the impact of these promises on voter processing of economic facts. In fact, Carter actually took pains to be sure that his program was seen as a "long-term" agenda for noninflationary economic expansion rather than as election-year manipulation of the economy.* In announcing the program, the president stated that "this is no time for an economic stimulus program nor for inflationary tax reductions. *We must be responsible,* and make careful investments in American productivity."[39] If Carter's intention was to rapidly expand the macroeconomy prior to the 1980 election, neither the timing given for the program's enactment nor his own way of characterizing it would lead one to that conclusion.

Thus, there is no compelling evidence that President Carter acted to strategically manipulate the macroeconomy in PBC fashion during 1980. His macroeconomic decision making that year represented a continuation of his shift away from a partisan Democratic logic as he continued policies of fiscal and monetary austerity designed to fight inflation as a prerequisite for lessening unemployment. This is essentially the same program pursued by Eisenhower in 1955–56, although the latter did not face a macroeconomic crisis of Carter's magnitude during those years.

Carter's belated move toward recovery and expansion in fall 1980 appears to be an ill-timed attempt to assure the electorate that all would eventually be well with the macroeconomy if Carter were given the time necessary to enact his program during a second term. Since this program did not lead to an actual expansion of the economy in 1980, it is difficult to label it as PBC behavior. In any event, it obviously did not have the intended psychological effect, as Ronald Reagan won the White House. As will be shown below, President Reagan faced a very different macroeconomic scenario in 1984 and made decisions that allowed him to ride the crest of macroeconomic recovery to victory.

Reagan in 1984

President Reagan faced a more promising set of macroeconomic circumstances as he entered his reelection year. The inflation rate during 1982–83 was only 3.2 percent, the lowest consumer price index reading since 1967. In addition, by December, 1983, the economic recovery that the country was experiencing dropped the unemployment rate 2.5 percent from its level in the depths of the 1982 recession. The same period also experienced a 6.1 percent rise in real GNP.[40] The Fed's switch to a policy of moderate expansion of the money supply ensured that the recovery would continue into 1984.[41] Given these statistics, it is not all that surprising that President Reagan decided to do nothing to upset the recovery in 1984.

What was most unusual was the absence of major deficit reduction proposals on par with those proposed during the prior three years. The deficit was still hovering just under $200 billion, so one would expect Reagan to continue his succession of deficit reduction proposals. Instead, reflecting upon his disappointment that Congress had failed to enact his $239 billion deficit reduction program from 1983, Reagan decided to wait until after the election to make any further major decisions. He commented in his *Economic Report* for 1984 that "the unwillingness of the Congress to accept the proposals that I offered has made it clear to me that we must wait until after this year's election to enact spending reductions coupled with tax simplification that will eventually eliminate our budget deficit."[42] To this end, the fiscal 1985 budget (January, 1984) reflected two major themes: protection of the military buildup and what was left of the 1981 tax cut and a string of

$180 billion deficits for the following three fiscal years.[43] Reagan did, however, propose future negotiations on a three-year $100 billion "down payment" deficit reduction program.[44]

Thus, one might argue that Reagan acted strategically in an election year to ride the upswing in the business cycle to victory. Former OMB director Stockman made this argument in retrospect. He wrote, "What economic success there was had almost nothing to do with our original supply-side doctrine. Instead, Paul Volcker and the business cycle had brought inflation down and economic activity surging back. But there was nothing new, revolutionary, or sustainable about this favorable turn of events. The cycle of economic boom and bust had been going on for decades and by election day [1984] its oscillations had reached the high end of the charts. That was all."[45] If one accepts Stockman's argument, then it is possible to say that Reagan rode the business cycle to victory by not doing anything to alter its path, thereby engaging in a strategic *inactivity* of sorts. Yet elsewhere, Stockman contradicts his own argument by claiming that "the fundamental reality of 1984 was not the advent of a new day, but a lapse into fiscal undiscipline on a scale never before experienced in peacetime."[46] Stockman further argues that

> I was appalled by the false promises of the 1984 campaign. . . . No program that had a name or line in the budget would be cut; no taxes would be raised. Yet the deficit was pronounced intolerable and it was pledged to be eliminated. This was the essence of the unreality. The president and his retainers promised to eliminate the monster deficit with spending cuts when for all practical purposes they had already embraced or endorsed 95% of all the spending there was to cut. The White House itself had surrendered to the political necessities of the welfare state early on.[47]

One might argue, therefore, that Reagan's acceptance of federal spending and deficits during an election year (rhetoric notwithstanding) fits the notion that Republican presidents are sometimes more liberal in the fourth year of their terms. It is much harder to determine the extent to which Reagan's macroeconomic decision making purposefully manipulated the upswing in a business cycle that was already underway before 1984.

Conclusion

The case studies presented in this chapter suggest that a purely stimulative electoral incentive *does not* operate systematically on presidential decision making in the American political economy in years with incumbent presidents seeking reelection. The strategic, manipulative behavior hypothesized by the PBC model appears to be more situational in nature, sometimes clearly evident in the election-year decision making of presidents and other times virtually nonexistent. *Presidential decision making is clearly mediated by the presence of a president's institutional responsibility and the concomitant need for stabilization policy during an election year.*

When confronted with a vicious inflation cycle in an election year, Democrat Jimmy Carter emphasized fiscal austerity, in the belief that only by reducing inflation would he increase employment. When the macroeconomy was booming (on the upswing of the PBC) and inflation was not a pressing issue, both Democratic and Republican presidents (Johnson and Reagan) sought to provide more of a good thing. Johnson chose a continuation of fiscal stimulus in order to ride the already expanding macroeconomy to electoral victory, whereas Reagan adopted a hands-off approach to the same end. In both cases the dynamics of the business cycle were seen as beneficial if properly handled. Eisenhower, facing no vicious recessionary cycle, simply continued his partisan focus on inflation and budget balancing.

These election-year case studies suggest a systematic way of thinking about the relationship between presidential decision making, institutional responsibility, and election-year politics; the electoral incentive is institutionally, rather than behaviorally, grounded. Presidents are cognizant of the fact that part of their institutional responsibility is to watch over the nation's macroeconomic health and to act to stabilize it when necessary. In seeking reelection, they realize that their relative success or failure at this undertaking will undergo its most intense scrutiny during that year. *Thus, contingent upon the nature of the most pressing macroeconomic problem during a reelection year, presidents work to move the macroeconomy in a particular direction, one that will make them look fiscally responsible (and presidential) in the eyes of the public on election day.* To say that expansion of the macroeconomy in an election year is the only way to achieve this goal is to overlook much of the variation in macroeconomic context that confronts presidents as they seek reelection.

144   The case studies presented here substantially confirm the insights of the presidential decision-making model estimated in chapter 3. Presidents are willing to accept tradeoffs in the pursuit of partisan and electoral incentives, if the imperatives of sound macroeconomic management constrain them to do so, in order to exercise their requisite institutional responsibility for policy outcomes. The archival evidence demonstrates that each of the presidents (although to a lesser extent Reagan) was willing to go forward with these often dramatic shifts in policy objectives, even in the face of substantial opposition by members of the president's own party in Congress.

For each case, however, I conclude that in accepting these decision-making shifts away from partisan objectives, presidents also filter the electoral incentive through the lens of institutional responsibility. Recall from chapter 4 President Carter's need to be viewed in public as a "responsible visionary" by pursuing a lean and austere fiscal policy that clearly provoked the ire of his own partisans in Congress. Democrats feared that Carter's policies would alienate labor and other core Democratic constituencies leading into both the 1978 midterm and 1980 general elections. Similarly, recall from chapter 5 President Eisenhower's need to be seen by the public as "constantly at work and perpetually preoccupied" with the question of unemployment, despite substantial disagreement among Republicans in Congress (conservatives in particular) over his shift in policy-making objectives. In each case, presidents filter the electoral incentive through the constraint of institutional responsibility for sound macroeconomic management; they are particularly concerned about public perceptions that they are engaged in responsible decision-making behavior.

Interestingly, in three of these examples, presidential shifts away from core partisan objectives occurred under conditions of unified government. This circumstance fits perfectly with the findings of the institutional responsibility model in chapter 3. Under conditions of unified government, presidents are viewed as more directly responsible for the condition of the economy. Without the ability to point a finger at divided government grid-lock, presidents are substantially more likely to accept tradeoffs in partisan objectives for the good of an improved electoral position.

Even Ronald Reagan (with a Republican-leaning majority) received a great deal of skepticism from Republicans in Congress, who were unconvinced that the tax cut and spending priorities of the president's supply-side agenda could be met without a further ballooning of the deficit. I conclude that presidents are willing to incur the wrath of their own partisans in Congress, especially under unified government, if the concomitant tradeoff in decision making allows them to be seen by the electorate as pursuing responsible macroeconomic policy objectives. For Reagan, divided government provided him with the political cover to pursue partisan rhetoric, while in practice accepting important tradeoffs in the growth of spending.

This is a very different notion of presidential response to an electoral incentive, however, than the one suggested by the political business cycle literature. Chapter 6 makes clear that, while presidents may be careful not to upset a cycle on the upswing (as was true for Johnson and Reagan), they generally do not act to rapidly stimulate the economy for electoral purposes shortly before standing for reelection. If anything, the behavior of Eisenhower and Carter during their reelection years underscores precisely the reverse logic, one in which both presidents publicly condemned the potential for strategic expansionary decision making during an election year. The archival evidence demonstrates that both presidents were highly conscious of the need to be viewed by the public as pursuing responsible macroeconomic objectives while standing for reelection.

Interestingly, the archival record demonstrates that presidents are quite cognizant of those moments (sometimes expressed in their own words) in which they accept decision-making tradeoffs that require them to temporarily appropriate the macroeconomic policy-making logic of the opposition party. In chapter 4 we see President Carter condemn early in his administration the Republican macroeconomic logic that inflation must be brought under control before unemployment can be reduced. Yet he later adopts this very same logic as the paradigmatic centerpiece of his own anti-inflation initiatives. Similarly, the archival record in chapter 5 paints Eisenhower as a fiscal conservative focused on both deficit and debt reduction, only to show him born again as a countercyclical Keynesian during the 1954 recession.

In general, the archival record suggests that these shifts occur somewhat gradually over time and are indeed temporary, as presidents return to the pursuit of partisan objectives once the constraint of institutional responsibility loosens with improved macroeconomic conditions. This finding is again in keeping with the results of the institutional responsibility model presented in chapter 3. President Carter was never able to return to a Democratic calculus for decision making, however, due to the difficult macroeconomic conditions in which he found himself through the end of his term in office.

It is also evident in the case studies, however, that presidents may accept these decision-making tradeoffs as a means of salvaging some portion of their original partisan and electoral objectives. This would place the presidential decision-making calculus somewhere between the nodes of pure institutional responsibility and pure partisanship. Both Johnson and Eisenhower were in part constrained by their need to continue funding for the Vietnam and Korean Wars, respectively. These imperatives take the president, as commander-in-chief, into a somewhat different realm of institutional responsibility. So both presidents were in part willing to shift away from the pursuit of partisan objectives, in order to direct their fiscal resources toward various security commitments. In a sense, Reagan's commitment to substantially increase defense spending, despite the deficit, fits into this category as well.

Johnson and particularly Carter were also willing to accept these decision-making tradeoffs as a means of continuing the funding of a portion of their domestic policy agendas. By pursuing macroeconomic policy objectives that were not directly in keeping with the wishes of their core partisans in Congress, both presidents were actually able to create a little breathing room for some of their most cherished programs, many of which were established under Johnson's Great Society.

More generally, it is clear that all four presidents were constrained by the difficult tradeoffs implicit in fiscal policy. Budget deficits loomed as a substantial constraint on policy making for all four presidents, but particularly for Presidents Carter and Reagan. In each case, the president's desire to salvage some portion of his policy-making agenda, as represented in the federal budget, forced him to look elsewhere for help with macroeconomic management. To this end, all four presidents relied heavily on Federal Reserve policy at some point in their administrations, as a means of taking a responsible action to stabilize the macroeconomy while also continuing to pursue their partisan objectives at a reduced funding level. In each case, interest rates, and the housing market in particular, bore the brunt of restrictive macroeconomic policy.

So I conclude that presidents may actually shift away from broadly pursuing their partisan objectives as a means of salvaging at least some portion of their policy-making agenda for core constituencies while at the same time appearing to the public as taking responsible action to stabilize the macroeconomy. For Democratic presidents, these shifts in decision-making logic have largely entailed tradeoffs in their pursuit of demand-side spending priorities, while for Republican presidents these same shifts in decision-making logic have largely required tradeoffs with supply-side revenue policies. For presidents of both parties, Federal Reserve policy provides the ability to create additional space for the pursuit of partisan objectives; the Fed in essence allows the president to delay a complete shift away from, or return to, partisan decision making. We see exactly this behavior in Johnson's willingness to rely on tight monetary policy as a means of delaying the tax surcharge. This circumstance slightly loosens the constraint of institutional responsibility on presidential decision making. The case studies clearly underscore this type of presidential behavior, although it is less evident in the aggregate results in chapter 3.

Presidential Decision Making Reconsidered

The integration of presidential studies and political economy presented in this study demonstrates that the two disciplines need not talk past each other. Placing institutional constraints on par with exogenous incentives allows us to generalize more fruitfully about presidential decision making in the American political economy, based on connections to the archival record. The institutional responsibility model tells a systematic story about presidential behavior in the postwar period. The model demonstrates that presidents generally make partisan decisions early in their administrations, even in the face of ominous spikes in the macroeconomy. As presidents' time in office increases, however, they accrue institutional imperatives for macroeconomic policy management (as defined in chapter 2) so that the potential for tension with partisan incentives is greatly increased; the electorate's desire for macroeconomic stability acts as a significant constraint on presidential decision making. Presidents are likely to shift their decision-making logic at these moments away from the pursuit of partisan and electoral objectives; their behavior is increasingly shaped by institutional accountability rather than by partisan accountability. Only divided government shields the president from this political pressure. The model shows that the longer presidents remain in office, the more they internalize the notion of institutional responsibility.

The theory of institutional responsibility developed here also establishes the idea that presidential decision making in the American political economy is more dynamic than posited by current research. Not only are presidential decisions regarding macroeconomic outcomes *not* immutably partisan, but they respond systematically to changes in institutional context in ways that actually work against partisanship. When institutional constraints, tightened by deteriorating macroeconomic conditions, are of sufficient magnitude, presidents are highly likely to abandon partisan objectives. This conception of presidential decision making certainly could be expanded to incorporate other policy-making domains. In each case, assumptions about presidential behavior should be drawn from a close consideration of the historical record.

While other scholars have noted that the president has institutional responsibility for various policy domains, this book is the first to link it explicitly to decision-making paradigms in a particular policy domain. It is also the first to use the idea of institutional responsibility as a theoretical lens through which to systematically reconsider and model the historical record on presidential decision making in the American political economy. As such, my hope is that it will serve as one example of how theoretical insights from presidential studies can be more carefully integrated into rational choice models of presidential behavior.

Interestingly, the vicious cycle seems to have disappeared from view (at least temporarily) since the recession of the early 1990s. Our nation enjoyed record prosperity with high growth and low inflation for the better part of a decade. One may wonder whether presidents will ever again be forced to shift partisan logics in order to confront the cycle. It can be argued that President George H. W. Bush was essentially undone by the vicious cycle in 1990, when he was forced to move away from partisanship, break his "no new taxes" pledge, and sign the budget accord with congressional Democrats. After the decade of the 1980s, however, when presidential decision making was strongly circumscribed by astronomical budget deficits and the Federal Reserve was often viewed as the only policy-making game in town, President Bill Clinton seemed to have all but escaped the vicious cycle.

Yet President Clinton's decision making on the economy suggests several important considerations for theory. Might it be possible that the postwar notion of competing partisan logics for macroeconomic stabilization has permanently changed? Clinton's New Democratic economic policy borrowed liberally from both partisan logics rather than cycled between the two partisan decision-making nodes described in the political economy literature. It may also be the case, however, that since the nation experienced neither high inflation nor high unemployment for almost a decade, Clinton was simply able to avoid the sort of decision-making behavior triggered by the vicious cycle. In essence, he never felt the constraint of institutional responsibility on his decision-making calculus.

While small recessionary storm clouds gathered on the economic horizon in 2001, only time will tell whether the postwar notion of how to exercise institutional responsibility has been transformed into some new paradigm for the new century. In introducing his $1.6 trillion tax cut plan on February 8, 2001, President George W. Bush seemed to underscore the idea that institutional responsibility is still at work in the American presidency: "A president should not wait on events. He must try to shape them. And the warning signs are clear. . . . The President . . . [is] *responsible* to confront the danger of an economic slowdown and to blunt its effect."[1] President Bush's proposal of tax cuts as a short-term source of fiscal stimulus, and his suggestion that the cuts "will help jump-start the economy," present familiar Keynesian stabilization themes.[2] Perhaps the vicious cycle is set to reappear after an eight-year absence.

Political Economy, Presidential Studies, and the Rational Paradigm

The future notwithstanding, this study concludes with a systematic decision-making model based on realistic assumptions about presidential behavior and on the way in which a president's institutional role has shaped that behavior in the postwar world. I do not suggest, however, that rational partisan and political business cycle theories are not important heuristics for understanding presidential behavior. They provide an abstract and parsimonious account of how the political world might possibly function. For many social scientists, this is actually a more central undertaking than understanding how the political world actually functions. In fact, many political economists would argue (and have) that a dependent variable based on a subjective coding of presidential decisions (such as the one employed here) cannot hope to match the precise measurement standards of a typical economic indicator as dependent variable. Nonetheless, if we think about the loss in political insight resulting from the dependent variables traditionally used in political economy, I would argue that some measurement error is more than tolerable, given the potential for substantive new insights into presidential behavior. That this behavior can be shown to fit closely with the historical record should allay some of these methodological concerns.

If we think carefully about the institutional context for presidential decision making, and about the ideas and assumptions underlying that behavior, there is no reason why social scientists cannot continue to look at the importance of exogenous incentives, such as partisan and electoral concerns, on decision making. In the past, presidential scholars have been hesitant to fully embrace the rational paradigm precisely because of the sort of incongruities in the historical record and abstract model noted in this study. They have instead preferred to rely on contextual factors such as style or character as a means of remaining intellectually grounded in the presidential milieu. The task for presidential scholars now is to take the important insights of their archival work and present these insights in a way that is user friendly for modelers. If the econometric work of political economists (and other political scientists as well) can be more firmly based upon accurate assumptions about the behavior of political actors such as the president, then presidential scholars are likely to be more receptive to their insights as well.

To this end, *Vicious Cycle* has been an attempt to open a dialogue between the two sides and to allow the rich empirical findings of presidential studies to work hand-in-hand with the systematic theory building of rational choice models. It is quite possible that both sides of the debate will be dissatisfied with the synthesis of presidential studies, political economy, and rational choice presented in this study. If I am able to set scholars to thinking about these issues, however, then this book has accomplished a large part of its task.

Macroeconomic Initiatives of Presidents Eisenhower through Clinton, 1953–96

Dependent variables are coded as follows in this appendix: 0 = content of initiative represents consistent partisan decision making by the president; 1 = content of initiative represents a shift away from consistent partisan decision making by the president.

Data are taken from the Weekly Compilation of Presidential Documents, January 1, 1953, to March 17, 1997 (Office of the Federal Register, National Archives and Records Service, General Services Administration, Washington, D.C.)

Eisenhower

Number	Coding	Date	Initiative	Description
1	0	Feb. 2, 1953	Message to Congress on the state of the union	—Proposes a fiscal and economic policy designed to: 1. reduce the planned deficits and then balance the budget by reducing federal expenditures to a safe minimum 2. meet the huge costs of national defense (The president especially stresses meeting defense costs, addressing the nation solely on this topic on May 19, 1953.) 3. check inflation 4. work toward the earliest possible reduction of taxes (However, the president refrains from specifically proposing tax cuts at this time.)
2	1	Jan. 21, 1954	Annual budget message to Congress, fiscal year 1955	—Calls for reductions in government spending, pledging greater efficiency and economy in meeting the nation's security requirements and in maintaining the necessary functions of the government —Proposes tax reductions (The president elaborates on the tax plan in his Mar. 15 radio and television addresses.)

Number	Coding	Date	Initiative	Description
3	1	Jan. 25, 1954	Special message to Congress on housing	—Announces the development of conditions under which every American family can obtain good housing as a major objective of national policy —Calls for: 1. neighborhood rehabilitation and the elimination and prevention of slums by making available a program of loans and grants for the renovation of salvable areas and for the elimination of nonsalvable slums, authorizing the Federal Housing Administration to insure private credit used to rehabilitate homes in declining neighborhoods 2. the conservation and improvement of existing housing by providing loans on existing homes comparable to those available for new housing and increasing the maximum loan to repair and modernize single-family homes from $2,500 to $3,000 3. the adjustment of permissible terms of government-insured or guaranteed mortgages 4. the reorganization of the Federal National Mortgage Association
4	1	Mar. 30, 1954	Special message to Congress on foreign economic policy	—Announces a series of policies designed to: 1. reduce trade and payments barriers 2. simplify and make customs administration and procedures more efficient 3. encourage U.S. investment abroad 4. expand economic aid and technical assistance to developing nations
5	0	Jan. 17, 1955	Annual budget message to Congress, fiscal year 1956	—Cites increases in defense spending as the first priority of the budget —Pledges that the administration will advance human welfare and encourage economic growth —Calls for policies to curtail inflation —Announces no further reduction of taxes
6	0	Jan. 16, 1956	Annual budget message to Congress, fiscal year 1957	—Proposes balanced budget for 1957 —Calls for the continuation of increased spending for defense and for measures to prevent inflation
7	0	Jan. 16, 1957	Annual budget message to Congress, fiscal year 1958	—Proposes balanced budget —Indicates no tax reductions —Proposes a series of fiscal policies designed to fulfill the following objectives: 1. maintaining peace 2. providing for powerful armed forces 3. providing for a healthy and growing economy with prosperity widely shared

Number	Coding	Date	Initiative	Description
				4. conserving natural resources
				5. preserving fiscal integrity
				6. increasing international trade and investment
8	1	Jan. 23, 1957	Annual message transmitting the economic report to Congress	—Calls for the modification of present statutory minimum down payment requirements for the purchase of homes with FHA-insured loans —Makes additional funds availbale to the Federal National Mortgage Association —Adjusts the maximum permissible interest rate on VA-guaranteed home loans to a level competitive with the return on comparable investments —(These proposals were transmitted to Congress in February and are summarized in the White House press release of Mar. 29, 1957; they are embodied in the Housing Act of 1957.)
9	1	Jan. 13, 1958	Annual budget message to Congress, fiscal year 1959	—Calls for: 1. an immediate increase of $1.3 billion in spending authority for defense spending and a further increase of $2.5 billion in 1959 over 1958 spending levels 2. curtailments, revisions, or elimination of certain present civil programs and deferments of previously recommended new programs in order to restrain nonmilitary spending in 1959
10	1	Dec. 22, 1958	Statement by the president on the budget for fiscal year 1960	—Calls for a balanced budget —States that the budget will provide higher expenditures for national defense in peacetime than ever before —Maintains that domestic nondefense programs will also continue at record high levels —Maintains that reductions in total spending will be achieved in part by ending programs in agriculture, unemployment insurance, and housing —Requests increased receipts from higher postage rates, gasoline taxes, and some new user changes for government services but does not call for general tax increases
11	0	Jan. 20, 1959	Annual message presenting the economic report to Congress	—Announces that Congress will be requested to amend the Employment Act of 1946 to make reasonable price stability an explicit goal of federal economic policy

Number	Coding	Date	Initiative	Description
12	1	Feb. 12, 1959	Special message to Congress on increasing the resources of the International Bank for Reconstruction and Development and the International Monetary Fund	—Authorizes the U.S. governor of the IMF to request and consent to an increase of 50 percent in the quota of the United States in the IMF and authorizes the U.S. governor of the International Bank to vote for an increase of 110 percent in the capital stock of the bank, and, subject to said increase becoming effective, to subscribe on behalf of the United States to 31,750 additional shares of stock of the bank, amounting to a doubling of the U.S. subscription
13	0	May 13, 1959	Special message to Congress urging timely action regarding the highway trust fund, housing, and wheat	—Notes that in making his legislative recommendations in January (State of the Union address, Jan. 9), the president called attention to three matters that Congress had yet to act upon: 1. a recommendation for a temporary increase in the federal tax on motor fuels designed to avert a serious disruption of the Interstate Highway Program due to an impending deficit in the Highway Trust Fund 2. a recommendation for increased authorization for the insuring of home mortgages by the FHA 3. a recommendation for corrective legislation to halt the accelerated buildup of surplus agricultural commodities —Urges prompt consideration of these proposals
14	1	June 8, 1959	Special message to Congress on the management of the public debt	—Legislation provides for: 1. removal of the present 3.26 percent interest rate ceiling on savings bonds intended to reinvigorate the savings bond program 2. removal of the present 4.25 percent interest rate ceiling on new issues of Treasury bonds 3. an increase in the regular public debt limit from $283 billion to $288 billion and an increase in the temporary limit from $288 billion to $295 billion

Kennedy

Number	Coding	Date	Initiative	Description
15	1	Feb. 6, 1961	Special message to Congress on gold and the balance of payments deficit	—Proposes measures to correct the payments deficit and achieve longer-term equilibrium: 1. action by the Senate to approve the Organization for Economic Cooperation and Development 2. promotion of exports 3. cost and price stabilization 4. export guarantees and financing 5. promotion of foreign travel to the United States 6. expansion of agricultural exports 7. prompt removal of tariffs, restrictions, and discrimination against American exports 8. promotion of foreign investment in the United States 9. prevention of the abuse of foreign "tax havens" by American capital abroad as a means of tax avoidance 10. foreign assistance contributions to less developed countries and to the common defense 11. reduction of customs exemption for returning American travelers 12. centralization of the government's review of foreign dollar outlays
16	0	Mar. 24, 1961	Special message to Congress on budget and fiscal policy	—The administration intends to adhere to the following basic principles: 1. federal revenue and expenditure levels must be adequate to effectively meet the essential needs of the nation 2. the federal budget should, apart from any threat to national security, be in balance 3. federal expenditures and revenue programs should contribute to economic growth and maximum employment within a setting of reasonable price stability 4. as the nation, its needs, and its complexity continue to grow, no federal nondefense expenditures should be expected to increase, but expenditures should be allowed to rise of their own momentum without regard to value received, prospective revenues, economic conditions, the possibilities of closing out old activities when initiating new ones, and the weight of current taxes on the individual citizen and the economy
17	0	Apr. 20, 1961	Special message to Congress on taxation	—Proposes tax incentives for the modernization and expansion of private plant and equipment in the form of a tax credit of: 1. 15 percent of all new plant and equipment ex-

Number	Coding	Date	Initiative	Description
				penditures in excess of current depreciation allowances
				2. 6 percent of such expenditures below this level but in excess of 50 percent of depreciation allowance; with
				3. 10 percent of the first $5,000 of new investment as a minimum credit
				—Proposes reforms in tax treatment of foreign income, specifically in:
				1. the elimination of tax deferral privileges in developed countries and "tax haven" deferral privileges in all countries
				2. taxation of foreign investment companies
				3. taxation of American citizens abroad
				4. estate taxes levied on property located abroad
				5. allowances for foreign tax on dividends
18	0	Jan. 18, 1962	Annual budget message to Congress, fiscal year 1963	—Calls for the deferral of many new projects due to increases in defense spending, education, and technological research —Reveals a modest surplus of $500 million
19	0	Jan. 22, 1962	Economic report of the president	—Cites goals of economic policy as: 1. the achievement of full employment and sustained prosperity without inflation 2. the acceleration of economic growth 3. the extension of equality of opportunity 4. the restoration of balance of payments equilibrium
20	0	July 12, 1962	Statement by the president on new tax depreciation schedules	—Announces new tax depreciation schedules that permit more rapid depreciation than is currently taken on 70 to 80 percent of the machinery and equipment used by American business operators and farmers —Indicates that the "tax cut" these changes make possible amounts to $1.5 billion in the first year
21	0	Jan. 17, 1963	Annual budget message to Congress, fiscal year 1964	—Proposes a major program of tax reductions and reform designed to help spur full employment and a higher growth rate —Severely limits 1964 expenditure proposals in order to prevent excessive revenue loss —Calls for expenditure increases in national defense and space programs
22	0	July 18, 1963	Special message to Congress on balance of payments	—Proposes stepping up short-run efforts to reduce balance of payments deficits while augmenting long-range efforts to improve economic performance over a period of several years to achieve internal expansion

Number	Coding	Date	Initiative	Description
				—Indicates long-run policies will include:
				1. continuing price-cost stability
				2. limiting wage and profit increases by urging business and labor to recognize and use reasonable wage-price guideposts
				—Indicates short-run policies will include:
				1. export expansion
				2. tourism
				3. continuing expenditures abroad
				4. reducing the outflow of short-term capital

Johnson

Number	Coding	Date	Initiative	Description
23	0	Jan. 21, 1964	Annual budget message to Congress, fiscal year 1965	—Calls for a reduction from the preceding year in total administrative budget expenditures —Cuts the deficit in half —Provides for increases in defense spending
24	0	Oct. 26, 1964	Presidential statement no. 1 on economic issues: maintaining prosperity	—Proposes to avoid recessions by a continued partnership of government and private enterprise to: 1. continue restraint in costs and prices 2. continue reduction of taxes 3. enact monetary policy that provides adequate credit for steady expansion without inflation —States that if recession were to threaten, a well-timed tax cut would be an effective measure for redressing the country's economic state
25	0	Oct. 16, 1964	Presidential statement no. 2 on economic issues: monetary policy for stability and growth	—States that in the future, as in the past, the country's monetary system must remain flexible and not be bound by any rigid rules
26	0	Oct. 26, 1964	Presidential statement no. 3 on economic issues: strengthening the balance of payments	—States that the administration must work toward expanding exports, creating conditions that attract more capital into domestic investment, and pursuing responsible fiscal and monetary policies that will retain the world's confidence in the American economy and the American dollar

Number	Coding	Date	Initiative	Description
27	0	Oct. 27, 1964	Presidential statement no. 4 on economic issues: responsible and effective fiscal policy	—Proposes countering "fiscal drag" through the enactment of further tax reduction, increases in expenditures for top-priority federal programs, and increases in the flow of funds to state and local authorities
28	0	Oct. 27, 1964	Presidential statement no. 5 on economic issues: further tax reduction	—States that the administration has already pledged excise tax cuts in 1965 and backs further income tax reductions for both individuals and businesses in the years ahead
29	0	Oct. 28, 1964	Presidential statement no. 6 on economic issues: strengthening state-local government	—States that the administration favors the development of fiscal policies designed to provide revenue sources to state and local governments —Advocates the strengthening of existing programs of federal-state-local cooperation in public assistance, public health, urban renewal, highways, recreation, and education
30	0	Oct. 29, 1964	Presidential statement no. 8 on economic issues: expanding world trade	—States that the administration seeks trade liberalization
31	1	Oct. 29, 1964	Presidential statement no. 9 on economic issues: promoting price-wage controls	—Supports price-wage guideposts as a sound basis for continued price stability
32	0	Oct. 30, 1964	Presidential statement no. 10 on economic issues: achieving full employment	—Identifies a policy of expanding demand while simultaneously devising special measures to deal with youth, the long-term unemployed, and other disadvantaged groups —States that the administration's employment goal is to provide job opportunities for all persons willing and able to work
33	0	Jan. 25, 1965	Annual budget message to Congress, fiscal year 1966	—Announces budget based on five principles: 1. government fiscal policies must promote national strength, economic progress, and individual opportunity 2. the tax system must continue to be made less burdensome, more equitable, and more conducive to continued economic expansion

Number	Coding	Date	Initiative	Description
				3. the Great Society must be a bold society
				4. the Great Society must be a compassionate society
				5. the Great Society must be an efficient society
				—Substantially reduces excise taxes
				—Increases Social Security benefits
				—Supports increases in defense spending
34	0	Mar. 25, 1965	Special message to Congress on area and regional economic development	—Supports a maximum effort to providing conditions under which the private market can provide jobs and increased income —States that federal assistance projects will not be originated at the federal level; rather, they will come from state and local authorities
35	1	Jan. 24, 1966	Annual budget message to Congress, fiscal year 1967	—Maintains that apart from the special costs of operations in Southeast Asia, increases in federal expenditures for high priority Great Society programs and for unavoidable workload growth have been largely offset by reductions in lower priority programs, management improvements, and other measures —Proposes to supplement the expansion of federal revenues by a series of tax measures, including: 1. a plan for improving pay-as-you-go effectiveness of the withholding system on personal income taxes 2. a corresponding plan to accelerate the transition of corporate income tax payments to a full pay-as-you-go basis 3. a temporary reinstatement of the excise taxes on passenger automobiles and telephone services that were reduced at the beginning of the calendar year
36	1	Jan. 24, 1967	Annual budget message to Congress, fiscal year 1968	—Proposes a temporary 6 percent surcharge on both corporate and individual income taxes with exemptions for individuals in the lower income tax brackets —States that the tax should remain in effect for two years —Pledges not to reduce federal programs in defense, education, health, the rebuilding of cities, and the War on Poverty

Number	Coding	Date	Initiative	Description
37	1	Jan. 1, 1968	Statement by the president outlining a program of action to deal with the balance of payments problem	—Proposes the following short-term measures to reduce the balance of payments deficit: 1. establishing a mandatory program to restrain direct investment abroad 2. requesting that the Federal Reserve Board tighten its program of restraining foreign lending by banks and other financial institiutions 3. asking the American people to defer for the next two years all nonessential travel outside the western hemisphere 4. directing the secretary of state to initiate negotiations with NATO allies to minimize the foreign exchange costs of keeping U.S. troops in Europe —Proposes the following long-term measures to reduce the balance of payments deficit: 1. asking Congress to support a five-year, $200 million Commerce Department program to promote the sale of American goods overseas 2. asking Congress to earmark $500 million of the Export-Import Bank authorization to provide better export insurance, expand guarantees for export financing, and broaden the scope of government financing of our exports 3. supporting non-tariff barriers 4. encouraging foreign investment and travel in the United States
38	1	Jan. 29, 1968	Annual budget message to Congress, fiscal year 1969	—Proposes the selective expansion of existing programs or the inauguration of new programs in defense only as necessary to meet urgent requirements —Proposes delays and deferments in existing programs when doing so is possible without sacrificing vital national objectives —Proposes basic changes, reforms, or reductions designed to lower the budgetary costs of federal programs

Nixon

Number	Coding	Date	Initiative	Description
39	0	Mar. 26, 1969	Special message to Congress on fiscal policy	—States that the country must come to grips with the problem of inflation that has been allowed to run into its fourth year; notes that only a policy of a strong budget surplus combined with monetary restraint can be effective in cooling inflation and, ultimately, in reducing interest rates —States that cutting expenditures while maintaining revenues is necessary to produce a budget that will stop inflation

Number	Coding	Date	Initiative	Description
				—Urges the postponement of scheduled reductions in telephone and passenger car excise taxes —Notes the administration's commitment to establishing a more equitable and efficient tax structure
40	0	Apr. 4, 1969	Statement on balance of payments	—Calls for export expansion, fair trade policies, the encouragement of more foreign travel to the United States, and the encouragement of international investment in the United States
41	0	Feb. 2, 1970	Annual budget message to Congress, fiscal year 1971	—Provides for a balanced budget, yielding a surplus of $1.3 billion —Calls for anti-inflationary measures —Notes that for the first time in two decades, the federal government will spend more money on human resource programs than on national defense —Supports continuing the income tax surcharge at 10 percent until Dec. 31, 1969, and at 5 percent until June 30, 1970 —Supports repealing the investment tax credit and the extension of selected excise taxes and user charges
42	0	Mar. 17, 1970	Statement on the combating inflation in the construction industry and on meeting future construction needs	—Reduces the cost of mortage money —Stabilizes the cost of building materials —Moderates severe increases in the cost of labor
43	1	Jan. 29, 1971	Annual budget message to Congress, fiscal year 1972	—Increases spending for defense —Provides a new balance of responsibility and power in America by proposing the sharing of federal revenues with states and communities on a large scale —Favors the development of national strategies designed to improve health care and the distribution of wealth —Adopts the idea of a "full employment budget," in which spending does not exceed the revenues the economy could generate under the existing tax system at a time of full employment —Calls for increased restraint in wage and price decisions by labor and business

Number	Coding	Date	Initiative	Description
44	1	July 21, 1971	Statement about the Emergency Employment Act of 1971	—Creates 150,000 jobs for the unemployed and underemployed
45	1	Aug. 15, 1971	Address to the nation outlining a new economic policy: "The Challenge of Peace"	—Proposes combating unemployment by asking Congress to consider as its first priority the enactment of the Job Development Act of 1971 —Proposes the repeal of the 7 percent excise tax on automobiles —Proposes to speed up the personal income tax exemptions scheduled for Jan. 1, 1972, to Jan. 1, 1973 —Launches an economic stabilization program designed to curtail inflation through a system of price controls
46	0	Jan. 24, 1972	Annual budget message to Congress, fiscal year 1972	—Diminishes economic stimulation as an economic priority and, by so doing, is designed to act as a barrier against the renewal of inflationary pressure —Spends more on federal programs than will be collected in taxes —Urges Congress to enact a rigid ceiling on outlays that will prevent the government from spending more than the $246 billion requested in the budget to guard against inflation
47	0	Jan. 29, 1973	Annual budget message to Congress, fiscal year 1974	—Rejects tax increase —Supports proposals for a leaner federal bureaucracy —Increases reliance on state and local governments
48	0	June 13, 1973	Address to the nation announcing price control measures	—Orders an immediate freeze on prices —Notes that the only prices not affected by the price controls will be those of unprocessed agricultural products at the farm levels and rents —States that the freeze will last for a maximum of sixty days
49	1	Sept. 19, 1973	Special message to Congress proposing legislation and outlining administration actions to deal with federal housing policy	—Reaffirms the administration's commitment to achieving the objectives initially set forth in the Housing Act of 1949: "a decent home and a suitable living environment for every American family" —Proposes policies designed to resolve problems in providing adequate housing credit: 1. permitting home buyers to pay market-level interest rates and still be eligible for federal insurance

Number	Coding	Date	Initiative	Description
				2. authorizing more flexible repayment plans under federally insured mortgages 3. establishing a mortgage interest tax credit 4. furthering the development of private mortgage insurance companies —Indicates that program is specially designed to help low-income families secure suitable living conditions
50	0	Feb. 4, 1974	Annual budget message to Congress, fiscal year 1975	—Calls for: 1. maintaining a proper fiscal balance 2. providing for a strong defense force 3. reestablishing the nation's ability to be self-sufficient in energy production 4. strengthening the role of state and local governments 5. basic reforms in major domestic programs 6. efficient management of the federal government
51	1	Feb. 19, 1974	Special message to Congress proposing economic adjustment assistance legislation	—Objectives: 1. to help states provide smoother and more orderly adjustments to economic changes 2. to limit the number of new economically distressed areas designed to grant state and local officials greater flexibility in the way they spend federal funds within distressed areas

Ford

Number	Coding	Date	Initiative	Description
52	0	Oct. 8, 1974	Address to a joint session of Congress on the economy: "We must whip inflation right now"	—States that proposed inflation remedies not feasible unless joined in one package —Identifies areas for joint action between the executive and legislative branches to fight inflation: 1. producing more food to lower prices 2. fighting energy shortages 3. ending all restrictive and costly practices whether instituted by labor, industry, or government 4. producing more capital by reliberalizing investment tax credit, enacting tax legislation to provide that all dividends on preferred stocks issued for cash be fully deductible by the issuing company, and liberalizing capital gains tax legislation

Number	Coding	Date	Initiative	Description
				5. helping those hurt most by inflation 6. stimulating housing 7. mustering sufficient international cooperation to stabilize world economy 8. providing relief for savings and loan institutions hard hit by inflation 9. increasing tax revenues through one-year 5 percent surcharge on corporate and upper-level individual income taxes
53	1	Jan. 13, 1975	Address to the nation on energy and economic programs	—Proposes to wage a simultaneous three-front campaign against recession, inflation, and energy dependence —Uses the emergency powers of the president to reduce U.S. dependence on foreign oil by raising import fees on each barrel of foreign crude by one to three dollars over three months —Urges enactment of a more comprehensive program of energy conservation taxes on oil and natural gas —States that the country needs an immediate federal income tax cut of $16 billion, with $12 billion of the cut going to individual taxpayers in the form of a cash rebate and the other $4 billion going to business taxpayers to promote plant expansion and to create more jobs
54	1	Feb. 3, 1975	Annual budget message to Congress, fiscal year 1976	—Provides for 1. fiscal policy actions to increase purchasing power and stimulate economic revival, including tax reductions and increased aid to the unemployed 2. a new energy program to hold down energy use, accelerate the development of domestic energy resources, and promote energy research and development 3. an increase in outlays for defense 4. a one-year moratorium on new federal spending programs other than energy programs 5. a temporary 5 percent ceiling on increases in pay for federal employees
55	1	Oct. 6, 1975	Address to the nation on federal tax spending reductions	—Sets forth two proposals tied together in one package: 1. a substantial and permanent reduction in taxes 2. a substantial and permanent reduction in the growth of federal spending —States that "the tax reductions, totaling $28 billion, constitute the biggest tax cut in history with chief benefits concentrated among working people":

Number	Coding	Date	Initiative	Description
				1. raises personal tax exemption from $750 to $1,000 a year
				2. makes the standard deduction for single taxpayers a flat $1,800 and for every married couple, $2,500
				3. lowers basic personal income tax rates
				—Proposes holding federal spending in the coming year to $395 billion
				—Supports a dollar-for-dollar cut in taxes and spending so that for every dollar that is returned to the American taxpayer, projected federal spending is cut by the same amount
56	1	Jan. 21, 1976	Annual budget message to Congress, fiscal year 1977	—Proposes to cut the rate of federal spending growth, year to year, to 5.5 percent
				—Proposes further, permanent income tax reductions
				—Provides for increases in defense spending

Carter

Number	Coding	Date	Initiative	Description
57	0	Jan. 31, 1977	Message to Congress proposing a two-year economic recovery package	—Calls for:
				1. an increase of $4 billion in authorization for local public works
				2. a $4 billion program of tax reform
				3. individual tax rebates and payments to Social Security, Supplemental Security Income, and Railroad Retirement beneficiaries totaling $11.4 billion
				4. an optional credit against income taxes equal to 4 percent of payroll taxes or an additional 2 percent investment tax credit for businesses
				—Committed to balancing the budget for fiscal year 1981
58	1	Apr. 15, 1977	Statement outlining actions to control and reduce inflation	—Announces a series of measures aimed at controlling and reducing inflation:
				1. fiscal discipline to ensure a balanced budget by fiscal year 1981
				2. an agreement with leaders of business and labor to establish a framework for consulting with government to create jobs
				3. incentives for business to increase investment
				4. regular monthly meetings between the chair of the Federal Reserve, the president, and chief economic advisers to achieve better coordination of monetary and fiscal policies

Number	Coding	Date	Initiative	Description
				5. reorganization of the federal government to streamline its operations and improve its efficiency
59	0	Nov. 14, 1977	Statement endorsing the Full Employment and Balanced Growth Act	—Endorses an act that proposes to: 1. establish the commitment of the federal government to achieve full employment 2. establish the commitment of the federal government to achieve price stability 3. establish for 1983 a goal of 4 percent unemployment 4. expand jobs in the private sector
60	0	Jan. 20, 1978	Economic report to Congress	—Outlines four major economic objectives and strategies for achieving them: 1. continuing to move toward a high-employment economy in which the benefits of prosperity are widely shared 2. relying principally on the private sector to stimulate economic expansion and create new jobs 3. containing and reducing inflation rate 4. acting in ways that contribute to the health of the world economy —Strategies for achieving the objectives: 1. adopting effective energy program 2. prudently managing federal expenditures 3. reducing taxes and reforming tax system 4. reducing federal deficit and balancing budget as rapidly as strength of the economy allows 5. improving programs to redress unemployment among the disadvantaged 6. adopting programs to reduce inflation 7. pursuing international economic policies that promote economic recovery throughout the world, encourage the expansion of world trade, and maintain a strong international monetary system
61	0	Jan. 20, 1978	Tax reduction and reform, message to Congress	—An elaboration of the administration's plans to reform the tax system, which were mentioned more generally in the president's economic report to Congress —Recommends that Congress enact a series of proposals to reform the tax system and provide $25 billion in tax reductions for individuals and businesses
62	0	Jan. 20, 1978	Annual budget message to Congress, fiscal year 1979	—An elaboration of the administration's budget priorities, which were outlined more generallly in the president's economic report to Congress: 1. providing an effective national energy plan

Number	Coding	Date	Initiative	Description
				2. providing for essential human needs of U.S. citizens 3. ensuring that the armed forces are sufficiently strong to guarantee U.S. security 4. protecting the environment 5. investing in the nation's technological future 6. increasing the efficiency of the federal government through reorganization and zero-base budgeting
63	1	Apr. 11, 1978	Remarks to members of the American Society of Newspaper Editors announcing anti-inflation policy	—Plan to fight inflation by: 1. lessening government expenditures and resisting pressures to increase government spending 2. working toward a balanced budget 3. urging each sector of the economy to voluntarily hold wage and price increases below the average wage increases for the next two years 4. pledging to freeze the pay of all executive appointees to the federal government
64	1	Jan. 22, 1979	Annual budget message to Congress, fiscal year 1980	—Gives priority to restraining federal spending by: 1. eliminating programs that are unworkable 2. seeking to make remaining federal programs more effective and efficient 3. focusing assistance on the disadvantaged 4. reorganizing and consolidating federal activities to improve efficiency
65	1	Jan. 25, 1979	Economic report to Congress	—Declares reducing inflation to be the administration's top economic priority —Calls for budgetary austerity —Announces intention of not reducing inflation at the expense of the poor, elderly, and unemployed, and proposes the expansion of: 1. health programs 2. spending for education 3. public housing 4. job-related programs 5. welfare reform program
66	1	May 22, 1979	Message to Congress on financial reform legislation	—Recommends that Congress enact a comprehensive financial reform program, calling for: 1. an orderly transition period that will permit all deposit interest rates to rise to market-rate levels 2. the power to offer variable rate mortgages to all federally chartered savings institutions 3. all federally chartered savings institutions being permitted to invest up to 10 percent of their assets on consumer loans

Number	Coding	Date	Initiative	Description
				4. all federally insured institutions being permitted to offer interest-bearing transaction accounts to individuals
67	1	Jan. 21, 1980	State of the Union address	1. cites inflation as the country's most serious economic problem 2. calls for the continuation of public and private restraint in the short run and for a program to attack the structural causes of inflation over the long run
68	1	Mar. 14, 1980	Remarks announcing anti-inflation program	—Calls for: 1. a balanced budget for 1981 2. the implementation of credit controls to moderate the expansion of credit 3. improved compliance with existing voluntary wage and price controls 4. cutting oil imports

Reagan

Number	Coding	Date	Initiative	Description
69	0	Feb. 5, 1981	Address to the nation on the economy	—Notes that the federal budget is out of control and federal spending is a major cause of the nation's high levels of inflation —States that he could raise taxes but that the people's tolerance of an increase in the tax burden has already been exceeded —States that the United States is declining in international competitiveness —States that the United States has reached a turning point and must increase productivity —Proposes budget cuts and a 10 percent across the board reduction in personal income tax rates for the next three years
70	0	Feb. 18, 1981	Address before a joint session of Congress transmitting the proposed package on the program for economic recovery	—Elaborates on the administration's specific economic policies outlined in the president's address to the nation on the economy, presenting four key elements of the package: 1. a budget reform plan to cut the rate of growth in federal spending 2. a series of proposals to reduce personal income tax rates by 10 percent a year over three years and to create jobs by accelerating depreciation for business investment in plants and equipment 3. a program of regulatory relief 4. a commitment to a monetary policy aimed at restoring a stable currency and healthy financial markets

Number	Coding	Date	Initiative	Description
71	0	Sept. 24, 1981	Address to the nation on the program for economic recovery	—Proposes to move on to a second round of budget savings to keep nation on the road to a balanced budget —Calls for additional federal savings of $6 billion in 1982 and a total of $80 billion spread over the next three years by: 1. asking Congress to reduce the 1982 appropriation for most government agencies and programs by 12 percent 2. shrinking the size of the nondefense payroll over the next three years by 6.5 percent 3. dismantling the Cabinet Departments of Energy and Education 4. making reductions of $20 billion in federal loan guarantees 5. forwarding to Congress a new package of entitlement and welfare reform measures saving the federal government $27 billion over the next three years 6. urging Congress to enact proposals to eliminate abuses in the tax code 7. urging Congress to approve proposals for user fees
72	0	Feb. 8, 1982	Annual budget message to Congress, fiscal year 1983	—Proposes a continuation of the 1981 economic plan of spending and tax cuts designed to reduce the federal deficit $239 billion over the next three years —Pledges to continue the restoration of national defense
73	0	Feb. 10, 1982	Message to Congress transmitting the annual economic report of the president	—Elaborates on the economic policies the administration plans to pursue through the 1980s: 1. leave to private initiative all the functions that individuals can perform privately 2. use the level of government closest to the community involved for all the public functions it can handle 3. reserve federal government action for functions that only the national government can undertake —Seeks to shrink the federal deficit in 1982 and beyond through a continuation of the administration's policies of stimulating economic growth, lowering interest rates, and controlling spending
74	0	Oct. 13, 1982	Address to the nation on the economy	—Urges Congress to: 1. control government spending 2. pass a constitutional amendment to balance the budget 3. act on regulatory reform to help make the federal government more economical and efficient

Number	Coding	Date	Initiative	Description
				4. pass the enterprise zone initiatives to revive declining inner city and rural communities by providing new incentives to develop businesses and jobs 5. pass the Clean Air Bill
75	0	Jan. 31, 1983	Annual budget message to Congress, fiscal year 1984	—Commits to continuing the four fundamentals of the economic program by: 1. limiting tax burdens to the minimum levels necessary to finance essential government services 2. reducing the federal regulatory burden in areas where the federal government intrudes unnecessarily 3. supporting a moderate monetary policy to bring inflation under control —Proposes a four-part plan of fiscal policy changes designed to enhance prospects for sustained economic recovery and lower unemployment and to reduce growing federal deficits by: 1. recommending a federal spending freeze 2. asking Congress to adopt measures to control the growth of "uncontrollable" spending programs 3. proposing $55 billion in defense savings over the next five years 4. proposing a stand-by tax limited to no more than 1 percent of the gross national product to start in fiscal year 1986
76	1	Feb. 2, 1983	Message to Congress transmitting the annual economic report of the president	—States that the administration will propose many additional measures over the next several years to strengthen economic incentives, reduce regulations, increase capital formation, and raise the standard of living
77	1	Mar. 11, 1983	Message to Congress transmitting proposed employment legislation	—Proposes assisting the long-term unemployed by: 1. extending federal supplemental compensation 2. inducing more employment through job vouchers 3. creating enterprise zones to increase employment in distressed inner cities and rural towns —Proposes assisting displaced workers by: 1. requesting an appropriation of $240 million for the Job Training Partnership Act 2. using unemployment insurance for reemployment assistance —Proposes assisting youth by establishing a youth employment opportunity wage of $2.50 an hour

Number	Coding	Date	Initiative	Description
78	0	Sept. 9, 1983	Statement on international investment policy	—States that fundamental premise motivating policy is that foreign investment flows that respond to private market forces will lead to more efficient international production, thereby benefiting both home and host countries —Presents policy objectives: 1. strengthening multilateral and bilateral discipline over government actions that affect investment decisions 2. reducing unreasonable and discriminatory barriers to establishment 3. creating an international environment in which direct investment can make a greater contribution to the development process 4. fostering a domestic economic climate in the United States that is conducive to investment
79	0	Feb. 1, 1984	Annual budget message to Congress, fiscal year 1985	—Proposes fiscal policy action to break the momentum of entrenched spending programs and the implementation of a restrained monetary policy —Calls for limited measures to increase receipts in order to make the tax system fairer and for substantial reductions in federal spending
80	0	Feb. 2, 1984	Message to Congress transmitting the economic report of the president	—Plans to continue economic policy of reduced spending and tax cuts
81	0	Mar. 15, 1984	Remarks to reporters announcing a deficit reduction plan	—Proposes a balanced budget package comprising three elements: 1. saving $43 billion over three years from the nondefense portion of the budget 2. closing certain tax loopholes to raise revenues by $48 billion over three years 3. making reductions in defense spending —Estimates that the enactment of all three proposals will save $18 billion in interest payments on the federal debt, bringing the three-year total savings to $150 billion
82	0	Feb. 4, 1985	Annual budget message to Congress, fiscal year 1986	—Proposes one-year freeze in total spending other than debt service —Outlines cost savings in the Medicare program, in federal payroll costs, in agricultural and other subsidies to businesses and upper-income groups, and numerous other programs —Calls for tax reform and simplification

Number	Coding	Date	Initiative	Description
				—Calls for comprehensive management improvements and administrative reforms designed to increase the efficiency of the federal government
83	0	Feb. 5, 1985	Message to Congress transmitting the annual economic report of the president	—States that principle behind economic policy is that the primary economic responsibility of the federal government is not to make choices for people but to provide an environment in which people can make their own choices —Calls for: 1. reducing federal deficit by cutting federal spending 2. further reduction in personal tax rates to encourage stronger economic growth 3. reducing and eliminating federal regulation of economic activity
84	0	Feb. 5, 1986	Annual budget message to Congress, fiscal year 1987	—Continues to explain the administration's economic policies set forth in the economic report of the president —States that major objective is implementing spending cuts and other reforms designed to set the deficit on a downward path to a balanced budget by 1991 —Seeks reforms in the budget process
85	0	Jan. 5, 1987	Annual budget message to Congress, fiscal year 1988	—Presents budget proposals, including: 1. lowering the deficit primarily through the curtailment of domestic spending 2. maintaining adequate funding for high priority programs 3. changing the incentive structure of federal programs to promote efficiency 4. operating federal credit programs through private markets 5. increasing the role of state and local governments 6. better managing federal activities 7. maintaining modest and sustained growth in defense spending 8. reforming the budget process
86	1	Feb. 19, 1987	Message to Congress transmitting proposed Trade, Employment, and Productivity Act of 1987	—Presents series of steps to ensure American competitiveness: 1. investment in human capital 2. doubling the budgetary commitment to the National Science Foundation 3. omnibus intellectual property and copyright reform 4. statutory reforms to reduce the product liabil-

Number	Coding	Date	Initiative	Description
				ity spiral, amend antitrust laws, and deregulate surface transportation and the pricing and transportation of natural gas 5. reform of national banking laws 6. reform of trade laws, including the establishment of reciprocal access to foreign markets
87	0	Feb. 26, 1987	Message to Congress transmitting proposed low-income opportunity legislation	—Encourages state-sponsored and community-based demonstrations in public assistance policy
88	0	July 3, 1987	Remarks announcing America's Economic Bill of Rights	—Underscores need to support: 1. freedom to work 2. freedom to enjoy the fruits of one's labor 3. freedom to own and control one's property 4. freedom to participate in a free market —Presents centerpiece of the Economic Bill of Rights: constitutional amendment requiring the federal government to balance the budget

Bush

Number	Coding	Date	Initiative	Description
89	0	Feb. 9, 1989	Address on administration goals before a joint session of Congress	—Proposes cutting the federal budget deficit by: 1. attention to urgent priorities 2. investment in the future 3. no new taxes —Seeks reforms of problems hampering the savings and loan industry
90	1	July 25, 1989	Proposed legislation to amend the Job Training Partnership Act	—Maintain the successful cornerstones of the current JTPA system —Target youth and adults most at risk of failure in the job market —Achieve a comprehensive, coordinated human resource system —Enhance program quality by individualizing JTPA services —Encourage local JTPA programs to invest in program strategies and practices that are known to be effective in helping at-risk youth —Increase accountability by establishing achievement objectives for participating in the program

Number	Coding	Date	Initiative	Description
91	1	Feb. 1, 1990	Remarks transmitting proposed savings and economic growth legislation	—Indicates that legislation is designed to increase national savings, lower the cost of capital, create jobs, increase international competitiveness, and improve the national standard of living —Presents the three elements of the act: 1. family savings accounts to encourage Americans to save for their future 2. permanent tax-rate reduction for long-term capital gains to lower the cost of capital and provide an incentive for long-term investment 3. a home ownership initiative that allows individuals to withdraw without penalty up to $10,000 from an individual retirement account prior to retirement if the funds are used to purchase a first home
92	0	Feb. 6, 1990	Message to Congress transmitting the 1990 economic report	—Presents administration's primary economic goal: to achieve the highest possible rate of sustainable economic growth —To achieve this goal, the administration proposes: 1. reducing government borrowing by slowing the growth of federal spending 2. supporting a systematic monetary policy program that sustains maximum economic growth while controlling and reducing inflation 3. removing barriers to innovation, investment, work, and saving in the tax, legal, and regulatory system 4. avoiding unnecessary regulations and designing necessary regulatory programs in a way that effectively utilizes market forces 5. continuing to lead the world to freer trade and more open markets
93	0	Feb. 4, 1991	Annual budget message to Congress, fiscal year 1992	—Remains consistent with five-year deficit reduction law enacted the previous fall —Recommends discretionary spending levels that fall within the statutory caps for defense, international, and domestic discretionary programs —Holds the overall rate of growth of federal government spending to approximately 2.6 percent —Proposes tax incentives to increase savings and long-term investment
94	0	May 1, 1991	Letter to congressional leaders on the North American Free Trade Agreement	—Claims that NAFTA would expend national economic growth and enhance the well-being of the American people —Pledges: 1. to work toward close bipartisan cooperation in NAFTA negotiations

Number	Coding	Date	Initiative	Description
				2. to address concerns about dislocated workers
				3. to support environmental protection
				4. to enforce labor standards
95	0	Dec. 26, 1991	Statement on foreign direct investment policy	—Reaffirms unequivocal and long-standing support for a policy of free and open foreign direct investment among all nations —Asserts that U.S. open investment policy is based on the principle of national treatment: foreign investors should not be treated differently from domestic investors
96	1	Jan. 28, 1992	Address before a joint session of Congress on the state of the union	—Proposes long- and short-term economic stimulus package to create jobs and spur investment and growth —Proposes a constitutional amendment for a balanced budget
97	1	Apr. 18, 1992	Address to the nation on Job Training 2000	—Presents a series of legislative initiatives aimed at helping to advance workers' education and sharpen their job skills —Calls for the implementation of the "lifetime education and training account," a package of grants and a line of credit worth $35,000 to every eligible American to use to further their education or acquire new job skills to make the most of their abilities —Calls for the implementation of the "Youth Apprentice Act," which proposes that the employee and employer work together to devise a feasible course of study and a job schedule that will keep the employee on track to graduation
98	1	Sept. 16, 1992	Remarks and an exchange with reporters on family leave legislation	—Calls for a tax credit for employees of all small and medium-sized businesses

Clinton

Number	Coding	Date	Initiative	Description
99	0	Feb. 15, 1993	Address to the nation on the economic program	—Outlines proposals to deflate the federal deficit, including such measures as: 1. cutbacks in federal spending 2. increases in taxes 3. restructuring of the tax system with the wealthy paying a greater proportion of the tax burden

Number	Coding	Date	Initiative	Description
				—Outlines proposals to stimulate the economy, including: 1. the creation of millions of long-term jobs 2. incentives to business 3. investments in education and job training 4. welfare reform
100	0	Mar. 9, 1994	Remarks on proposed re-employment system legislation	—Outlines four points of program: 1. replacing the existing fragmented reemployment programs with one comprehensive program 2. offering more choices for reemployment services 3. putting the private sector in charge of ensuring that reemployment training actually prepares people for real jobs 4. establishing accountability in the program
101	0	Jan. 6, 1995	Remarks on the economy	—Calls for continued reductions in federal spending and in the size of the federal work force —Calls for middle-class bill of rights to ensure more investments in better education and more disposable income for working families by pledging to reward investments in education, the rearing of children, health care, retirement costs, and paying for training
102	0	Feb. 6, 1995	Annual budget message to Congress, fiscal year 1996	—Elaborates on ideas outlined a month earlier in president's remarks on economy —Presents budget proposals: 1. add $81 billion more to deficit reduction 2. eliminate or consolidate 400 federal programs —Presents centerpiece of budget proposal, a "middle-class Bill of Rights" comprising four provisions: 1. a tax deduction for the cost of education and training after high school 2. a $500 tax credit for children under thirteen 3. the ability to put money into an individual retirement account and withdraw the money tax-free for education, health care costs, the care of an elderly parent, or the purchase of a home for the first time 4. a "GI bill" for American workers that eliminates 70 federal training programs, instead giving a voucher worth $2,600 a year in cash to workers who are unemployed or who have low wages and are eligible for federal training assistance

Number	Coding	Date	Initiative	Description
103	0	Mar. 17, 1996	Annual budget message to Congress, fiscal year 1997	—Presents proposals, including: 1. balancing the budget in seven years 2. shrinking and reforming the federal government 3. opening foreign markets 4. reforming welfare 5. protecting Medicare and Medicaid 6. continuing investment in education and the environment 7. cutting taxes for working families and small businesses

APPENDIX B
Overview of Institutions and the Macroeconomy

Year	President	Party	Divided Government	Unemployment (U_t)	Inflation (I_t)
1953	Eisenhower	R	No	2.9	0.8
1954	Eisenhower	R	No	5.5	0.7
1955	Eisenhower	R	Yes	4.4	−0.4
1956	Eisenhower	R	Yes	4.1	1.5
1957	Eisenhower	R	Yes	4.3	3.3
1958	Eisenhower	R	Yes	6.8	2.8
1959	Eisenhower	R	Yes	5.5	0.7
1960	Eisenhower	R	Yes	5.5	1.7
1961	Kennedy	D	No	6.7	1.0
1962	Kennedy	D	No	5.5	1.0
1963	Kennedy	D	No	5.7	1.3
1964	Johnson	D	No	5.2	1.3
1965	Johnson	D	No	4.5	1.6
1966	Johnson	D	No	3.8	2.9
1967	Johnson	D	No	3.8	3.1
1968	Johnson	D	No	3.6	4.2
1969	Nixon	R	Yes	3.5	5.5
1970	Nixon	R	Yes	4.9	5.7
1971	Nixon	R	Yes	5.9	4.4
1972	Nixon	R	Yes	5.6	3.2
1973	Nixon	R	Yes	4.9	6.2
1974	Nixon	R	Yes	5.6	11.0
1975	Ford	R	Yes	8.5	9.1
1976	Ford	R	Yes	7.7	5.8
1977	Carter	D	No	7.1	6.5
1978	Carter	D	No	6.1	7.6
1979	Carter	D	No	5.8	11.3
1980	Carter	D	No	7.1	13.5
1981	Reagan	R	Yes	7.6	10.3
1982	Reagan	R	Yes	9.7	6.2
1983	Reagan	R	Yes	9.6	3.2
1984	Reagan	R	Yes	7.5	4.3
1985	Reagan	R	Yes	7.2	3.6
1986	Reagan	R	Yes	7.0	1.9

Year	President	Party	Divided Government	Unemployment (U_t)	Inflation (I_t)
1987	Reagan	R	Yes	6.2	3.6
1988	Reagan	R	Yes	5.5	4.1
1989	Bush	R	Yes	5.3	4.8
1990	Bush	R	Yes	5.5	5.4
1991	Bush	R	Yes	6.7	4.2
1992	Bush	R	Yes	7.4	2.9
1993	Clinton	D	No	6.8	2.7
1994	Clinton	D	No	6.1	2.7
1995	Clinton	D	Yes	5.6	2.5
1996	Clinton	D	Yes	5.3	3.3

APPENDIX C
Distribution of Variables

Variable	Mean	Standard Deviation	Minimum	Maximum	Valid N
decision	0.38	0.49	0.00	1.00	103
midterm	0.52	0.50	0.00	1.00	103
divided	0.59	0.49	0.00	1.00	103
$(I_t - I_{ma3})$	0.60	2.40	−4.80	7.00	103
$(U_t - U_{ma3})$	1.63	1.18	0.00	4.40	103
presyr	3.50	1.90	1.00	8.00	103
tbill	5.70	2.93	0.95	14.03	103
outecon	39.20	13.68	18.30	78.40	103
prespop	56.16	12.76	26.00	76.00	103
concur	71.07	14.22	43.00	93.10	103
unifed	0.41	0.49	0.00	1.00	103

Notes

PREFACE

1. The one exception here is the Reagan case study. Due to the recent proximity of the Reagan administration (in archival time), and thus the unavailability of some records, recourse is made to the memoirs of key Reagan officials and to Reagan's own words, whenever available in the public record.

PART ONE INTRODUCTION

1. Minutes of Cabinet Meeting of Feb. 5, 1954, p. 2, Box 3, Cabinet Series, Papers of Dwight D. Eisenhower as President, 1953–61, Dwight D. Eisenhower Library, Abilene, Kans. (hereafter cited as DDE Papers).

2. DDE Diary, Apr. 8, 1954, pp. 1–2, Diary Series, January-November, 1954, Box 4, DDE Papers.

3. Letter, Lodge to Eisenhower, July 22, 1954, pp. 1–3, Lodge 1954, Folder 5, Box 24, Administration Series, DDE Papers.

4. Fact Sheet, President's Anti-Inflation Program, Oct. 24, 1978, p. 1, Box 102, Chief of Staff-Butler, Jimmy Carter Library, Atlanta, Ga.

5. Memo, Eizenstat to Carter, Mar. 22, 1978, p. 3, BE4-2, Jan. 20, 1977, to Aug. 16, 1978, Box 16, White House Central Files (hereafter cited as WHCF), Carter Library.

CHAPTER 1

1. See Spiliotes 2000 for an initial consideration of these paradigmatic issues.

2. Moe 1993, 346.

3. George 1980, 5, 6.

4. Warshaw 1997, 218.

5. See Miroff 1997 for one of the more direct responses to Moe's sustained criticism of presidential studies.

6. Moe 1993 and 1997, 1. For a relatively complete view of the chronological development of Moe's critique of presidential studies, see Moe 1985, 1993, 1997; Moe and Wilson 1994.

7. Moe 1997, 2.

8. Ibid. See also Ragsdale and Rusk 1999, 101–103. Hult and Walcott 1998 levels a similar critique at presidential studies, but, in contrast to Moe, draws on organizational theory to propose a "process tracing" approach to understanding presidential decision making. Hult and Walcott argue that a rational choice approach focusing on decisions may "over-concretize the rather ambiguous, uncertain processes of change and underplay the continual redefinition, reshaping, and reformulation which commitments to action constantly undergo" (1998, 3). This approach is only partially responsive to Moe's critique, for it opens the door to more complex, rather than more parsimonious, models of presidential behavior.

9. It should be noted that this book is *not* motivated by a desire to revisit the history of stabilization policy per se. Presidential involvement in this policy domain has already been well documented by Herbert Stein, John Sloan, James Anderson, and many other scholars of economic policy making. My goal is instead to use this political history as a foundation upon which to reconcile a rational choice ap-

proach to the presidency and political economy with the vexing problems in the critique of presidential studies. Thus, I traverse familiar historical terrain for a somewhat different analytic purpose. See Stein 1996, 1988; Sloan 1999; and Anderson and Hazleton 1986 among others for the historical development of macroeconomic policy making in the presidency.

10. Moe 1993, 344.

11. Hult 1993, 140.

12. Walcott and Hult 1995, 4.

13. Weatherford and McDonnell 1997, 8.

14. Hibbs 1992 provides a useful fifteen-year review of rational partisan theory.

15. For research on the partisan cycle that takes the basic theory in a variety of additional directions, see McGregor 1996, Roemer 1995, and Schmidt 1996. Rob Ray McGregor (1996) looks for partisan cycles in the voting records of Federal Reserve Board governors and finds some confirming evidence. John Roemer (1995) tests the partisan cycle implications of changes in proportional tax rates on income, the revenues from which are used to finance a public good. Manfred Schmidt (1996) takes a comparative approach to determine the impact of party composition and state structure on the potential for partisan influence on public policy.

16. Alt and Chrystal 1983, 125.

17. Moe and Wilson 1994, 11.

18. Moe and Wilson 1994, 12.

CHAPTER 2

1. Harding's 1921 statement is quoted Bailey 1950, 6.

2. U.S. Congress, *Employment Act of 1946,* Public Law 304, 79th Cong., 2nd sess., Feb. 20, 1946, sec. 2.

3. Pemberton 1979, 20.

4. Skowronek 1982, 4, 9.

5. Ibid., 9; Orloff 1988, 80.

6. Weir 1992, xiii.

7. Ibid., 19.

8. For more on the interbranch struggle ar-

gument, and the resultant "managerial" presidency, see Marini 1992; Hart 1987; Pemberton 1979; Hess 1988; and Karl 1963.

9. Bailey 1950, 5.

10. Brownlow et al. 1941, 107; more generally, see Mosher 1984.

11. Marini 1992, 4.

12. Savage 1988, 144.

13. Ibid. Scholars often place this initial transition in institutional responsibility from legislative to executive in 1905, when Theodore Roosevelt appointed a Commission on Executive Departments under Charles Hallam Keep. The Keep Commission studied ways of making the executive branch function more efficiently as an organization of personnel processing information. The commission was the first on executive reorganization to report to the president, rather than to the legislature, and is believed to have paved the way for congressional appropriation of funds for the Taft Commission. See Karl 1963, 187; and Marini 1992, 60.

14. Brownlow et al. 1941, 108.

15. Mosher 1984, 20–21.

16. Smith 1993, 20; Karl 1963, 182; Savage 1988, 145.

17. Mosher 1984, 20; Savage 1988, 144.

18. Mosher 1984, 26.

19. See President's Commission on Economy and Efficiency 1912.

20. Marini 1992, 62.

21. Mosher 1984, 25.

22. Smith 1993, 2.

23. Mosher 1984, 25.

24. Kimmel 1959, 4–5.

25. Marini 1992, 65.

26. Veto Message, House Document No. 804, 66th Cong., 2nd sess., 1920, cited in Marini 1992, 64–65.

27. Buck and Mansfield 1937, 21; Marini 1992, 5.

28. Stein 1996, 16; Bach 1971, 155; Kimmel 1959, 153.

29. Buck and Mansfield 1937, 4.

30. Kimmel 1959, 190.

31. Savage 1988, 169.

32. Stein 1988, 63; Savage 1988, 174; Kimmel 1959, 182, 215–17.

33. Nourse 1953, 55; Polenberg 1966, 9.

34. Karl 1963, 143–44.

35. Stein 1988, 60.

36. Nourse 1953, 57.

37. Bach 1971, 74; Stein 1988, 91.

38. Bailey 1950, 17–18; Stein 1988, 167; See also Collins 1981 and Lekachman 1975.

39. Weir 1992, 9; Stein 1996, 167; Bailey 1950, 17.

40. Smith 1993, 104; Weir 1992, 40–41.

41. President's Committee on Administrative Management 1937; Polenberg 1966, 26–27.

42. President's Committee on Administrative Management 1937, 139–67.

43. Mosher 1984, 65; Karl 1963, 234.

44. Polenberg 1966, 132.

45. Stein 1988, 129–30.

46. Smith 1993, 103; Bach 1971, 17.

47. Bach 1971, 17.

48. Bailey 1950, 26–27.

49. Nourse 1953, 65 n. 23.

50. Marini 1992, 92; Stein 1988, 177.

51. Bailey 1950, 41.

52. Flash, 1965, 9.

53. Bailey 1950, 13–14.

54. Nourse 1953, 72. See also Bailey 1950, for a comprehensive legislative history of the Full Employment Bill's transformation into the Employment Act of 1946.

55. Nourse 1953, 72.

56. U.S. Congress, *Employment Act of 1946,* sec. 2; Flash 1965, 10–12.

57. That both partisan interpretations were consistent with the broader paradigm of macroeconomic stabilization is confirmed in Coleman 1996.

58. U.S. Congress, *Employment Act of 1946,* sec. 4(a).

59. Ibid., sec. 4(c), para. 5.

CHAPTER 3

1. See Alt and Woolley 1982 for a discussion of reaction function models.

2. Weatherford 1988, 110.

3. See Aldrich and Nelson 1984 for a general discussion of discrete choice models and of probit and logit in particular. In practice, there is very little difference in the results of discrete choice models estimated with probit and logit. The logit model simply employs a logistic distribution rather than a normal distribution.

4. Macroeconomic decision data are taken from *Public Papers of the Presidents of the United States,* 1953–96. Shull (1983) and Kessel (1974, 1975) establish a precedent for using this source as a systematic compilation of presidential decisions on a variety of public policy issues. Initial intercoder reliability for the aggregate data was 93 percent, with two independent coders agreeing on the characterization of 96 of 103 presidential decisions. Appropriate characterization of the seven decisions in disagreement was resolved through addition archival research to clarify presidential decision. See appendix A for complete information on each of the initiatives.

5. All statistical analysis presented in this chapter was conducted using Limdep 7.0.

6. Since calculation of marginal effects here involves taking the partial derivative of the variable of interest at its mean with respect to the other variables at their means, marginal effects calculated for dichotomous independent variables that only take the values zero and one (0,1) are not as precise as those calculated for continuous variables. Still, the marginal effect reported for divided government is a useful rough estimate of the impact of the variable on the probability of presidential deviation. The predicted probabilities presented later in this book, however, provide a more accurate measure of the divided government variable's impact on probability, since in that calculation an actual value of the divided government variable is included in the equation. For more on this issue and on probability calculations in discrete choice models, see Liao 1994.

7. One could also set both macroeconomic

variables at their third quartile values or higher in order to simulate the impact of stagflation on the probability of deviation from partisan decision making.

CHAPTER 4

1.   Interview with Gardner Ackley in Hargrove and Morley 1984, 217.

2.   Memo, C. Douglas Dillon (Treasury), Kermit Gordon (Budget), and Gardner Ackley (CEA) to LBJ, Dec. 7, 1964, p. 1, BE5-4, Nov. 1, 1964, to Dec. 15, 1964, Box 32, WHCF, Lyndon Baines Johnson Library, Austin, Tex. (hereafter LBJ Library).

3.   Ibid., 2.

4.   Ibid., 4.

5.   Memo, Ackley to LBJ, Dec. 13, 1964, pp. 2–3, BE5-4, Nov. 1, 1964, to Dec. 15, 1964, Box 32, WHCF, LBJ Library.

6.   Memo, Ackley to LBJ, Jan. 26, 1964, p. 2, BE5-4, Dec. 16, 1964, to Feb. 28, 1965, Box 32, WHCF, LBJ Library.

7.   Hargrove and Morley 1984, "Ackley," 246–47.

8.   Ibid., 247.

9.   Ibid., 218.

10.   Memo, Ackley to LBJ, June 2, 1965, p. 1, FG11-3, May 27 to June 22, 1965, Box 57, WHCF, LBJ Library.

11.   Ibid., 1.

12.   Ibid., 2.

13.   Memo, Ackley to LBJ, July 30, 1965, p. 4, FG11-3, June 23 to Aug. 7, 1965, Box 57, WHCF, LBJ Library.

14.   Ibid., 1.

15.   Ibid., 2–3.

16.   Ibid., 1.

17.   Memo, Ackley to LBJ, Oct. 5, 1965, p. 2; Memo, Ackley to LBJ, Nov. 13, 1965, pp. 2–3, both in FI Finance, Aug. 26, 1965, to Mar. 8, 1966, Box 1, WHCF, LBJ Library.

18.   Memo, Ackley to LBJ, Nov. 13, 1965, 3.

19.   Hargrove and Morley 1984, "Ackley," 218.

20.   Memo, Califano to LBJ, Dec. 17, 1965, p. 1, FI Taxation, June 29, 1965, to Mar. 16, 1966, Box 55, WHCF, LBJ Library.

21.   Memo, Ackley to LBJ, Dec. 17, 1965, pp. 1–2, FI Taxation, June 29, 1965, to Mar. 16, 1966, Box 55, WHCF, LBJ Library.

22.   Ibid., 1.

23.   Ibid., 2.

24.   Lyndon Baines Johnson, *The Vantage Point* (New York: Holt, Reinhart and Winston, 1971), cited in Hargrove and Morley 1984, "Ackley," 248.

25.   Ibid., 248; see also Memo, Ackley to LBJ, Feb. 22, 1966, FI Finance, Aug. 26, 1965, to Mar. 8, 1966, Box 1, WHCF, LBJ Library, for former Johnson and Kennedy CEA chairman Walter Heller's concurrence with Ackley's recommendation of a tax increase.

26.   Memo, Franklin B. Dryden (acting director, OEP) to LBJ, Jan. 21, 1966, pp. 1–3, BE5-2, Cost of Living (1966), Box 3, Confidential File, WHCF, LBJ Library.

27.   Ibid., 2.

28.   Memo, Ackley to LBJ, Mar. 4, 1966, FG11-3, Council of Economic Advisers, Feb. 8 to Mar. 26, 1966, pp. 1–2, Box 58; Memo, Ackley, Okun, and Duesenberry to LBJ, Mar. 12, 1966, pp. 1–5, FI11 Taxation, Box 44, Confidential File, both in WHCF, LBJ Library.

29.   Memo, Ackley, Okun, and Duesenberry to LBJ, Mar. 12, 1966, 2.

30.   Ibid., 1–3.

31.   Ibid., 3.

32.   Ibid., 5.

33.   Memo, Califano to LBJ, Mar. 5, 1966, FI Taxation, June 29, 1965, to Mar. 16, 1966, p. 1, Box 55, WHCF, LBJ Library.

34.   Memo, Wirtz to LBJ, Mar. 17, 1966, p. 4, FI Taxation, Box 44, Confidential File, WHCF, LBJ Library.

35.   Ibid., 3.

36.   Ibid.

37.   Memo, Okun to LBJ, Mar. 16, 1966, p. 1, FG11-3, Council of Economic Advisers, Feb. 8 to Mar. 26, 1966, Box 58, WHCF, LBJ Library.

38.   Ibid.

39. Memo, Ackley to LBJ, May 10, 1966, p. 2, FI11, Mar. 17 to Aug. 20, 1966, Box 56, WHCF, LBJ Library.

40. Ibid.

41. Ibid.

42. Ibid., 3.

43. Memo, Schultze to LBJ, May 11, 1966, pp. 1–3, FI11, Mar. 17 to Aug. 20, 1966, Box 56, WHCF, LBJ Library.

44. Memo, Heller to LBJ, May 13, 1966, p. 2, FI11–4, Income Tax (1964–66), Box 44, Confidential File, WHCF, LBJ Library.

45. Letter, Heller to *New York Times*, May 11, 1966, p. 1, FI11–4, Income Tax (1964–66), Box 44, Confidential File, WHCF, LBJ Library; for additional administration background on the case for a tax increase see Memo, Martin (Fed chairman) to Fowler, June 6, 1966, FI11–4, Income Tax (1964–66), Box 44, Confidential File; and, Memo, Fowler to LBJ, May 11, 1966, FI11, Mar. 17 to Aug. 20, 1966, Box 56, both in WHCF, LBJ Library.

46. Hargrove and Morley 1984, "Ackley," 251 (emphasis added).

47. Ibid., 251–53.

48. Ibid., 254.

49. Letter, Ullman to LBJ, June 27, 1966, pp. 1–2, BE5–3, Inflation-Money Scarcity, Nov. 23, 1963, to July 7, 1966, Box 31, WHCF, LBJ Library.

50. Ibid., 2.

51. Mills quoted in Memo, Ackley to LBJ, Aug. 17, 1966, p. 1, FI, June 17 to Oct. 10, 1966, Box 1, WHCF, LBJ Library.

52. Ibid.

53. Javits quoted in Memo, Ackley to LBJ, July 18, 1966, p. 1, FG11–3, June 22 to Aug. 2, 1966, Box 58, WHCF, LBJ Library.

54. Memo, Califano to LBJ, Sept. 1, 1966, pp. 1–3, FI11 Taxation, Box 44, Confidential File, WHCF, LBJ Library. For a look at the concerns of particular advisers on this package prior to Califano's consensus memo, see Memo, Ackley to LBJ, Aug. 9, 1966, FI11, Mar. 17 to Aug. 20, 1966, Box 56; Memo, Ackley to LBJ, Aug. 22, 1966, FI11, Aug. 21, 1966, to Jan. 2, 1967, Box 56; Memo, Kermit

Gordon to LBJ, Aug. 22, 1966, FI11, Aug. 21, 1966, to Jan. 2, 1967, Box 56; Memo, Heller to Ackley, Aug. 22, 1966, FI11, Aug. 21, 1966, to Jan. 2, 1967, Box 56; Memo, Schultze to Ackley, Aug. 19, 1966, FI11, Aug. 21, 1966, to Jan. 2, 1967, Box 56; Memo, Fowler to LBJ, Aug. 27, 1966, FI11, Aug. 21, 1966, to Jan. 2, 1967, Box 56; Memo, Wirtz to LBJ, Sept. 1, 1966, FI Taxation, Box 44, Confidential File, all in WHCF, LBJ Library. These memos clearly express the general policy choice consensus of the Califano memo. The debate was primarily over Fowler's opposition to suspension of the investment tax credit, a proposal that, to enact, would require the strong support of the Treasury secretary. There was also substantial discussion of the size of a potential tax surcharge on individual and corporate incomes, a proposal that was largely moot, as LBJ was still not prepared to go in that direction and thus it was not even recommended to the president in the Califano memo.

55. Hargrove and Morley 1984, "Ackley," 219, 253; Letter, Paul Popple (assistant to the president for correspondence) to Nora Burke (constituent), Sept. 28, 1966, p. 1, BE5–3, July 27 to Nov. 23, 1966, Box 31, WHCF, LBJ Library; "The CEA Role in Fiscal Policy," in Administrative History of the Council of Economic Advisers, 1:16–17, Box 1, Administrative Histories/Council of Economic Advisers, LBJ Library; Memo, Joseph Barr (undersecretary of Treasury) to LBJ, Nov. 30, 1966, pp. 2–3, FI11, Aug. 21, 1966, to Jan. 2, 1967, Box 56, WHCF, LBJ Library.

56. Barr memo to LBJ, Nov. 30, 1966, pp. 48–49; Memo, Ackley to LBJ, Nov. 23, 1966, p. 1, FG11–3, Nov. 16 to Dec. 15, 1966, Box 59, both in WHCF, LBJ Library.

57. Telex, Califano to LBJ, Dec. 23, 1966, pp. 1–2, FI11–4, Income Tax (1964–66), Box 44, Confidential File, WHCF, LBJ Library. This telex provided an up-to-the-minute account to LBJ, at his ranch, of the tax position of each adviser and of the Fed's board of governors. The lack of enthusiasm among those favoring an increase, as depicted by Califano, stands in bold contrast to the strong pro–tax increase positions held by LBJ's advisers in the spring and summer of 1966. See also Memo, Fowler, Schultze, and Ackley (the

troika) to LBJ, Dec. 30, 1966, FI11–4, Income Tax (1964–66), Box 44, Confidential File, WHCF, LBJ Library.

58. Memo, Heller to LBJ, Nov. 23, 1966, pp. 2–3; see also Memo, Heller to LBJ, Dec. 14, 1966, both in FI11, Aug. 21, 1966, to Jan. 2, 1967, Box 56, WHCF, LBJ Library.

59. Memo, Francis Bator to LBJ, Dec. 21, 1966, pp. 2–3, FI11–4, Income Tax (1964–66), Box 44, Confidential File, WHCF, LBJ Library.

60. Memo, Robert Kintner to LBJ, Dec. 10, 1966, p. 2, Aug. 21, 1966, to Jan. 2, 1967, Box 56, WHCF, LBJ Library.

61. Telex, Califano to LBJ, Dec. 23, 1966, 1, 3–4.

62. "The CEA Role in Fiscal Policy," 20. See also two joint decision memos from LBJ's advisers recommending this fiscal program: Memo, Califano to LBJ, Jan. 4, 1967, FI11, Jan. 3 to Mar. 22, 1967, Box 56; and, Memo, McNamara, Fowler, Wirtz, Connor, Schultze, Ackley, Clifford, and Califano to LBJ, Jan. 9, 1967, FG11–3, Jan. 6 to Feb. 4, 1967, Box 59, both in WHCF, LBJ Library.

63. Newswire, Associated Press, Jan. 11, 1967, p. 1, FI11, Jan. 3 to Mar. 22, 1967, Box 56, and BE5–3, Oct. 9, 1966, to May 31, 1968, Box 31, both in WHCF, LBJ Library; Memo, Fred Panzer (staff assistant) to Kintner, Jan. 26, 1967, p. 1, FI11–4 Income Tax (1967–68), Box 44, Confidential File, WHCF, LBJ Library.

64. "The CEA Role in Fiscal Policy," 21.

65. Memo, Ackley to LBJ, Feb. 24, 1967, p. 1, FI11, Jan. 3 to Mar. 22, 1967, Box 56, WHCF, LBJ Library.

66. "The CEA Role in Fiscal Policy," 21; Hargrove and Morley 1984, "Ackley," 219, 255–57. For the decision to postpone the tax proposal beyond the July 1 date, see Memo, Califano to LBJ, June 12, 1967, FG11–3, May 16 to June 15, 1967, and Memo, Califano to LBJ, June 17, 1967, FG11–3, June 16 to July 3, 1967, both in Box 60, WHCF, LBJ Library. The June 12 memo contains Califano's summary of the various timing concerns of LBJ's advisers but notes their general agreement on the need for a tax surcharge. The June 17 memo notes that

all advisers agreed that a proposal should not go forward until after the congressional recess and until after McNamara returned from Vietnam with a better feel for the costs of the war. LBJ marked his approval of the strategy at the bottom of the page.

67. Memo, Ackley to LBJ, May 22, 1967, p. 2, FG11–3, May 16 to June 15, 1967, Box 60, WHCF, LBJ Library.

68. Memo, Ackley to LBJ, June 3, 1967, p. 3, FI, Jan. 25 to July 15, 1967, Box 2, WHCF, LBJ Library.

69. Ibid.

70. Memo, Heller to LBJ, July 11, 1967, p. 1, BE5–4, June 1 to Sept. 10, 1967, Box 34, WHCF, LBJ Library.

71. Memo, Fowler, Wirtz, Trowbridge, McNamara, Schultze, Ackley, and Califano to LBJ, July 22, 1967, p. 1, FI11, Mar. 23, 1967, to Jan. 19, 1968, Box 56, WHCF, LBJ Library; "The CEA Role in Fiscal Policy," 26.

72. "The CEA Role in Fiscal Policy," 26.

73. Ibid., 27.

74. Memo, Ackley to LBJ, Oct. 6, 1967, p. 1, FG11–3, Sept. 14 to Nov. 15, 1967, Box 60, WHCF, LBJ Library.

75. Memo, Panzer to LBJ, Oct. 13, 1967, p. 1, BE5–3, Oct. 9, 1967, to May 31, 1968, Box 31, WHCF, LBJ Library.

76. Ibid.

77. Memo, Ackley to LBJ, Oct. 13, 1967, p. 1, FG11–3, Sept. 14 to Nov. 15, 1967, Box 60, WHCF, LBJ Library.

78. Memo, Califano to LBJ, Nov. 20, 1967, p. 11, Box 11, Cabinet Papers, LBJ Library. The memo provided LBJ with talking points for a November 20 Cabinet meeting on the administration's November effort to get the tax package through Congress.

79. "The CEA Role in Fiscal Policy," 30, 34.

80. Hargrove and Morley 1984, "Ackley," 220.

81. Interview with Charles Schultze, in Hargrove and Morley 1984, 459–60.

82. Ibid., 459; Memo, Schultze to the Economic Policy Group, Jan. 22, 1977, p. 8, BE4 (Executive), Jan. 20–31, 1977, Box 13, WHCF,

Carter Library. The Economic Policy Group was a working committee established in the Carter White House to consider all economic issues of importance to the administration. It had broader range on economic issues than the traditional troika of earlier administrations but often served the same function of researching and making policy recommendations for the president on macroeconomic policy. In addition to the EPG, an informal troika met on occasion in the Carter White House; it usually included Vice President Walter Mondale and Stu Eizenstat, chief of the domestic policy staff, in addition to the other three traditional members. Schultze has noted that the membership of the EPG constantly shifted in the Carter White House, depending upon the issue under consideration. It did, however, have a fairly stable executive committee under the chairmanship of Michael Blumenthal (see Hargrove and Morley 1984, "Schultze," 468–69).

83. Interview with James McIntyre (including Hubert Harris and Van Ooms), Oct. 28–29, 1981, Miller Center Interviews, 5:16, Carter Presidency Project, Carter Library.

84. Ibid., 5:4.

85. Hargrove and Morley 1984, "Schultze," 476.

86. Ibid., 478.

87. Transcript, "Statement by the President on Inflation," Apr. 15, 1977, p. 1, Anti-Inflation [O/A 6338][5], Box 144, Domestic Policy Staff–Eizenstat, Carter Library.

88. Memo, Eizenstat and Ginsburg to Carter, Apr. 7, 1977, pp. 1–2, Anti-Inflation [O/A 6338][6], Box 144, Domestic Policy Staff–Eizenstat, Carter Library.

89. Ibid., 1.

90. Ibid., 2. For more on the development of the anti-inflation initiative see Memo, Schultze to Eizenstat, Apr. 4, 1977, Anti-Inflation [O/A 6338][8], Box 144, Domestic Policy Staff–Eizenstat, Carter Library.

91. Memo, Executive Committee, Economic Policy Group, to Carter, Apr. 8, 1977, p. 1, Anti-Inflation [O/A 6338][8], Box 144, Domestic Policy Staff–Eizenstat, Carter Library.

92. Testimony, W. Michael Blumenthal, Sec-

retary of the Treasury, before the Subcommittee on Economic Stabilization of the House Committee on Banking, Finance, and Urban Affairs, Apr. 20, 1977, p. 2, Anti-Inflation [O/A 6338][6], Box 144, Domestic Policy Staff–Eizenstat, Carter Library.

93. Ibid., 1–2.

94. Transcript, "Statement by the President on Inflation," 7.

95. Transcript, Press Conference No. 5 of the President of the United States, Apr. 15, 1977, p. 4, Anti-Inflation [O/A 6338][6], Box 144, Domestic Policy Staff–Eizenstat, Carter Library.

96. Ibid., 5.

97. Transcript, "Statement by the President on Inflation," 3.

98. The *Economic Stimulus Appropriation Act* (H.R. 4876) was signed into law by President Carter on May 14, 1977. The act appropriated $20.1 billion for revitalizing the economy through public works and public employment. See Report, Congressional Action on the Economy, May 17, 1977, BE4 (Executive), May 1–31, 1977, Box 13, WHCF, Carter Library.

99. Hargrove and Morley 1984, "Schultze," 460, 483.

100. Ibid., 483.

101. Memo, Bosworth to Blumenthal, Eizenstat, et al., Mar. 2, 1978, pp. 1–5, Anti-Inflation Program thru July 1978, Feb. 8 to May 31, 1978, Box 89, Chief of Staff–Butler, Carter Library.

102. Ibid., 1, 5.

103. Memo, Schultze to Carter, Mar. 14, 1978, pp. 4–5, Anti- Inflation Program, Mar. 14 to June 6, 1978, Box 89, Chief of Staff–Butler, Carter Library.

104. Memo, Blumenthal and Schultze to Carter, Mar. 15, 1978, pp. 3–6, Anti-Inflation, March, 1978 [O/A 7432], Box 144, Domestic Policy Staff–Eizenstat, Carter Library.

105. Memo, Francis to Moore, Mar. 20, 1978, pp. 1, 3, Anti-Inflation March, 1978 [O/A 7432], Box 144, Domestic Policy Staff–Eizenstat, Carter Library.

106. Ibid., 1–2.

107. Memo, Eizenstat to Carter, Mar. 22, 1978, p. 3, BE4-2, Jan. 20, 1977, to Aug. 16, 1978, Box 16, WHCF, Carter Library, 3.

108. Transcript, Address of the President to the American Society of Newspaper Editors, Apr. 11, 1978, p. 1, Anti-Inflation April, 1978 [O/A 7432][1], Domestic Policy Staff–Eizenstat, Carter Library.

109. Ibid., 3–4

110. Ibid., 5–6.

111. Statement on Inflation, AFL-CIO Executive Council, May 10, 1978, p. 2, Anti-Inflation 1978–79 [CF, O/A 748][2], Box 50, Staff Offices Press–Powell, Carter Library.

112. Ibid.

113. Memo, Cutter (assistant director, OMB) to Jordan (assistant to the president), May 30, 1978, p. 1, Anti-Inflation Program thru July, 1978, Feb. 8 to May 31, 1978, Box 89, Chief of Staff–Butler, Carter Library.

114. Ibid., 2.

115. Ibid.

116. Memo, Stern (Domestic Policy Staff) to Eizenstat, May 20, 1978, p. 2, Anti-Inflation [O/A 6338][5], Box 144, Domestic Policy Staff–Eizenstat, Carter Library.

117. Ibid.

118. Memo, Blumenthal to Carter, Sept. 13, 1978, pp. 1, 10, Inflation, Aug. 23 to Sept. 30, 1978, Box 102, Chief of Staff–Butler, Carter Library.

119. Ibid., 14.

120. Memo, Rafshoon to Carter, Sept. 1, 1978, p. 1, Anti-Inflation, 1978–79 [CF, O/A 748][1], Box 50, Staff Offices Press–Powell, Carter Library.

121. Ibid.

122. Memo, Blumenthal to Carter, Sept. 13, 1978, 1–4.

123. Ibid., 14.

124. See Memo, Schultze to Carter, Sept. 26, 1978, Inflation 1 of 2: Presidential Memoranda and Statements, September, 1978, to March, 1979, Box 21, Staff Offices Counsel–Lipschutz, Carter Library. On this decision

memo, Carter gave his approval of each component of the new initiative, roughly corresponding to the program suggested by the EPG. Of note is the fact that attached to the memo as tabs are additional memos by a number of Carter's advisers, including Jack Watson (Cabinet secretary), Roberts B. Owen, Mondale, Eizenstat, Blumenthal, Califano, OMB, and Defense. The administration's decision-making process has often been criticized for allowing members excessive access to the president, thereby circumventing any hierarchy in the policy selection process. Thus, although the advisers were in general agreement over the nature of the anti-inflation initiative, as evidenced in the September 26 Schultze memo, each felt compelled to provide Carter with his own personal take on the program. Carter did not particularly discourage this practice, although it often made the selection of a final program unwieldy and tedious.

125. Memo, Schultze to Carter, Sept. 18, 1978, p. 2, Anti-Inflation, September, 1978, [O/A 7432][1], Box 145, Carter Library.

126. Memo, Eizenstat to Carter, Oct. 19, 1978, p. 1, Anti-Inflation, October, 1978, [O/A 7432][5], Box 145, Domestic Policy Staff–Eizenstat, Carter Library.

127. Memo, Califano to Carter, Sept. 18, 1978, p. 4, Inflation 1 of 2: Presidential Memoranda and Statements, September, 1978, to March, 1979, Box 21, Staff Offices Counsel–Lipschutz, Carter Library.

128. Transcript, Remarks of the President in His Address to the Nation on Inflation, Oct. 24, 1978, p. 2, Inflation 1 of 2: Presidential Memoranda and Statements, September, 1978, to March, 1979, Box 21, Staff Offices Counsel–Lipschutz, Carter Library. See also Memo, Eizenstat to Carter, Oct. 19, 1978, 1.

129. Memo, Eizenstat to Carter, Oct. 19, 1978, 1.

130. Transcript, Remarks of the President, Oct. 24, 1978, 1.

131. Ibid.; Fact Sheet, President's Anti-Inflation Program, Oct. 24, 1978, Anti-Inflation Program, June 28 to Oct. 31, 1978, Box 89; Report, Carter Administration—Inflation: An Update, Oct. 24, 1978, Inflation/

CWPS, Oct. 24 to Dec. 28, 1978, Box 102, both in Chief of Staff-Butler, Carter Library.

132. Interview with James McIntyre (including Hubert Harris and Van Ooms), 51.

133. Ibid., 116.

134. Fact Sheet, President's Anti-Inflation Program, Oct. 24, 1978, 1.

135. Anti-Inflation Report 3, Jan. 26, 1979, p. 1, Inflation 1 of 2: Miscellaneous Pending November, 1978, to January, 1979, Box 21, Staff Offices Counsel–Lipshutz, Carter Library.

136. Ibid.

137. Memo, Schultze to Carter, Mar. 16, 1979, pp. 1, 4, Inflation 1 of 2: Presidential Memoranda and Statements, September, 1978, to March, 1979, Box 21, Staff Offices Counsel–Lipshutz, Carter Library.

138. Ibid., 1.

139. Ibid., 5–6.

140. Memo, Blumenthal to EPG Steering Group, May 15, 1979, pp. 3–4, BE4 (Confidential), Jan. 20, 1977, to Jan. 20, 1981, Box 13, WHCF, Carter Library (memo forwarded to Carter; see attached Memo, Blumenthal to Carter, May 25, 1979). See also Memo, Blumenthal and Kahn to Carter, May 24, 1979, BE4 (Confidential), Jan. 20, 1977, to Jan. 20, 1981, Box 13, WHCF, Carter Library.

141. Memo, Blumenthal to EPG Steering Group, May 15, 1979, 1, 4.

142. Memo, Alfred Kahn (special adviser on inflation) to Carter, May 23, 1979, p. 2, BE4 (Confidential), Jan. 20, 1977, to Jan. 20, 1981, Box 13; Memo, Bosworth and Russell to Blumenthal, Eizenstat, Kahn, McIntyre, and Schultze, June 1, 1979, pp. 3–4, BE4–2, Aug. 18, 1978, to Jan. 20, 1981, Box 16, both in WHCF, Carter Library.

143. Memo, Bosworth and Russell to Blumenthal et al., June 1, 1979, 4.

144. Memo, Moore to Carter, June 4, 1979, p. 1, BE4–2, Aug. 18, 1978, to Jan. 20, 1981, Box 16, WHCF, Carter Library.

145. Ibid.

146. Ibid., 2.

147. Ibid., 4.

148. Interview with James McIntyre (including Hubert Harris and Van Ooms), 88.

149. *Economic Report of the President,* 1980, 8.

150. Ibid., 44, 54, 68.

CHAPTER 5

1. Interview with Arthur Burns, "The Council of Economic Advisers under Chairman Arthur F. Burns, 1953–1956," in Hargrove and Samuel A. Morley 1984, 92.

2. Supplementary Notes, Legislative Leadership Meeting, Feb. 9, 1953, p. 1, Diary Series, January–December, 1953, Box 4, DDE Papers.

3. Minutes of Cabinet Meeting of May 1, 1953, p. 2, Box 2, Cabinet Series, DDE Papers.

4. Notes, Legislative Leadership Meeting, Apr. 30, 1953, pp. 3, 6, Diary Series, January–December, 1953, Box 4; Minutes of Cabinet Meeting of May 22, 1953, p. 3, Box 2, Cabinet Series, both in DDE Papers.

5. Notes, Legislative Leadership Meeting, Apr. 30, 1953, 5.

6. Ibid., 9.

7. Supplementary Notes, Legislative Leadership Meeting, May 19, 1953, p. 1, Diary Series, January–December, 1953, Box 4, DDE Papers.

8. Ibid.

9. Hargrove and Morley 1984, "Burns," 92. For an example of the administration's legislative push for the tax proposals, see Eisenhower's excess profits tax extension request in Letter, Eisenhower to Speaker of the House Joseph W. Martin, Jr. (R-Massachusetts), June 29, 1953, Martin, Joseph W., Speaker of the House, Box 26, Administration Series, DDE Papers.

10. Letter, Eisenhower to Gruenther, May 4, 1953, pp. 1–2, Diary Series, January, 1952–July, 1953, Folder 1, Box 3, DDE Papers.

11. DDE Diary Entry, June 1, 1953, p. 2, Personal Diary 1953–54, Folder 2, Box 9, Diary Series, DDE Papers.

12. Ibid.; Letter, Eisenhower to Gen. Benjamin F. Caffey, July 27, 1953, pp. 1–2, Personal

Diary, January, 1952–July, 1953, Folder 1, Box 3, Diary Series, DDE Papers.

13. Letter, Eisenhower to Gen. Benjamin F. Caffey, July 27, 1953, 2.

14. Hargrove and Morley 1984, "Burns," 92.

15. Memo, Hauge to Humphrey, Mar. 25, 1953, p. 2, Memos to George Humphrey, 1953–56, Box 1, Records of Gabriel Hauge, Eisenhower Library.

16. Ibid., 3.

17. Hargrove and Morley 1984, "Burns," 92.

18. Minutes of Cabinet Meeting of Sept. 25, 1953, p. 2, Box 2, Cabinet Series, DDE Papers.

19. Ibid., 1. On the nature of the coming recession, see also Memo, Hauge to Eisenhower, Oct. 9, 1953, Hauge 1952–55, Folder 6, Box 18, Administration Series, DDE Papers.

20. Memo, Burns to Eisenhower, Oct. 13, 1953, pp. 1, 2, White House Correspondence—DDE 1953, Box 103, Papers of Arthur F. Burns, 1930–69, Eisenhower Library.

21. Ibid., 1.

22. Memo, Eisenhower to Humphrey (Ayres memo attached), Dec. 16, 1953, p. 1, Humphrey, G., 1953, Folder 1, Box 20, Administration Series, DDE Papers.

23. Ibid. (Ayres memo), 1.

24. Ibid., 4.

25. Memo, Lodge to Eisenhower, Feb. 19, 1954, p. 1, Lodge 1954, Folder 8, Box 24, Administration Series, DDE Papers.

26. Letter, Dwight D. Eisenhower to Milton Eisenhower, Jan. 6, 1954, p. 1, DDE Diary 1954, Folder 2, Box 5, Diary Series, DDE Papers.

27. Ibid., 2.

28. Ibid., 3.

29. Letter, Leffingwell to Eisenhower, Feb. 9, 1954, pp. 1–2, Humphrey, G., 1954, Folder 2, Box 20, Administration Series, DDE Papers.

30. Letter, Eisenhower to Leffingwell, Feb. 16, 1954, p. 1, DDE Diary, February, 1954 (1), Box 5, Diary Series, DDE Papers.

31. Ibid.

32. *Economic Report of the President,* 1954; Hargrove and Morley 1984, "Burns," 93.

33. Hargrove and Morley 1984, "Burns," 93.

34. Minutes of Cabinet Meeting of Feb. 5, 1954, p. 3, Box 3, Cabinet Series, DDE Papers.

35. Minutes of Cabinet Meeting of Mar. 26, 1954, p. 2, Box 3, Cabinet Series, DDE Papers.

36. DDE Diary Entry, Apr. 8, 1954, pp. 1–2, DDE Diary, January–November, 1954, Box 4, Diary Series, DDE Papers.

37. Minutes of Cabinet Meeting of Apr. 2, 1954, pp. 2–3, Box 3, Cabinet Series, DDE Papers. For the initial list of options presented by Burns to the president and Cabinet, see Minutes of Cabinet Meeting of Mar. 26, 1954, p. 1, Box 3, Cabinet Series, DDE Papers.

38. DDE Diary Entry, Apr. 8, 1954, 2.

39. Hargrove and Morley 1984, "Burns," 118.

40. Minutes of Cabinet Meeting of May 14, 1954, p. 1, Box 3, Cabinet Series, DDE Papers; Memo, Budget Director Rowland Hughes to Eisenhower, May 21, 1954, p. 2, DDE Diary, May, 1954, Folder 1, Box 7, Diary Series, DDE Papers.

41. Minutes of Cabinet Meeting of June 11, 1954, p. 2, Box 3, Cabinet Series, DDE Papers. For Arthur Burns's background report on the administration's countercyclical program see, Report, "The Administration Program for Economic Expansion," June 9, 1954, Cabinet Meeting of June 11, 1954, Box 3, Cabinet Series, DDE Papers.

42. Report, "The Administration Program for Economic Expansion," 93–94.

43. Letter, Eisenhower to Craig, Mar. 26, 1954, p. 2, DDE Diary, March, 1954, Folder 1, Box 5, Diary Series, DDE Papers.

44. Letter, Eisenhower to William E. Robinson, Mar. 12, 1954, p. 2, DDE Diary, March, 1954, Folder 3, Box 5, Diary Series, DDE Papers.

45. Memo, Hauge to Eisenhower, Sept. 27, 1954, p. 1; Letter, Eisenhower to Hauge, Sept. 30, 1954, p. 1, both in Hauge 1952–55, Box 18, Administration Series, DDE Papers.

46. Letter, Lodge to Eisenhower, July 22, 1954, pp. 1–3, Lodge, 1954, Folder 5, Box 24, Administration Series, DDE Papers.

47. Minutes of Cabinet Meeting of July 23, 1954, p. 2, Box 3, Cabinet Series, DDE Papers.

48. Minutes of Cabinet Meeting of Nov. 19, 1954, p. 1, Box 4, Cabinet Series, DDE Papers.

49. Minutes of Cabinet-Legislative Conference of Jan. 3, 1955, p. 2, Box 4, Cabinet Series, DDE Papers.

50. Ibid.

51. Memo, Hughes to Eisenhower, May 15, 1955, pp. 2–3, Budget 1957, Folder 2, Box 9, Administration Series; Minutes of Cabinet Meeting of May 13, 1955, p. 1, Box 5, Cabinet Series, both in DDE Papers.

52. Minutes of Cabinet Meeting of May 13, 1955, 2.

53. Ibid.

54. Memo, Burns to Eisenhower, Aug. 1, 1955, p. 2, White House Correspondence 1955, Folder 1, Box 103, Papers of Arthur F. Burns, 1930–69, Eisenhower Library.

55. Minutes of Cabinet Meeting of Aug. 12, 1955, p. 9, Box 5, Cabinet Series, DDE Papers.

56. Minutes of Cabinet Meeting of Aug. 5, 1955, pp. 1–2, Box 5, Cabinet Series, DDE Papers; Memo, Burns to Eisenhower, Aug. 1, 1955, 1.

57. Interview with Neil Jacoby, OH 141, p. 83, Columbia Oral History Project, 1970, Eisenhower Library.

58. *Economic Report of the President*, 1982, 24, 271, 295.

59. Boskin 1987, 1.

60. Stockman 1986, 3.

61. Boskin 1987, 9.

62. Ibid., 9–10.

63. *Economic Report of the President*, 1982, 23.

64. Ibid., 119, 122; Boskin 1987, 58–59.

65. Boskin 1987, 54.

66. Ibid.

67. *Economic Report of the President*, 1982, 24–25.

68. Ibid., 119; Boskin 1987, 59; *Budget of the United States Government*, FY 1983, M8–M9.

69. Meese 1992, 129.

70. Ibid; Congressional Quarterly 1985, *Members of Congress since 1789*, 182.

71. Meese 1992, 129.

72. Ibid., 16.

73. Stockman 1986, 54.

74. Ibid.

75. Ibid., 97.

76. Boskin 1987, 65.

77. Quoted in Meese 1992, 143.

78. Boskin 1987, 65.

79. Ibid., 65–66; *Budget of the United States Government*, FY 1983, M17; *Economic Report of the President*, 1982, 94–95.

80. *Economic Report of the President*, 1982, 6.

81. Meese 1992, 143–44.

82. Ibid., 146; Boskin 1987, 66.

83. Meese 1992, 145.

84. Boskin 1987, 66.

85. Meese 1992, 147–48.

86. Stockman 1986, 97.

87. Meese 1992, 17.

88. *Economic Report of the President*, 1983, 3–4.

89. Ibid., 4.

90. Ibid., 26.

91. Boskin 1987, 66–67.

92. *Budget of the United States Government*, FY 1984, M10; Boskin 1987, 67.

93. Boskin 1987, 3.

94. Meese 1992, 134.

CHAPTER 6

1. Memo (Highlights of the Cabinet Meeting of Nov. 4, 1955), Maxwell Rabb (secretary to the Cabinet) to Eisenhower, Cabinet Meeting of Nov. 4, 1955, p. 2, Box 6, Cabinet Series, DDE Papers; *Economic Report of the President*, 1956, 101.

2. Memo, Rabb to Eisenhower, Nov. 4, 1955, 2.

3. Teletype, Eisenhower to Adams, Jan. 1, 1956, p. 1, Adams, Sherman, Folder 4, Box 1, Administration Series, DDE Papers.

4. Minutes of Cabinet Meeting of Jan. 1, 1956, p. 2, Box 6, Cabinet Series, DDE Papers.

5. *Economic Report of the President,* 1956, 76.

6. Memo, Presentation to the President on Acceleration Planning, May 19, 1956, pp. 1–2, Miscellaneous, May, 1956, Folder 2, Box 15, Diary Series, DDE Papers.

7. Memo, Ann Whitman (Eisenhower's personal secretary) to Colonel Goodpaster (staff secretary), Apr. 27, 1956, p. 1, Miscellaneous, April, 1956, Folder 1, Box 14, Diary Series, DDE Papers. This memo records Eisenhower's agreement with Humphrey's letter to the Fed chairman recommending action "through open market operations to make money and credit more plentiful."

8. Memo, Burns to Eisenhower, May 10, 1956, p. 1, Burns, Arthur, 1956–57, Folder 3, Box 9, Administration Series, DDE Papers.

9. Minutes of Cabinet Meeting of June 1, 1956, pp. 2–3, Box 7, Cabinet Series, DDE Papers.

10. Memo, Burns to Eisenhower, Oct. 15, 1956, p. 1, White House Correspondence, DDE 1956, Folder 1, Box 103, Papers of Arthur F. Burns, 1930–69, Eisenhower Library.

11. Memo, Heller to LBJ, Nov. 23, 1963, p. 1, FG11–3, Council of Economic Advisers, Nov. 22, 1963, to Jan. 31, 1964, Box 56, WHCF, LBJ Library.

12. Memo, Heller to LBJ, Jan. 9, 1964, p. 1, FG11–3, Council of Economic Advisers, Nov. 22, 1963, to Jan. 31, 1964, Box 56, WHCF, LBJ Library.

13. *Economic Report of the President,* 1965, 63.

14. *Economic Report of the President,* 1964, 6–7.

15. Ibid., 6.

16. Ibid., 7.

17. Ibid., 7–8; Memo, Heller to LBJ, Jan. 9, 1964, 1.

18. Campaign briefing materials, p. 20,

attached to Memo, Heller to George Reedy (White House press secretary), Oct. 14, 1964, BE5–4, Oct. 6–31, 1964, Box 32, WHCF, LBJ Library.

19. Ibid.

20. Ibid.

21. Memo, Heller to LBJ, Sept. 24, 1964, p. 3, FG11–3, Aug. 21 to Sept. 24, 1964, Box 56, WHCF, LBJ Library.

22. Memo, Heller to LBJ, Oct. 6, 1964, p. 1, FG11–3, Sept. 25 to Nov. 24, 1964, Box 56, WHCF, LBJ Library.

23. Ibid.

24. Memo, Bobbitt to Cutler, Mar. 3, 1980, p. 6, Inflation, Mar. 1–11, 1980, Box 80, Staff Offices Counsel–Cutler, Carter Library.

25. Boskin 1987, 51.

26. Ibid.

27. Memo, Eizenstat to Carter, Mar. 26, 1980, p. 1, BE4 (Confidential) Jan. 20, 1977, to Jan. 20, 1981, Box 13, WHCF, Carter Library.

28. Memo, Eizenstat to Carter, Mar. 6, 1980, p. 1, BE4–2, Mar. 1–31, 1980, Box 20, WHCF, Carter Library.

29. Ibid., 1–3.

30. Report, National Anti-Inflation Program, Mar. 17, 1980, p. 1, Inflation [5], Box 35, Staff Offices Administration–Carter, Hodding, Carter Library.

31. Ibid.

32. Report, Revisions to the 1981 Budget, Mar. 31, 1980, p. 2, Inflation [4], Box 35, Staff Offices Administration–Carter, Hodding, Carter Library.

33. Inflation-related guidance materials, p. 3, attached to Memo, Wexler and McDonald to the Cabinet, June 6, 1980, Anti-Inflation 1980 [CF, O/A 748][1], Box 50, Staff Offices Press–Powell, Carter Library.

34. Attachment, p. 1, with Memo, McDonald to Senior Staff and Cabinet, May 7, 1980, Inflation, Apr. 1 to July 31, 1980, Box 12, Speechwriter's Office—Subject File, Carter Library.

35. "Talking Points on Tax Cuts," p. 1, attached to Memo, Wexler and McDonald to Cabinet, June 28, 1980, Inflation [4], Box 35,

Staff Offices Administration–H. Carter, Carter Library.

36. Talking Points on the Mid-Session Review, July 18, 1980, p. 1, Anti-Inflation 1980 [CF, O/A 748][1], Box 50, Staff Offices Press–Powell, Carter Library.

37. Inflation Report, Aug. 28, 1980, p. 1, BE4–2, Aug. 1, 1980, to Jan. 21, 1981, Box 20, WHCF, Carter Library.

38. Ibid.

39. Ibid., 2.

40. *Economic Report of the President,* 1984, 3.

41. Ibid., 5.

42. Ibid., 8.

43. Boskin 1987, 67.

44. *Economic Report of the President,* 1984, 8.

45. Stockman 1986, 377–78.

46. Ibid., 379.

47. Ibid., 380.

CHAPTER 7

1. Remarks by the President [George W. Bush] on Tax Cut Proposal, Feb. 8, 2001, <www.whitehouse.gov/news/releases/20010208.html>, p. 2.

2. Ibid.

Bibliography

ARCHIVAL MATERIALS

Burns, Arthur. Papers. National Archives and Records Administration, Dwight D. Eisenhower Library, Abilene, Kans.

Carter, Hodding. Staff Offices Administration-H. Carter. National Archives and Records Administration, Jimmy Carter Library, Atlanta, Ga.

Carter, Jimmy. Chief of Staff File. National Archives and Records Administration, Jimmy Carter Library, Atlanta, Ga.

———. Speechwriter's Office-Subject File. National Archives and Records Administration, Jimmy Carter Library, Atlanta, Ga.

———. White House Central Files. National Archives and Records Administration, Jimmy Carter Library, Atlanta, Ga.

Columbia Oral History Project. National Archives and Records Administration, Dwight D. Eisenhower Library, Abilene, Kans.

Eisenhower, Dwight D. Papers of the President. 1953–61. National Archives and Records Administration, Dwight D. Eisenhower Library, Abilene, Kans.

Eizenstat, Stuart. Domestic Policy Staff-Eizenstat. National Archives and Records Administration, Jimmy Carter Library, Atlanta, Ga.

Hauge, Gabriel. Records. National Archives and Records Administration, Dwight D. Eisenhower Library, Abilene, Kans.

Johnson, Lyndon B. Administrative Histories. National Archives and Records Administration, Lyndon Baines Johnson Library, Austin, Tex.

———. Cabinet Papers. National Archives and Records Administration, Lyndon Baines Johnson Library, Austin, Tex.

———. White House Central Files. National Archives and Records Administration, Lyndon Baines Johnson Library, Austin, Tex.

Lipschutz, Robert J. Staff Offices Counsel-Lipschutz. National Archives and Records Administration, Jimmy Carter Library, Atlanta, Ga.

Miller Center Interviews. Presidency Project. National Archives and Records Administration, Jimmy Carter Library, Atlanta, Ga.

Powell, Jody. Staff Offices Press-Powell. National Archives and Records Administration, Jimmy Carter Library, Atlanta, Ga.

BOOKS, ARTICLES, AND PAPERS

Aldrich, John H., and Forrest D. Nelson. 1984. *Linear Probability, Logit, and Probit Models.* Beverly Hills, Calif.: Sage Publications.

Alesina, Alberto. 1987. "Macroeconomic Policy in a Two-Party System as a Repeated Game." *Quarterly Journal of Economics* 102 (August): 615–78.

———. 1988. "Macroeconomics and Politics." *NBER Macroeconomics Annual 1988*. Cambridge, Mass.: MIT Press: 13–52.

———. 1991. "Evaluating Rational Partisan Business Cycle Theory: A Response." *Economics and Politics* 3, no. 1 (March): 63–71.

Alesina, Alberto, John Londregan, and Howard Rosenthal. 1993. "A Model of the Political Economy of the United States." *American Political Science Review* 87, no. 1 (March): 12–33.

Alesina, Alberto, and Howard Rosenthal. 1989. "Partisan Cycles in Congressional Elections and the Macroeconomy." *American Political Science Review* 83, no. 2 (June): 373–98.

———. 1995. *Partisan Politics, Divided Government, and the Economy*. Cambridge: Cambridge University Press.

Alesina, Alberto, and J. Sachs. 1988. "Political Parties and the Business Cycle in the United States, 1948–1984." *Journal of Money, Credit, and Banking* 20 (February): 63–82.

Alt, James E. 1985. "Political Parties, World Demand, and Unemployment: Domestic and International Sources of Economic Activity." *American Political Science Review* 79, no. 4: 1016–40.

Alt, James E., and K. Alec Chrystal. 1983. *Political Economics*. Berkeley: University of California Press.

Alt, James E., and John T. Woolley. 1982. "Reaction Functions, Optimization, and Politics: Modeling the Political Economy of Macroeconomic Policy." *American Journal of Political Science* 26, no. 4: 709–40.

Alvarez, Michael R., Geoffrey Garrett, and Peter Lange. 1991. "Government Partisanship, Labor Organization, and Macroeconomic Performance." *American Political Science Review* 85, no. 2: 539–56.

Anderson, James E., and Jared E. Hazleton. 1986. *Managing Macroeconomic Policy: The Johnson Presidency*. Austin: University of Texas Press.

Arecelus, Francisco, and Allan H. Meltzer. 1975. "The Effect of Aggregate Economic Variables on Congressional Elections." *American Political Science Review* 69, no. 4: 1232–39.

Bach, G. L. *Making Monetary and Fiscal Policy*. 1971. Washington, D.C.: Brookings Institution.

Bailey, Stephen Kemp. 1950. *Congress Makes a Law: The Story behind the Employment Act of 1946*. New York: Columbia University Press.

Barber, James David. 1972. *The Presidential Character: Predicting Performance in the White House*. Englewood Cliffs, N.J.: Prentice-Hall.

Beck, Nathaniel. 1982a. "Parties, Administrations, and American Macroeconomic Outcomes." *American Political Science Review* 76, no. 1: 83–93.

———. 1982b. "Presidential Influence on the Federal Reserve in the 1970s." *American Journal of Political Science* 26:415–45.

———. 1984. "Domestic Political Sources of American Monetary Policy: 1955–1982." *Journal of Politics* 46:786–817.

———. 1987. "Elections and the Fed: Is There a Political Monetary Cycle?" *American Journal of Political Science* 31:194–216.

Bloom, Howard S., and H. Douglas Price. 1975. "Voter Response to Short-Run Economic Conditions: The Asymmetric Effect of Prosperity and Recession." *American Political Science Review* 69, no. 4: 1240–54.

Bond, Jon R., and Richard Fleisher. 1990. *The President in the Legislative Arena.* Chicago: University of Chicago Press.

Boskin, Michael J. 1987. *Reagan and the Economy: The Successes, Failures, and Unfinished Agenda.* San Francisco: ICS Press.

Brownlow, Louis, Harold D. Smith, Charles E. Merriam, William H. McReynolds, Lowell Mellett, and Luther Gulick. 1941. "The Executive Office of the President." *Public Administration Review* 1, no. 2: 101–40.

Buck, A. E., and Harvey C. Mansfield. 1937. "Fiscal Management in National Government." *Studies on Administrative Management in the Government of the United States,* vol. 2. Report prepared for the President's Committee on Administrative Management. Washington, D.C.: Government Printing Office.

Budget of the United States Government. Fiscal Years 1945–97. Washington, D.C.: Government Printing Office.

Burke, John P. 1992. *The Institutional Presidency.* Baltimore, Md.: Johns Hopkins University Press.

Campagna, Anthony S. 1994. *The Economy in the Reagan Years: The Economic Consequences of the Reagan Administrations.* Westport, Conn.: Greenwood Press.

Campbell, James E. 1993. *The Presidential Pulse of Congressional Elections.* Lexington: University Press of Kentucky.

Chappell, Henry W., Jr. 1983. "Presidential Popularity and Macroeconomic Performance: Are Voters Really So Naive?" *Review of Economics and Statistics* 65 (August): 385–92.

Chappell, Henry W., Jr., and William R. Keech. 1985. "A New View of Political Accountability for Economic Performance." *American Political Science Review* 79, no. 1: 10–27.

———. 1986a. "Party Differences in Macroeconomic Policies and Outcomes." *American Economic Review* 76, no. 2: 71–74.

———. 1986b. "Policy Motivation and Party Differences in a Dynamic Spatial Model of Party Competition." *American Political Science Review* 80, no. 3 (September): 881–99.

———. 1988. "The Unemployment Rate Consequences of Partisan Monetary Policies." *Southern Economic Journal* 55:107–21.

Cohen, Jeffrey E. 1997. *Presidential Responsiveness and Public Policy-Making: The Public and the Policies That Presidents Choose.* Ann Arbor: University of Michigan Press.

Coleman, John J. 1996. *Party Decline in America: Policy, Politics, and the Fiscal State.* Princeton, N.J.: Princeton University Press.

Collins, Robert M. 1981. *The Business Response to Keynes, 1929–1964.* New York: Columbia University Press.

Congressional Quarterly. 1985. *Members of Congress since 1789.* 3rd ed. Washington, D.C.: Congressional Quarterly.

Cox, Gary W., and Samuel Kernell, eds. 1991. *The Politics of Divided Government.* Boulder, Colo.: Westview Press.

Cox, Gary W., and Mathew D. McCubbins. 1991. "Divided Control of Fiscal Policy."

In *The Politics of Divided Government,* ed. Gary W. Cox and Samuel Kernell. Boulder, Colo.: Westview Press.

Downs, Anthony. 1957. *An Economic Theory of Democracy.* New York: Harper.

Eccles, Marriner S. 1951. *Beckoning Frontiers: Public and Personal Recollections.* Edited by Sidney Hyman. New York: Knopf.

Economic Report of the President, Together with the Annual Report of the Council of Economic Advisers. 1946–97. Washington, D.C.: Government Printing Office.

Edwards, George C., III. 1983. *The Public Presidency: The Pursuit of Popular Support.* New York: St. Martin's Press.

Edwards, George C., III, Andrew Barrett, and Jeffrey Peake. 1997. "The Legislative Impact of Divided Government." *American Journal of Political Science* 41 (April): 545–63.

Fair, Ray C. 1978. "The Effect of Economic Events on Votes for President." *Review of Economics and Statistics* 60, no. 2: 159–73.

———. 1984. *Specification, Estimation, and Analysis of Macroeconomic Models.* Cambridge, Mass.: Harvard University Press.

Fiorina, Morris P. 1981. *Retrospective Voting in American National Elections.* New Haven, Conn.: Yale University Press.

———. 1992. *Divided Government.* New York: Macmillan.

Fischer, Gregory W., and Mark Kamlet. 1984. "Explaining Presidential Priorities: The Competing Aspiration Levels Model of Macrobudgetary Decision Making." *American Political Science Review* 78:356–71.

Fisher, Louis. 1975. *Presidential Spending Power.* Princeton, N.J.: Princeton University Press.

Flash, Edward S., Jr. 1965. *Economic Advice and Presidential Leadership.* New York: Columbia University Press.

Frendreis, John P., and Raymond Tatalovich. 1994. *The Modern Presidency and Economic Policy.* Itasca, Ill.: F. E. Peacock Publishers.

Frey, Bruno S. 1978. "Politico-Economic Models and Cycles." *Journal of Public Economics* 9:203–20.

Frey, Bruno S., and Friedrich Schneider. 1975. "On the Modeling of Politico-Economic Interdependence." *European Journal of Political Research* 3:339–60.

———. 1978. "An Empirical Study of Politico-Economic Interaction in the United States." *Review of Economics and Statistics* 60:174–83.

———. 1979. "An Econometric Model with an Endogenous Government Sector." *Public Choice* 34:29–43.

Friedman, Milton, and Anna Jacobson Schwartz. 1963. *A Monetary History of the United States, 1867–1960.* Princeton, N.J.: Princeton University Press.

George, Alexander L. 1979. "Case Studies and Theory Development: The Method of Structured, Focused Comparison." In *Diplomacy: New Approaches in History, Theory, and Policy,* edited by Paul Gordon Lauren. New York: Free Press.

———. 1980. *Presidential Decisionmaking in Foreign Policy: The Effective Use of Information and Advice.* Boulder, Colo.: Westview Press.

George, Alexander L., and Juliette George. 1998. *Presidential Personality and Performance.* Boulder, Colo.: Westview Press.

Golden, David G., and James M. Poterba. 1980. "The Price of Popularity: The Political Business Cycle Reexamined." *American Journal of Political Science* 24, no. 4: 696–714.

Gordon, Robert J. 1987. *Macroeconomics.* Boston: Little, Brown.

Graves, W. Brooke. 1949. *Basic Information on the Reorganization of the Executive Branch, 1912–1948.* Public Affairs Bulletin No. 66. Washington, D.C.: Library of Congress.

Greenstein, Fred. 2000. *The Presidential Difference: Leadership Style from FDR to Clinton.* Princeton, N.J.: Princeton University Press.

Grier, Kevin. 1989. "On the Existence of a Political Monetary Cycle." *American Journal of Political Science* 33, no. 2: 376–89.

Hargrove, Erwin C., and Samuel A. Morley, eds. 1984. *The President and the Council of Economic Advisers: Interviews with CEA Chairmen.* Boulder, Colo.: Westview Press.

Hart, John. 1987. *The Presidential Branch.* New York: Pergamon Press.

Havrilesky, Thomas M. 1987. "A Partisan Theory of Fiscal and Monetary Regimes." *Journal of Money, Credit, and Banking* 19, no. 3: 308–25.

Hawley, Ellis W. 1966. *The New Deal and the Problem of Monopoly.* Princeton, N.J.: Princeton University Press.

Heclo, Hugh. 1977. *A Government of Strangers: Executive Politics in Washington.* Washington, D.C.: Brookings Institution.

Hess, Stephen. 1988. *Organizing the Presidency.* Rev. ed. Washington, D.C.: Brookings Institution.

Hibbs, Douglas A. 1977. "Political Parties and Macroeconomic Policy." *American Political Science Review* 71, no. 4: 1467–87.

———. 1983. "Comment on Beck." *American Political Science Review* 77: 447–51.

———. 1986. "Political Parties and Macroeconomic Policies and Outcomes in the United States." *American Economic Review* 76, no. 2: 66–70.

———. 1987. *The American Political Economy: Macroeconomics and Electoral Politics.* Cambridge, Mass.: Harvard University Press.

———. 1992. "Partisan Theory after Fifteen Years." *European Journal of Political Economy* 8:361–73.

———. 1994. "The Partisan Model of Macroeconomic Cycles: More Theory and Evidence for the United States." *Economics and Politics* 6, no. 1 (March): 1–23.

Hult, Karen M. 1993. "Advising the President." In *Researching the Presidency: Vital Questions, New Approaches,* edited by George C. Edwards, John H. Kessel, and Bert Rockman. Pittsburgh: University of Pittsburgh Press.

Hult, Karen M., and Charles E. Walcott. 1998. "Decisionmaking in the Presidency: A Way Out of the Thicket." *PRG Report* 21, no. 1: 1–5.

Johnson, Richard Tanner. 1974. *Managing the White House: An Intimate Study of the Presidency.* New York: Harper & Row.

Karl, Barry Dean. 1963. *Executive Reorganization and Reform in the New Deal: The Genesis of Administrative Management, 1900–1939.* Cambridge, Mass.: Harvard University Press.

Katznelson, Ira, and Mark Kesselman. 1987. *The Politics of Power: A Critical Introduction to American Government.* 3rd ed. San Diego: Harcourt Brace Jovanovich.

Keech, William. 1980. "Elections and Macroeconomic Policy Optimization." *American Journal of Political Science* 24, no. 2: 345-67.

———. 1995. *Economic Politics: The Costs of Democracy*. Cambridge: Cambridge University Press.

Keller, Robert R., and Ann Mari May. 1984. "The Presidential Political Business Cycle of 1972." *Journal of Economic History* 44, no. 2: 265-79.

Kernell, Samuel. 1978. "Explaining Presidential Popularity." *American Political Science Review* 72, no. 2: 506-22.

———. 1997. *Going Public: New Strategies of Presidential Leadership*. 3rd ed. Washington, D.C.: CQ Press.

Kessel, John H. 1974. "Parameters of Presidential Politics." *Social Science Quarterly* 55 (June): 8-24.

———. 1975. *The Domestic Presidency: Decision-Making in the White House*. North Scituate, Mass.: Duxbury Press.

Keynes, John Maynard. 1964. *The General Theory of Employment, Interest, and Money*. 1936. Reprint, San Diego: Harcourt Brace Jovanovich, First Harvest/HBJ Edition.

Kiewe, Amos, ed. 1994. *The Modern Presidency and Crisis Rhetoric*. Westport, Conn.: Praeger.

Kiewiet, D. Roderick. 1983. *Macroeconomics and Micropolitics: The Electoral Effects of Economic Issues*. Chicago: University of Chicago Press.

Kimmel, Lewis H. 1959. *Federal Budget and Fiscal Policy, 1789-1958*. Washington, D.C.: Brookings Institution.

King, Gary, Robert O. Keohane, and Sidney Verba. 1994. *Designing Social Inquiry: Scientific Inference in Qualitative Research*. Princeton, N.J.: Princeton University Press.

Kingdon, John. 1984. *Agendas, Alternatives, and Public Policies*. Boston: Little, Brown.

Kramer, Gerald H. 1971. "Short-Term Fluctuations in U.S. Voting Behavior, 1896-1964." *American Political Science Review* 65:131-43.

———. 1975. "Comment on Meltzer and Vellrath's 'The Effects of Economic Policies on Votes for the Presidency: Some Evidence from Recent Elections.'" *Journal of Law and Economics* 18 (December): 799-800.

Laney, Leroy O., and Thomas D. Willett. 1983. "Presidential Politics, Budget Deficits, and Monetary Policy in the United States, 1960-1976." *Public Choice* 40:53-69.

Lekachman, Robert. 1975. *The Age of Keynes*. New York: McGraw-Hill.

LeLoup, Lance T. 1977. *Budgetary Politics: Dollars, Deficits, Decisions*. Brunswick, Ohio: King's Court Communications.

———. 1980. *The Fiscal Congress: Legislative Control of the Budget*. Westport, Conn.: Greenwood Press.

LeLoup, Lance T., and Steven A. Shull. 1979. "Congress versus the Executive: The Two Presidencies Reconsidered." *Social Science Quarterly* 59, no. 4: 704-19.

Liao, Tim Futing. 1994. *Interpreting Probability Models: Logit, Probit, and Other Generalized Linear Models*. Thousand Oaks, Calif.: Sage Publications.

Light, Paul. 1991. *The President's Agenda: Domestic Policy Choice from Kennedy to Reagan*. Rev. ed. Baltimore, Md.: Johns Hopkins University Press.

Lindbeck, Assar. 1976. "Stabilization Policy in Open Economies with Endogenous Politicians." *American Economic Review* 66 (May): 1–19.

Lindberg, Leon N., and Charles S. Maier, eds. 1985. *The Politics of Inflation and Economic Stagnation.* Washington, D.C.: Brookings Institution.

Link, Arthur S. 1956. *Wilson: The New Freedom.* Princeton, N.J.: Princeton University Press.

Lowery, David. 1985. "The Keynesian and Political Determinants of Unbalanced Budgets: U.S. Fiscal Policy from Eisenhower to Reagan." *American Journal of Political Science* 29:428–60.

MacRae, C. Duncan. 1977. "A Political Model of the Business Cycle." *Journal of Political Economy* 85, no. 2: 239–63.

Maddala, G. S. 1983. *Limited-Dependent and Qualitative Variables in Econometrics.* Cambridge: Cambridge University Press.

Manski, Charles F., and Daniel McFadden, eds. 1981. *Structural Analysis of Discrete Data with Econometric Applications.* Cambridge, Mass.: MIT Press.

Marini, John. 1992. *The Politics of Budget Control: Congress, the Presidency, and the Growth of the Administrative State.* New York: Crane Russak.

Mayhew, David R. 1991. *Divided We Govern: Party Control, Lawmaking, and Investigations, 1946–1990.* New Haven: Yale University Press.

McClelland, Peter D. 1984. "Discussion of 'The Presidential Political Business Cycle of 1972' (Robert R. Keller and Ann Mari May)." *Journal of Economic History* 44, no. 2: 273–76.

McCraken, Paul W. 1973. "The Practice of Political Economy: Comment on Stigler's General Economic Conditions and National Elections." *American Economic Review* 63, no. 2: 168–71.

McGregor, Rob Ray. 1996. "FOMC Voting Behavior and Electoral Cycles: Partisan Ideology and Partisan Loyalty." *Economics and Politics* 8, no. 1 (March): 17–32.

Meese, Edwin, III. 1992. *With Reagan: The Inside Story.* Washington, D.C.: Regnery Gateway.

Meltzer, Allan H., and Marc Vellrath. 1975a. "The Effects of Economic Policies on Votes for the Presidency: Some Evidence from Recent Elections." *Journal of Law and Economics* 18:781–98.

———. 1975b. "Reply to Kramer's and Stigler's Comments on 'The Effects of Economic Policies on Votes for the Presidency: Some Evidence from Recent Elections.'" *Journal of Law and Economics* 18:803–805.

Milkis, Sidney M. 1999. "Political Parties and Divided Democracy." In *Presidential Policymaking: An End-of-Century Assessment,* edited by Steven A. Shull. Armonk, N.Y.: M. E. Sharpe.

Minford, Patrick, and David Peel. 1982. "The Political Theory of the Business Cycle." *European Economic Review* 17:253–70.

Miroff, Bruce. 1997. "Let a Hundred Theories Bloom: Theory and Presidency Research." *PRG Report* 20, no. 2: 4–5.

Moe, Terry. 1985. "The Politicized Presidency." In *The New Direction in American Politics,* edited by John E. Chubb and Paul E. Peterson. Washington, D.C.: Brookings Institution.

———. 1993. "Presidents, Institutions, and Theory." In *Researching the Presidency:*

Vital Questions, New Approaches, edited by George C. Edwards, John H. Kessel, and Bert Rockman. Pittsburgh: University of Pittsburgh Press.

———. 1997. "Theory and the Future of Presidential Studies." *PRG Report* 20, no. 2: 1–3.

Moe, Terry, and Scott Wilson. 1994. "Presidents and the Politics of Structure." *Law and Contemporary Problems* 57, no. 2: 1–44.

Mosher, Frederick C. 1984. *A Tale of Two Agencies: A Comparative Analysis of the General Accounting Office and the Office of Management and Budget.* Baton Rouge: Louisiana State University Press.

Mosley, Paul. 1984. *The Making of Economic Policy: Theory and Evidence from Britain and the United States since 1945.* New York: St. Martin's Press.

Mowery, David C., Mark S. Kamlet, and John P. Crecine. 1980. "Presidential Management of Budgetary and Fiscal Policymaking." *Political Science Quarterly* 95, no. 3: 395–425.

Murray, Robert K. 1969. *The Harding Era: Warren G. Harding and His Administration.* Minneapolis: University of Minnesota Press.

Myers, Margaret G. 1970. *A Financial History of the United States.* New York: Columbia University Press.

Neustadt, Richard E. 1990. *Presidential Power and the Modern Presidents: The Politics of Leadership from Roosevelt to Reagan.* New York: Wiley.

Nordhaus, William D. 1975. "The Political Business Cycle." *Review of Economic Studies* 42, no. 2: 169–90.

Nourse, Edwin G. 1953. *Economics in the Public Service: Administrative Aspects of the Employment Act.* New York: Harcourt, Brace.

Okun, Arthur M. 1970. *The Political Economy of Prosperity.* New York: Norton.

———. 1973. "Comments on Stigler's 'General Economic Conditions and National Elections.'" *American Economic Review* 63, no. 2: 172–77.

———. 1983. *Economics for Policymaking: Selected Essays of Arthur M. Okun.* Edited by Joseph A. Pechman. Cambridge, Mass.: MIT Press.

Orloff, Ann Shola. 1988. "The Political Origins of America's Belated Welfare State." In *The Politics of Social Policy in the United States,* ed. Margaret Weir, Ann Shola Orloff, and Theda Skocpol. Princeton, N.J.: Princeton University Press.

Orren, Karen, and Stephen Skowronek. 1999. "Regimes and Regime Building in American Government: A Review of Literature on the 1940s." *Political Science Quarterly* 113, no. 4: 689–702.

Palmer, John L., and Isabel V. Sawhill, eds. 1982. *The Reagan Experiment: An Examination of Economic and Social Policies under the Reagan Administration.* Washington, D.C.: Urban Institute Press.

Pemberton, William E. 1979. *Bureaucratic Politics: Executive Reorganization during the Truman Administration.* Columbia: University of Missouri Press.

Peretz, Paul. 1983. *The Political Economy of Inflation in the United States.* Chicago: University of Chicago Press.

Peterson, Mark A. 1990. *Legislating Together: The White House and Capitol Hill from Eisenhower to Reagan.* Cambridge, Mass.: Harvard University Press.

Pfiffner, James P. 1996. *The Strategic Presidency: Hitting the Ground Running.* 2nd ed., rev. Lawrence: University Press of Kansas.

Pious, Richard M. 1979. *The American Presidency.* New York: Basic Books.

Polenberg, Richard. 1966. *Reorganizing Roosevelt's Government: The Controversy over Executive Reorganization, 1936–1939.* Cambridge, Mass.: Harvard University Press.

Porter, Roger B. 1980. *Presidential Decision Making: The Economic Policy Board.* New York: Cambridge University Press.

———. 1983. "Economic Advice to the President: From Eisenhower to Reagan." *Political Science Quarterly* 98, no. 3: 403–26.

President's Commission on Economy and Efficiency. 1912. *The Need for a National Budget.* Washington, D.C.: Government Printing Office.

President's Committee on Administrative Management. 1937. *Report of the Committee.* Washington, D.C.: Government Printing Office.

Public Papers of the Presidents of the United States, Containing the Public Messages, Speeches, and Statements of the President. 1953–96. Washington, D.C.: Government Printing Office.

Ragsdale, Lyn. 1996. *Vital Statistics on the Presidency: Washington to Clinton.* Washington, D.C.: Congressional Quarterly.

Ragsdale, Lyn, and Jerrold G. Rusk. 1999. "Elections and Presidential Policymaking." In *Presidential Policymaking: An End-of-Century Assessment,* edited by Steven A. Shull. Armonk, N.Y.: M. E. Sharpe.

Ragsdale, Lyn, and John J. Theis III. 1997. "The Institutionalization of the American Presidency, 1924–1992." *American Journal of Political Science* 41, no. 4 (October): 1280–1318.

Ranney, Austin. 1954. *The Doctrine of Responsible Party Government.* Urbana: University of Illinois Press.

Regan, Donald T. 1988. *For the Record: From Wall Street to Washington.* San Diego: Harcourt Brace Jovanovich.

Roemer, John. 1995. "Political Cycles." *Economics and Politics* 7, no. 1 (March): 1–20.

Rogoff, Kenneth. 1988. "Comment on Alesina's 'Macroeconomics and Politics.'" *NBER Macroeconomics Annual 1988.* Cambridge, Mass.: MIT Press: 52–56.

Rossiter, Clinton. 1960. *The American Presidency.* 2nd ed. New York: Harcourt Brace.

Savage, James D. 1988. *Balanced Budgets and American Politics.* Ithaca, N.Y.: Cornell University Press.

Schattschneider, E. E. 1942. *Party Government.* New York: Farrar and Rinehart.

Schmidt, Manfred. 1996. "When Parties Matter: A Review of the Possibilities and Limits of Partisan Influence on Public Policy." *European Journal of Political Research* 30 (September): 155–83.

Schultz, Kenneth A. 1995. "The Politics of the Political Business Cycle." *British Journal of Political Science* 25:79–99.

Schultze, Charles L. 1992. *Memos to the President: A Guide through Macroeconomics for the Busy Policymaker.* Washington, D.C.: Brookings Institution.

Shepsle, Kenneth A. 1988. "Comment on Alesina's 'Macroeconomics and Politics.'" *NBER Macroeconomics Annual 1988.* Cambridge, Mass.: MIT Press: 57–60.

Shull, Steven A. 1983. *Domestic Policy Formation: Presidential-Congressional Partnership?* Westport, Conn.: Greenwood Press.

———, ed. 1999. *Presidential Policymaking: An End-of-Century Assessment.* Armonk, N.Y.: M. E. Sharpe.

Skowronek, Stephen. 1982. *Building a New American State: The Expansion of Na-*

tional Administrative Capacities, 1877–1920. Cambridge: Cambridge University Press.

———. 1993. *The Politics Presidents Make: Leadership from John Adams to George Bush.* Cambridge, Mass.: Belknap Press, Harvard University Press.

———. 1995. "Order and Change." *Polity* 28, no. 1 (fall): 91–96.

Slesinger, Reuben E. 1968. *National Economic Policy: The Presidential Reports.* Princeton, N.J.: Van Nostrand.

Sloan, John W. 1999. *The Reagan Effect: Economics and Presidential Leadership.* Lawrence: University Press of Kansas.

Smith, James Allen. 1993. *The Idea Brokers: Think Tanks and the Rise of the New Policy Elite.* New York: Free Press.

Spiliotes, Constantine J. 2000. "Partisanship and Institutional Responsibility in Presidential Decision Making." *Presidential Studies Quarterly* 30, no. 3: 485–513.

Stein, Herbert. 1988. *Presidential Economics: The Making of Economic Policy from Roosevelt to Reagan and Beyond.* 2nd ed. Washington, D.C.: AEI Press.

———. 1996. *The Fiscal Revolution in America: Policy in Pursuit of Reality.* 2nd rev. ed. Washington, D.C.: AEI Press.

Stigler, George J. 1973. "General Economic Conditions and National Elections." *American Economic Review* 63, no. 2: 160–67.

———. 1975. "Comment on Meltzer and Vellrath's 'The Effects of Economic Policies on Votes for the President: Some Evidence from Recent Elections.'" *Journal of Law and Economics* 18 (December): 801–802.

Stockman, David A. 1986. *The Triumph of Politics: How the Reagan Revolution Failed.* New York: Harper & Row.

Sundquist, James L. 1981. *The Decline and Resurgence of Congress.* Washington, D.C.: Brookings Institution.

———. 1988. "Needed: A Political Theory for the New Era of Coalition Government in the United States." *Political Science Quarterly* 103, no. 1: 613–35.

Tufte, Edward R. 1975. "Determinants of the Outcomes of Midterm Congressional Elections." *American Political Science Review* 69:812–26.

———. 1978. *Political Control of the Economy.* Princeton, N.J.: Princeton University Press.

Tulis, Jeffrey K. 1987. *The Rhetorical Presidency.* Princeton, N.J.: Princeton University Press.

U.S. Congress. *Employment Act of 1946.* Public Law 304. 79th Cong., 2nd sess., February 20, 1946.

Walcott, Charles E., and Karen Hult. 1995. *Governing the White House: From Hoover through LBJ.* Lawrence: University Press of Kansas.

Warshaw, Shirley Anne. 1997. *The Domestic Presidency: Policy Making in the White House.* Boston: Allyn and Bacon.

Weatherford, M. Stephen. 1978. "Economic Conditions and Electoral Outcomes: Class Differences in the Political Response to Recession." *American Journal of Political Science* 22, no. 4: 917–38.

———. 1988. "Political Business Cycles and the Process of Economic Policymaking." *American Politics Quarterly* 16, no. 1: 99–136.

Weatherford, M. Stephen, and Lorraine M. McDonnell. 1997. "Do Presidents Make a Difference in the Economy (And If So, How?)." Paper presented at the Annual Meeting of the American Political Science Association, Washington, D.C.

Weir, Margaret. 1992. *Politics and Jobs: The Boundaries of Employment Policy in the United States.* Princeton, N.J.: Princeton University Press.

Weir, Margaret, Ann Shola Orloff, and Theda Skocpol, eds. 1988. *The Politics of Social Policy in the United States.* Princeton, N.J.: Princeton University Press.

Weko, Thomas J. 1995. *The Politicizing Presidency: The White House Personnel Office, 1948–1994.* Lawrence: University Press of Kansas.

Wilber, Charles K., and Kenneth P. Jameson. 1990. *Beyond Reaganomics: A Further Inquiry into the Poverty of Economics.* Notre Dame, Ind.: University of Notre Dame Press.

Wildavsky, Aaron. 1988. *The New Politics of the Budgetary Process.* Glenview, Ill.: Scott, Foresman.

Willett, Thomas D., ed. 1988. *Political Business Cycles: The Political Economy of Money, Inflation, and Unemployment.* Durham, N.C.: Duke University Press.

Williams, John T. 1990. "The Political Manipulation of Macroeconomic Policy." *American Political Science Review* 84, no. 3: 767–95.

Willoughby, William Franklin. 1918. *The Problem of a National Budget.* New York: Appleton.

———. 1927. *The National Budget System, with Suggestions for Its Improvement.* Baltimore, Md.: Johns Hopkins Press.

Woolley, John T. 1984. *Monetary Politics: The Federal Reserve and the Politics of Monetary Policy.* Cambridge: Cambridge University Press.

———. 1988. "Partisan Manipulation of the Economy: Another Look at Monetary Policy with Moving Regression." *Journal of Politics* 50, no. 2: 335–60.

Index

BOSE, MEENA.
Shaping and Signaling Presidential Policy:
The National Security Decision Making of
Eisenhower and Kennedy. 1998.

CALIFANO, JOSEPH A., JR.
The Triumph and Tragedy of Lyndon Johnson:
The White House Years. 2000.

CAMPBELL, JAMES E.
The American Campaign:
U.S. Presidential Campaigns and the National Vote. 2000.

FISHER, LOUIS.
Congressional Abdication on War and Spending. 2000.

FISHER, LOUIS.
The Politics of Shared Power:
Congress and the Executive. 4th ed. 1998.

GARRISON, JEAN A.
Games Advisors Play: Foreign Policy
in the Nixon and Carter Administrations. 1999.

PFIFFNER, JAMES P., ED.
The Managerial Presidency. 2d ed. 1999.

PONDER, DANIEL E.
Good Advice: Information and Policy Making
in the White House. 2000.

Constantine J. Spiliotes is an assistant professor of government at Dartmouth College and earned his Ph.D. at the University of Chicago.

ISBN 1-58544-142-2